Preaching the Great Themes of the Bible

CHEVIS F. HORNE

Preaching the Great Themes of the Bible

Broadman Press
Nashville, Tennessee

© Copyright 1986 • Broadman Press
All rights reserved
4222-62
ISBN: 0-8054-2262-5

Dewey Decimal Classification: 251.02
Subject Heading: SERMONS—OUTLINES, SYLLABI, ETC.
Library of Congress Catalog Card Number: 86-6865

Printed in the United States of America

Library of Congress Cataloging-in-Publication Data

Horne, Chevis F.
  Preaching the great themes of the Bible.

  1. Bible—Homiletical use.   2. Preaching.
I. Title.
BS534.5.H67   1986   251'.02   86-6865
ISBN 0-8054-2262-5 (pbk.)

To Dr. A. C. Reid,
my great teacher,
who is gifted of mind,
gentle of spirit,
reverent in the presence of truth,
faithful in friendship,
and devoted to Christ his Lord.

Contents

Foreword

One of the maladies of much current preaching is a theological homelessness. Many sermons speak in a thin contemporary voice but have no overtones of the eternal. An effective sermon must always look to "the rock from which it is hewn." The author's avowed intent in this volume is to offer a "homiletical approach to theology." His book constitutes a compelling invitation to the preacher to declare "the whole counsel of God" and to avoid the pursuit of paltry themes—what Charles Spurgeon called "holy trifling."

Theology is the reflective clarification of the *content* of the Christian faith. It is concerned with the major realities and symbols of our faith as they interpret, illumine, and clarify the basic nature of our human existence and history. Preaching at its best is anchored in the redeeming revelation and activity of that God who is the ultimate point of reference beyond which we cannot move in imagination, thought, and devotion. From that point it moves to such terms as church, covenant, grace, faith, love, reconciliation, salvation, redemption, evil, and suffering that spin from the full web of that grounding reality. Theology is the conscience of the sermon. It is the self-test by which the church measures its language and its life. It monitors the church's proclamation of the gospel.

No person is better equipped to look at theology from the pulpit than Chevis F. Horne. His preaching has always been rooted in a serious engagement with biblical sources and an intellectual comradeship with the fathers and theologians of the church. Few preachers understand so perceptively the contemporary human situation. In reading and observation Dr. Horne's eye is generous, and thus the whole man is full of light. One will find in these pages an absence of parochial thinking and an explorative thrust that leads us beyond pedestrian trails. These chapters reflect all the felicities of oral style in words that are freshly minted, and in the woven pattern of thought, irony, and mood they create a happy fusion of the abstract and the concrete. The author does not wrap himself in clerical vapors. One will find here organization, clarity, and the simplicity of mastery.

Dr. Horne's preaching carries a dual appeal—the power of the prophetic voice and the therapeutic offering of the "balm of Gilead." He has consistently lifted up his voice against the cultural captivity of the church and has challenged every form of human exploitation. This has been done in the spirit of the true prophet—more *anguish* than anger. He has also been attuned to the "still, sad music of humanity" and has brought to his hearers the consolations of grace.

Chevis F. Horne is a man who in mind and spirit has always magnified his office. As a professor of preaching at the Southeastern Baptist Theological Seminary following his retirement from a thirty-two year pastorate of the First Baptist Church, Martinsville, Virginia, he was a veritable Pied Piper on the campus as a large number of students sought his instruction and counsel. He exemplified the largeness of the preacher's culture and championed standards of excellence that filled vocational form with substance. He expounded and personfied for students and colleagues the minister's role as servant expressed as the total bent of a loving life in stewardship and serviceability. Others discerned in him one who could define his own space, savour his own solitude, and sculpt the contours of his own individuality. He seemed instinctively to divine where the treasures of life are to be found and thus was delivered from our little games of getting on and cashing in. He is totally uncluttered—a man of simplicity whose horizons are unblurred by the petty assertions of a sovereign ego. The readers of this volume will be grateful heirs of that spirit and achievement.

JOHN W. CARLTON

Professor of Preaching
Southeastern Baptist Theological Seminary
Wake Forest, North Carolina

Introduction

This book might be called a homiletical approach to theology. It is looking at theology from the pulpit. Or, to put it differently, it is an attempt to discover preaching values in the great biblical themes and theological truths.

I have discussed the great themes of the Bible which are like the main theme of a symphony—they occur over and over again. I have resisted the temptation to deal with novel truths that might appeal to the fancy of congregations. Such themes are like water eddies that whirl and churn and may be more interesting than the mainstream. Yet, no cargo sails on them. Only the mainstream is capable of such a load. Just so with the Bible. Great truths are found in its main themes, and I hope I have been faithful to them.

Theological ideas are often clothed in technical and abstract language that is very difficult. The ideas seem removed from our common life and the language from our common parlance. I have tried to escape this weakness and have searched for fresh, simple language which can be easily understood.

The discussion of each theme is followed by thought starters for sermons, appropriate Scriptures and texts, and, finally, pertinent biblical illustrations. I do not offer sermon outlines which can be crutches for lazy minds, but even the most responsible preachers often need stimulating ideas to get their sermons started.

For over forty years I have faced the challenging, but laborious, task of preparing sermons each week, and I have needed all the help I could get. While I have shied away from easy preparation helps, I have looked for responsible sources. I hope this book will be such a resource.

Let me say a word about the illustrations. We sometimes feel that an illustration must be a story, and it is true that stories can make good illustrations. But anything that can focus a truth and set it in a clearer light is an illustration. It may be as simple as a simile or a metaphor. You will remember that Jesus was a master of both. It is hoped that these illustrations will give a greater visibility to characters, truths, and experiences. It is also hoped that these illustrations will serve a larger purpose—that of opening up vistas of thought and suggesting sermon ideas and topics.

I hope you will use your imagination to help touch to life these Scriptures, texts, and illustrations. Let your imagination transpose you into the historical situation. Be there, see, hear, feel, and handle again the original experience. You will be surprised the difference it makes.

The origin of this book goes back to a day in August 1980, when I attended the Passion Play at Oberammergau, Germany. It was one of the great days of my life, filled with luminous moments, when the truth was clear and compelling. Under the inspiration of that day, while in the Passion Playhouse, I outlined a course to be given later at Southeastern Baptist Seminary using the title, "Preaching the Great Themes of the Bible." Little did I dream that it would someday become a book.

As I have written this book, I have been looking in two directions. I have been seeing busy pastors, many of whom are tired and discouraged, whose idealism of early years for their pulpits has been blunted, yet who want their preaching to be biblical, fresh, and in touch with life. And, I immodestly confess, I have been looking in the direction of classrooms where professors of preaching are offering courses in biblical preaching. I hope this book will be of some help to them and their students.

CHEVIS F. HORNE

1
Creation,
Fallen Creation, New Creation

I am always looking for keys that unlock the meaning of the Bible. Here are three—creation, fallen creation, and new creation. These are primary themes of the Bible. They are so basic that other themes are either subsumed under them or inextricably bound up with them.

Creation

Creation was not an accident. It was not the result of blind and random forces. There is purpose back of the universe since God created it. Genesis begins like this: "In the beginning God created the heavens and the earth" (1:1). I had a college professor who used to say that this is the sublimest sentence in the English language.

God was not like a tired craftsman beneath the burden of creation. He created with ease and did it by the power of His Word. God spoke and creation happened. There is a kind of refrain that runs through the creation story: "And God said . . . and God said . . . and God said."

It is a very interesting and profitable study to compare the first chapter of Genesis with the first fourteen verses of John's Gospel. Genesis tells about the original creation while John tells about the new creation, and in both cases God created by the power of His Word. In John's account the Word was Jesus Christ.

John begins his Gospel like this: "In the beginning was the Word, and the Word was with God, and the Word was God.

He was in the beginning with God; all things were made through him, and without him was not anything made that was made" (1:1-3). It is made unmistakably clear that the Word was Jesus Christ: "And the Word was made flesh and dwelt among us" (v. 14, KJV). The agent of creation was Christ.

Christ didn't create the universe and then get locked out of it, and He was not so transcendent that He disdained to enter it. In Christ, God made a strange, new radical entrance into the world. He took upon Himself our frail and fragile form and dwelt among us. He clothed Himself in flesh and assumed our humanity so He could touch with our hands, see with our eyes, and feel our hurt and pain. This was the incarnation. God was on a mission of creation, to make all things new in Christ.

According to the Genesis account, God's creation moved in an orderly and progressive way, and the climactic and most creative act was to bring forth a creature called man. He was like everything God created. He was grounded in nature and went through the cycle of birth, growth, maturity, and death. Yet he was different, radically different: God stamped upon man His own image. Because of that, man was an immensely complex, gifted, and powerful creature. In a sense, man was both the center and zenith of God's creation.

Let us make four observations about creation.

1. Creation has a theological meaning. The Genesis account of creation is theological. The purpose is told in the opening sentence of the story: "In the beginning God created." The purpose is not to tell how but who. Science is concerned with the how, theology with the who.

The plain truth is the Bible has no science in the modern sense of the term, and that is true because the Bible has no concept of natural law which is the basis of modern science. Let us use the Bible as a story of God's revelation of Himself in an effort to seek, find, and save us and our world. Thus the Bible is like an impregnable fortress. It needs no defense. It is our privilege to declare it, knowing the Bible will fight and win its own battles.

2. Because God created, our life and existence have meaning.

This is a message our world badly needs to hear. There is a shadow of meaninglessness that lies heavy over the modern mind. For a lot of people, life doesn't make sense. It is like a jigsaw puzzle where the pieces do not fit into a pattern of meaning. It is as if we were caught in revolving doors that go round and round, leading nowhere. It seems sometimes as if we have been pushed into blind alleys or up dead-end streets. The fact that God created speaks to this mood of doubt. God has created us, planned a high destiny for us, and put our feet in ways that lead somewhere.

Despite the feeling of meaninglessness that creeps over many of us, most people find at least a relative and tentative meaning for life. Obviously we find some meaning for the week that lies ahead, else we would not enter it. We would stay in bed on Monday morning. We achieve meaning in terms of human relations, with people whom we love and who love us. We find meaning in our work, in our vocational commitments. We discover meaning in causes we espouse, causes that we feel are worth risking our lives for. We find purpose in all of these, but the meaning is relative and tentative. What about the people whom we have loved when they walk no more with us, when from faltering hands we drop our vocational skills and our work is done, when the causes we have espoused fail, and when our lives seem to be fulfilled no longer, having become empty and hollow? It is in these experiences, which all of us have, that we learn how relative and tentative these meanings are. It is then that we know how badly we need some final and ultimate meaning, a meaning that continues when the more relative ones lie in shambles about our feet. Where will we find it? In our Christian faith that tells us a loving God has created us and that He intends good for us.

3. God is not nature. He is nature's God.

As we know, most of the ancient religions were nature religions. The gods were the forces of nature personified. For example, the Canaanitish gods, Baalim, which Israel found in

Canaan, were fertility gods, and the religion was fertility cults. But you do not find anything like that in Israel's religion. Yahweh is not nature. He is not the forces of nature personified, not even in subtle and sophisticated ways. Yahweh is nature's God.

Augustine once wrote: "And what is this? I asked the earth, and it answered me, 'I am not He'; and whatsoever things are in it confessed the same. I asked the sea and the deeps, and the living creeping things, and they answered, 'We are not thy God; seek above us.' I asked the moving air, and the whole air with its inhabitants answered, 'Anaximenes was deceived; I am not God.' I asked the heavens, sun, moon, stars, and they say, 'nor are we the God whom thou seekest.' And I replied unto all the things which encompass the door of my flesh, 'Ye have told me of my God that ye are not He; tell me something of Him! And they cried out with a loud voice, 'He made us' ... I asked the whole frame of the world about my God; and it answered me, 'I am not He, but He made me.' "[1]

Joseph Addison, in his hymn, "The Spacious Firmament on High," writes of the stars:

> In reason's ear they all rejoice,
>   And utter forth a glorious voice;
> Forever singing, as they shine,
>   "The hand that made us is divine."

4. Creation was good.

When God had completed His creation, He looked out upon it and was pleased with what He saw. There was no evil in it, and it was not marred or flawed in any sense. There was no moral shadow across it as a result of its being physical and finite. God was not afraid to touch it lest His hands be soiled by it. No, it was good, and God saw it as such. Twice the goodness of creation is acclaimed. "And God saw that it was good" (Gen. 1:12). And again, "And God saw everything that he had made, and behold, it was very good" (v. 31).

Fallen Creation

Something went radically wrong with God's creation. The God who looked out on His creation and saw that it was very good, looked out upon it another day and saw that it was bad, very bad. His creation had fallen. The basic relations in God's creation became broken. The third and fourth chapters of Genesis tell of this tragic fall.

What happened? What went wrong? Who or what turned against the Creator? Did earth or heaven revolt against its maker? No, creation fell from its zenith. It became corrupt, not at the bottom but at the top. Man, the fairest of all God's creation, rebelled, disobeyed, sinned.

You remember the story, set in a garden, so simply and vividly told that it is arresting to a child and yet so profound that theologians cannot fathom its deepest meanings. Adam and Eve, our ancient forebears, were the caretakers of that garden. There was a tree in the middle of the garden the fruit of which they were forbidden to eat. They had been solemnly warned that if they ate it they would die. The serpent, the representative of evil in our world, tempted Adam and Eve. The temptation seemed to have appealed to the pride and desire for power in their lives. The serpent said: "For God knows that when you eat of it your eyes will be opened, and you will be like God, knowing good and evil" (Gen. 3:5). They yielded, and God drove them out of the garden. They who had been the proud keepers of a beautiful garden became homeless and roving vagabonds on earth.

On that fateful day, man and woman took a terrible tumble. Down from their pinnacle they came. We are the Humpty Dumpties of our world. We've had a great fall. We are the broken ones. And all our power, knowledge, science, technology, and know-how cannot put us back together again.

More than men and women are fallen. The original sin set off a kind of chain reaction. Nature is fallen, and creation is marred.

Creation is like a seamless robe. Cut it anywhere and the whole garment is damaged. Our universe has about it a wholeness and unity. It is one verse, a uni-verse. Anything that affects one part of it affects the whole.

It is only in recent years that I have been aware of how prominent nature is in the fall. God said: "Cursed is the ground because of you; in toil you shall eat of it all the days of your life; thorns and thistles it shall bring forth to you; and you shall eat the plants of the field" (Gen. 3:17-18).

Men and women are flawed and nature is flawed. I think of how ruthless and destructive nature can be with its floods, tornados, earthquakes, famine, and disease. It is indeed red in tooth and claw. It is so careless of human life and human values. I am shocked, sometimes horrified, when I see babies born without limbs. It is even more frightening to see them born with limited or no mental capacity.

Not only are human beings and nature flawed, but all of creation is broken. There seems to be conflict, brokenness, and fragmentation beyond our world and human history. The cosmos seems to be cracked. The split that lies across all human existence appears to be extended out into the universe. Paul, in the eighth chapter of Romans, sees the whole creation, like human existence, in need of being redeemed. Thus he writes: "For the creation waits with eager longing for the revealing of the sons of God; for the creation was subjected to futility, not of its own will but by the will of him who subjected it in hope, because the creation itself will be set free from its bondage to decay and obtain the glorious liberty of the children of God" (Rom. 8:19-21).

But how do you preach about the fall? It is so far back in such a remote past. It stands in the predawn of our history. You have to do two things. First, you have to contemporize its message, bringing it from the remote past into the present. Second, you have to preach its truth existentially; you preach it to people in their historical, personal, concrete situation.

Eden is where we live. The fall is something that happens to us.

A good many years ago I preached a sermon on "My Name Is Adam." I told the congregation that was their name, too. The thing that happened to Adam happens to me and to them.

If I were preaching on Eden, my topic might well be: "Eden Is At 716 Windsor Lane." There is where I live.

New Creation

The Christian message runs in a kind of cycle. First, God has created a good world. Because He has, life has meaning and possibilities. Then, there is bad news. God's good world has become a bad world. It is a fallen world. The basic relationships that sustain us have been broken. Finally, there is good news. Someone has come who can mend our brokenness, reconcile us to God and our brother, and give us new life. He is Jesus Christ.

In a world where so much of the news is bad, we have good news. A preacher standing in his pulpit with a week behind him in which the headlines of the newspaper have told of war, tragedy, and suffering, can say to his people: "I've got good news for you."

The Christian gospel speaks of new creation in three ways—new life, a new humanity, and a new order.

Can God change human life? Any religion that survives must give a positive answer to that question. If it cannot, it will pass. Christianity gives a resounding yes.

Paul talked about how Christ can give new life. His classical statement was: "If any one is in Christ, he is a new creation; the old has passed away, behold, the new has come" (2 Cor. 5:17). Paul was not speculating or theorizing. He was telling what had happened to him. He had met Christ along the Damascus way and the risen Lord had spun him around in his tracks, causing him to pivot on a 180-degree angle. His face was set in a new direction and his feet in a new path. He loved that which he had hated and hated that which he had loved.

He called him Lord whom he had once cursed and despised. How would he tell of that? He was a new creation in Christ.

Saint Francis of Assisi said that the day he met Jesus Christ, his life was changed. He seemed to be looking at a new world through new eyes. The flowers were brighter, the sky was bluer, and the birds sang more sweetly.

When these new lives which Christ has created are brought together, we get a new humanity.

Paul looked out upon a world that was broken in many ways. Great cleavages divided it and threatening chasms made it dangerous. But a miracle was being wrought. God was bridging those chasms, bringing together people long separated and hostile in peace and love. Paul speaks specifically about this in Galatians 3:28: "There is neither Jew nor Greek"—the cultural-religious barrier had been removed; "there is neither slave nor free"—the socioeconomic barrier had been overcome; "there is neither male nor female"—the sexual barrier, where men were greatly superior to women, had been eliminated; "for you are all one in Christ Jesus."

Paul saw the greatest cleavage existing between Jew and Gentile. The possibility of their being brought together in peace and love staggered the imagination. It seemed impossible. But the impossible was happening before their eyes. "For he is our peace," Paul wrote, "who has made us both one, and has broken down the dividing wall of hostility, by abolishing in his flesh the law of commandments and ordinances, that he might create in himself one new man in place of the two, so making peace" (Eph. 2:14-15). A new humanity was being created. It was beyond dispute. They could see it being born. And the church, the body of Christ, was its habitat.

Finally, a part of the good news is that there is to be a new order with a new heaven, a new earth, and a new city. Revelation 21 begins with a startling announcement: "Then I saw a new heaven and a new earth; for the first heaven and the first earth had passed away, and the sea was no more. And I saw the holy city, new Jerusalem, coming down out of heaven from God, prepared as a bride adorned for her husband" (vv. 1-2).

In that new city, the chasm between God and men will have been completely overcome: "Behold the dwelling of God is with men. He will dwell with them, and they shall be his people, and God himself will be with them" (v. 3).

The new life in the new city will be very different: "[God] will wipe away every tear from their eyes, and death shall be no more, neither shall there be mourning nor crying nor pain any more, for the former things have passed away" (v. 4).

There we shall be able to do those things which we have not been able to do here. We shall render to God a pure service and offer Him perfect worship, and we shall love our fellows with perfect love. And there we shall have the deepest longing of the human heart fulfilled. With our poor vision healed, we shall see God face to face. "They shall see his face" (22:4).

When you study great biblical themes like these, it is like striking a homiletical anvil, with sparks flying everywhere.

Thought Starters

A series of three sermons: Creation, Fallen Creation, New Creation.

A series of three sermons on New Creation: A New Life, A New Humanity, A New Order.

Other sermons: No Dead-end Streets; Eden Is Where I Live; My Name Is Adam; We Are the Humpty-Dumpties; The Church and the New Humanity; A New Life Befitting the New Order; They Shall See His Face.

Scripture

Creation: Genesis 1:1-31; 2:1-24; John 1:1-5; Colossians 1:15-20.

Fallen Creation: Genesis 3:1-24; 4:1-26; Jeremiah 13:20-27; Romans 1:18-28; 2:1-29; 3:1-20.

New Creation: Psalm 51:1-14; Isaiah 42:5-9; 48:6-8; John

3:1-14; Romans 8:18-25; 2 Corinthians 5:16-21; Ephesians 2:11-22; 4:17-24; 1 Peter 1:22-25; Revelation 21:1-16.

Texts

1. Creation: Genesis 1:1,31; John 1:3; Colossians 1:16.
2. Fallen Creation: Genesis 3:6; 4:9; 6:5; Jeremiah 13:23; Romans 3:12,22-23.
3. New Creation: Psalm 51:10; Ezekiel 36:26; John 3:7; 2 Corinthians 5:17; Galatians 6:15; Ephesians 2:14-15; Colossians 3:9-10; 1 Peter 1:23; Revelation 21:1,5.

Illustrations

God, no tired craftsman (Gen. 1:1-31); Creation by the Word (Gen. 1:3; John 1:3); Light, God's first creation (Gen. 1:3); An ordered creation (Eccl. 3:1-9); Ownership by virtue of creation (Ps. 50:10-11).

Sin as pride (Gen. 3:1-7); Sin like a predatory animal (Gen. 4:1-7); Sin as the misuse of power (Gen. 11:1-9).

Nicodemus, a man who must be born again (John 3:7); New creation in Christ (2 Cor. 5:17); The new life (Col. 3:9-10); The new humanity (Eph. 3:7-10); New heaven and new earth (Isa. 65:17; 66:22; 2 Pet. 3:13; Rev. 21:1-4).

Note

1. John Baille, *A Diary of Readings* (New York: Charles Scribner's Sons, 1955), p. 191.

2
Persons:
Their Grandeur and Misery

We are paradoxical creatures. We are mortal, yet our hearts sing of eternal things; we are sinners, yet we are called to be saints in Christ. Pascal said man is the pride and refuse of the universe. He also spoke of the grandeur and misery of man. It is on that paradox that we are reflecting.

The Paradox

We are made in the image of God, yet we are sinners. The image has been blurred, marred, defaced, almost destroyed, but not quite. There is always a faint trace of that image. We live in the hope of its being retraced.

John Knox speaks of man as being both splendid and wretched. "In a word," he wrote, "man is fallen. God's good creation, while not destroyed, has been despoiled—corrupted, twisted, perverted, as by some terrible accident. Such is man, and to be a sinner is to share in the humanity—in the original and ineffable splendor of it and in the wretchedness which has overtaken it. Neither the splendor nor the wretchedness is our own in any separate or individual sense; they are the splendor and wretchedness of man. In Adam we were all created, in Adam we have all sinned; in Adam we all die."[1]

Dr. Ralph Sockman, one of the greatest preachers of the past generation, lived in New York City for over fifty years. During that period, he said two events moved that city more deeply than any other. They were the sinking of the *Titantic* and the assasination of President John F. Kennedy. The day of the sinking of the *Titantic,* two cartoons appeared in one of the city's newspapers. One showed the *Titantic* crashing into a giant iceberg and carried the caption: "The Primacy of Nature; the Weakness of Man." The other cartoon showed a man giving up his seat on a lifeboat, which was his last chance of survival, to a little girl. The caption of this cartoon was: "The Primacy of Man; the Weakness of Nature." Here we see again the paradox that marks our lives. We are both weak and strong.

Our modern world with its science and technology has not blurred this paradox but has thrown it into clearer focus.

Our astronauts find their power exhilirating. They have cut free of their earthboundness, transcended their earth, and are becoming masters of space. As they sail through the vastness of cosmic space they must feel as if they can reach out and almost touch the hand of God. From certain heights they look down upon their planet and see it as a small blue disc floating in space. It looks so small and insignificant. At times they would like to bear some good message of hope from earth to the larger universe. But they remember how troubled earth is. It is at war. It finds it hard to make peace, and the peace it achieves it cannot keep. Our space technology has outdistanced our human relations. The astronauts know that they are better at controlling their space craft than they are at managing their hearts. Therefore, the paradox, rather than being hidden, is revealed. We are strong, but weak; grand, but miserable.

Our Grandeur

Let us look briefly at one side of the paradox—our grandeur. Its recognition comes from many sources.

Shakespeare wrote of us: "What a piece of work is a man! how noble in reason! how infinite in faculty! In form and moving how express and admirable! in action, how like an angel! in apprehension, how like a god!"

Pascal wrote of us: "Man is but a reed, the most feeble thing in nature, but he is a thinking reed. The entire universe need not arm itself to crush him. A vapour, a drop of water suffices to kill him. But, if the universe were to crush him, man would still be more noble than that which killed him, because he knows that he dies and the advantage which the universe has over him; the universe knows nothing of this."[2]

But the Bible knows best of all our grandeur. We were the crowning act of God's creation. When God had created everything else, he said: "Let us make man in our image, after our likeness; and let them have dominion over the fish of the sea, and over the birds of the air, and over the cattle, and over all the earth, and over every creeping thing that creeps upon the earth" (Gen. 1:26).

The eighth Psalm, along with Genesis 1:26-28, is a fine statement of our grandeur. The psalmist sees grandeur emerging as a part of a paradox. Man is so small, yet so great. He is dwarfed by his universe. "When I look at thy heavens," the psalmist wrote, "the work of thy fingers, the moon and the stars which thou hast established; what is man that thou art mindful of him, and the son of man that thou dost care for him?" But his smallness must not deceive you.

So the psalmist continues: "Yet thou has made him a little less than God, and dost crown him with glory and honor. Thou hast given him dominion over the works of thy hands; thou hast put all things under his feet, all sheep and oxen, and also the beasts of the field, the birds of the air, and the fish of the sea, whatever passes along the paths of the sea" (vv. 3-8).

"Thou hast made him little less than God." Imagine it! Nothing surpasses that evaluation of us.

We find our grandeur and uniqueness in the fact that we have been created in the image of God, that God knows us, loves us, and cares for us.

What does it mean to be created in the image of God? Does it mean that we have rational powers? Animals can do rudimentary thinking, but only human beings can do conceptual and abstract thinking. Does it mean that we are free and therefore responsible for our actions in ways animals never can be? Does it mean that we can be self-transcendent, that in some real sense we can stand above ourselves and see ourselves think and act? Does it mean that we can transcend time at least partially, look back and remember, and also look forward and dare to predict the future? Only human beings can envision their death. Does it mean that we are religious, that we seek God and worship Him? Only men and women build altars and pray.

It is possible that being created in the image of God means any or all of these.

But these concepts seem to be a little too abstract for biblical thought. It more likely means God has given us semisovereignty, that He has entrusted to us the keeping of the world, that we are God's representatives on earth. After creating persons in His own image, God blessed them and said, "Be fruitful and multiply, and fill the earth and subdue it; and have dominion over the fish of the sea and over the birds of the air and over every living thing that moves upon the earth" (Gen. 1:28). The eighth Psalm says the same thing "Thou hast given him dominion over the works of thy hands; thou hast put all things under his feet" (Ps. 8:6).

Gerhard von Rad has written: "Just as powerful earthly kings, to indicate their claim to dominion, erect an image of themselves in the provinces of their empire where they do not personally appear, so man is placed upon earth in God's image as God's sovereign emblem. He is really only God's representative, summoned to maintain and enforce God's claim to dominion over earth. The decisive thing about man's similarity to God, therefore, is his function in the nonhuman world."[3]

One day Jesus asked for a coin. "Whose likeness and inscription is this?" He asked, and they replied, "Caesar's" (Matt. 22:20-21). The image on the coin obviously bore a likeness to Caesar. Just so with us. Because we are made in the image of God we bear a kind of likeness to God. That image, while probably telling something about our rationality, our freedom, our partial transcendence over self and time, and our religious nature tells essentially something, as has already been said, about our dominion over the created order. There is a sense in which God has turned it over to us.

This concept of the image of God gives a high seriousness to our life on this planet. If we keep earth beautiful, productive, and habitable, we are to be praised. However, if earth's beauty is marred, if her wealth is exploited and used up, if she becomes bare and nonproductive, if she becomes sick with our refuse and waste, we can blame nobody but ourselves. If we turn our vast technological power to humane ends, if we produce enough to feed and clothe our world, if we achieve peace and brotherhood, we are to be praised. However, if we tolerate social inequities where the rich have too much and the poor have too little, if we allow racial discrimination and bigotry, if we misuse the good resources of our earth in a mad armament race, if we destroy life on this planet in a nuclear holocaust, we are to be blamed. We cannot put the blame on nature, history, or God.

How does this grandeur express itself? In five ways.

1. Our grandeur appears in our carrying out God's commission to subdue the earth. We have done well here. We have shown how ingenious we are in making the earth productive, eliminating time and distance, and in the conquering of disease. Our science and technology, which are instruments of our conquest, are awesome in their versatility and power.

Not being satisfied in subduing our earth, we now turn to space. Our conquest there will no doubt be more impressive than our subduing of earth. We have overcome our earth-boundness in our time, having become cosmic. The Russians call their space fliers cosmonauts which means sailors of the cosmos. It is a lovely term, but we use even a lovelier and more poetic one. We call ours astronauts which means sailors of the stars. The late John F. Kennedy envisioned our conquest of space when he urged us "to set sail on this new sea." The new sea was the sea of space, the cosmic sea. We are becoming as comfortable there as we are on the seas of earth.[4]

2. Our grandeur appears in our intellectual and imaginative

powers. Because of these we are so apt in our conquest of earth and space. Our science and technology are the creations of our minds. Our minds explore the secrets and mystery of our universe. There are no off limits to our inquiring and probing rational powers.

Our imagination gives us great art and music before which we often stand in awe and reverence. Our imagination envisions that which is not, and we then proceed to create it with our ingenious powers.

We combine our intellectual and imaginative powers in creating great institutions that stand for centuries. We create great schools, great museums, great laboratories, and great research centers.

3. Our grandeur is seen in our moral power. We frequently do the courageous, heroic, and sacrificial thing.

I think of the prophet Nathan's confronting King David after David's great sin of committing adultery with Bathsheba and then having her husband Uriah slain in battle. You remember how he told the story about the rich man who had many flocks and herds and the poor man who had one little ewe lamb which was like a member of his family. A traveler visited the wealthy man and, rather than taking one of his own flock or herd, he took the poor man's ewe lamb, killed it, and prepared it for the stranger. David's anger was kindled against this kind of high-handed injustice. So David said: "As the Lord lives, the man who has done this deserves to die; and he shall restore the lamb fourfold, because he did this thing, and because he had no pity" (2 Sam. 12:5-6). Then Nathan, looking this powerful king straight in the eye, said: "You are the man" (v. 7). It required courage to do that. He took his life into his own hands. There is grandeur in courage like that.

I remember Robert Maxwell from World War II. Robert was from Oregon and had been reared by his grandmother. I have never known a finer young man. I recall the night in southern France when the enemy was counterattacking and threw a hand grenade into the midst of his communication crew. The group was immobile but Robert was not. He grabbed his blanket and fell on the grenade. When it went off, his body and his blanket absorbed the shrapnel. He was wounded but his buddies went free of injury. Procedures were begun immediately to get for him the Congressional Medal of Honor, the Army's highest award. I feel like falling on my knees before courage like that. There is grandeur in it.

Often people are ridiculed and rejected for positions they take because they believe them to be just. They had rather fight for causes they believe are right, but which they know will lose, than to champion wrong causes which are popular and will win.

4. Our grandeur can sometimes be seen in our social commitment. We can be loving, caring, and accepting. We can be good neighbors. We often reach across social and racial barriers, keep open communication when people are afraid or reluctant to talk. We build homes where there is mutual love and trust, communities where democracy is a reality, and courts that are faithful to justice. We often achieve a substantial degree of compassion and humaness in our society.

5. Grandeur can be seen in our spiritual devotion. There are men and women who walk with God and have as their supreme desire to love and serve Him. They give themselves to prayer, reflection, and meditation. They exult in the Word of God and hide it in their hearts. They are broken and contrite of heart, trusting not their own goodness but the grace of Christ. They long to be pure of heart.

I think of Saint Francis of Assisi, a gentle Christlike man who is still inspiring our world. When we remember him, we would like to offer God a pure devotion. I recall his famous prayer:

> Lord, make me an instrument of thy peace,
> Where there is hatred let me sow love;
> Where there is injury, pardon;
> Where there is doubt, faith;
> Where there is despair, hope;

Where there is darkness, light;
Where there is sadness, joy.

There is spiritual grandeur in that prayer.

Our Misery

We are grand but we are also miserable. Let us look at our misery.

Why this misery? Basically for three reasons: We are set in a decaying order, we have sensitive emotional natures, and we are sinful.

1. We are part of a transient, decaying, and perishing order.

In the second story of creation we read: "Then the Lord God formed man of dust from the ground, and breathed into his nostrils the breath of life; and man became a living being" (Gen. 2:7).

We are made of dust, and we are grounded like trees and animals in the physical order which changes and decays. We are born, grow, mature, become old, and eventually die. Our youth passes, our beauty fades, our strength ebbs into weakness, and we die too soon. Our skills fall from faltering hands and we die before our work is done.

One of the saddest and most painful things is to see a strong man or woman have their strength and vitality reduced by the years. It is sad to see someone lose their hearing and be cut off from the world of sound or to see someone lose their vision and be cut off from the world of sight. Many are obsessed with the fear of growing old. The aging process is painful.

Do you remember how the aging process is described in the twelfth chapter of Ecclesiastes? It is beautiful but the beauty serves to heighten the pathos and sadness of growing old. The writer begins like this: "Remember also your creator in the days of your youth, before the evil days come, and the years draw nigh, when you will say, 'I have no pleasure in them'" (v. 1).

Reinhold Niebuhr was a strong man in body, mind, and spirit, but he could not escape the devastation of time. When he was sixty he suffered a stroke which left him lame in his left side. He went through several severe depressions. Niebuhr had written the meaningful prayer used by Alcoholics Anonymous: "God, give us the grace to accept with serenity the things that cannot be changed, courage to change the things that should be changed, and the wisdom to distinguish the one from the other."

Over a period of time he received two letters a week inquiring about the prayer, whether the author was Francis of Assisi or even an admiral who had used it in a shipboard worship service. Every letter embarrassed him because he remembered that his life belied the serenity of which the prayer spoke. "I confessed my embarrassment to our family physician," he wrote, "who had a sense of humor touched with gentle cynicism. 'Don't worry,' he said, 'doctors and preachers are not expected to practice what they preach.' I had to be content with this minimal consolation."[5]

2. We have sensitive emotional natures. We know fear, anxiety, and depression. Sometimes life can be almost completely engulfed in darkness. Often the more brilliant and sensitive a person is the more he suffers.

Harry Emerson Fosdick was the great preacher of the generation just passed. Nobody could preach the way Fosdick could. He was without peer in the pulpit. While a middler in the seminary he suffered a nervous breakdown and had to go home for a year of rest. During that period he felt at times as if he were falling into a bottomless pit of darkness. He was severely depressed. In his autobiography, *For the Living of These Days*, he tells of the morning when he was tempted to commit suicide. He had a razor blade in his hand when from somewhere in the house he heard his father calling, "Harry! Harry! where are you?" Through the years he shuddered to think what might have happened if his father had not called him.

So much of our suffering is mental and emotional in nature.

3. We are sinful.

I have talked about Nathan's confrontation with King David. Nathan risked his life for a principle, and in him we see the moral grandeur of a man. But if we see the grandeur of a man in Nathan, we see moral misery in David. David had committed a great sin. Think of his moral wretchedness. While God forgave him, the memory of that sin must have burned in him like a consuming fire. He must have walked always in its terrible shadow.

But why does sin make us so miserable? For three reasons: It separates us, enslaves us, and destroys us.

Sin separates. If I could use only one word to describe the human tragedy, it would be *separation.* Sin separates us from God, the brother, the inner self, and nature. Sin cuts us off from the sources of life. Sin blocks the way to the springs of life.

Sin enslaves. It destroys our freedom and wastes our dignity. We know a moral and spiritual bondage just as real as prison bars, just as real as cuffs about our wrists and chains about our ankles. We are bound. We are slaves. We are captives just as much as prisoners of war and those who are hostages.

Sin destroys. As already stated, sin destroys us by cutting us off from the springs of life. It destroys our freedom and dignity by enslaving us. Sin brings death. Paul writes, "For the wages of sin is death" (Rom. 6:23). James says: "Then desire when it has conceived gives birth to sin; and sin when it is full-grown brings forth death" (Jas. 1:15).

Grandeur Restored

I talked in the first chapter about the cycle Christian faith runs. Here is another one—grandeur, misery, and grandeur restored.

The hope of the gospel is that God has acted in such a way in Christ that grandeur is restored.

The first Adam was a despoiler of life, bringing misery and death. The second Adam, Jesus Christ, brought grandeur and life. Paul could say, "For as in Adam all die, so also in Christ shall all be made alive" (1 Cor. 15:22). (See also Rom. 5:17 and 1 Cor. 15:45.)

Jesus told many stories, but none tells better of restored grandeur than the prodigal son. The young man obviously belonged to a fine family. He was well-born, well-bred, and well-loved. There was true grandeur in his relationship with his family. Then he besmirched and squandered it. But the father restored the grandeur of that relationship around a banquet table.

How does Christ, the second Adam, restore the faded grandeur? Let me suggest four ways.

1. Christ thrusts into the midst of the decaying order where death is inevitable, a quality of life which the New Testament calls eternal life. It is quality of life born of a new relationship with God, the primary spring of life, and the brother, the secondary spring of life.

Paul, in the closing part of the eighth chapter of Romans, runs the full gamut of changes, vicissitudes, and tragedy, and concludes that nothing "will be able to separate us from the love of God in Christ Jesus our Lord" (v. 39). Christ sets us in a new relationship with God and that is the one relationship that can never be broken. Herein is the real secret of eternal life.

2. Christ restores us to moral grandeur.

The great moral ideal is to love the way Jesus did. Jesus said this is how the world would identify his followers through the ages. (See John 13:35.) We are not to be known by the way we dress, nor by our religious words and pious gestures, nor by our denominational labels, not even by our theology. We would be known by our love. It is an ethical identification. Does this shock you?

Yet, here we face a real problem. We often cannot give plain, ordinary love. How often we don't love our spouses, our children, and our neighbors down the street the way we should. How can we love the way Jesus did? We can't unless our moral grandeur is restored, and then our love will be only an approximation of what we have seen in Jesus.

Christ restores our moral grandeur by giving us new hearts, by empowering us through the Holy Spirit, and setting our lives in a loving and redeemed fellowship which is the church.

We become new creations in Christ. Paul, out of his own experience, could say: "If any one is in Christ, he is a new creation; the old has passed away, behold the new has come" (2 Cor. 5:17). The new heart is congenial to the ethical ideal.

We are not asked to love the way Jesus did in our own strength. Power is given from beyond us. Paul could say: "God's love has been poured into our hearts through the Holy Spirit which has been given to us" (Rom. 5:5). When our heart is like a cup filled with anger, the Holy Spirit pours the love of God into it, displacing the hostility. The power to love like that is a gift, not an achievement.

The church, when it is authentic, helps us to love because it is a loving fellowship. Paul could write to the Ephesian Christians: "Let all bitterness and wrath and anger and clamor and slander be put away from you, with all malice, and be kind to one another, tenderhearted, forgiving one another, as God in Christ forgave you" (Eph. 4:31-32). Moral grandeur is restored as we become members of the body of Christ which is the church.

3. Christ restores us to social grandeur. Where does this take place? In the church. The church is His family. There we are loved, accepted, and affirmed. There we find brothers and sisters in Christ. They say to us: "We will not let you walk alone, we will walk with you. We will not let you be friendless anymore, we will be your friends, we will laugh with you and we will weep with you. We will not let you feel cheap and worthless anymore, we see great beauty and value in you."

4. Christ restores spiritual grandeur. Our broken relationship with God is healed. We who have been the enemies of God become His friends; we who have been far away are drawn near We who have been alien to His household become His

sons and daughters. Christ, with a finger of grace, retraces the image of God, that image that has been marred, blurred, almost defaced. Then we are able to know our real identity.

As we preach, let us run this cycle many times with its many variations—grandeur, misery, and grandeur restored. In so doing, we shall be in the midstream of biblical faith and at the heart of our gospel. And we shall be in touch with the anguish and hope of human life.

Thought Starters

A series of three sermons on a Basic Cycle of Faith: Grandeur, Misery, Grandeur Restored.

Three sermons on Our Sin and Misery: Sin Separates, Enslaves, Destroys.

Four sermons on Our Grandeur Restored: Physical, Moral, Social, Spiritual.

Other sermons: A Paradox of Our Existence; Whose Image? A Little Less Than God; Beneath Our Feet; God Has Turned It Over to Us; Sailors of the Stars; Where Our Grandeur Appears; Defaced, but Not Destroyed; The Image Restored; Connecting the Springs of Life Again; The One Relationship that Can Never be Broken.

Scripture

1. Grandeur: Genesis 1:26-30; 2:4-24; Psalm 8:1-9.
2. Misery: Genesis 3:22-24; 4:8-16; 6:5-8; 11:1-9; 2 Samuel 12:1-15; Psalms 39:1-13; 103:15-16; Isaiah 40:6-8; Romans 1:18-32; 3:9-20; 7:13-25.

Texts

1. Grandeur: Genesis 1:26-27; 2:15; 1 Samuel 10:9; 2 Samuel 3:38; Psalm 8:5.
2. Misery: 2 Samuel 12:7; Psalms 39:12b; 90:3-8; Proverbs 14:13; Jeremiah 10:23; 13:23; 17:9; Romans 7:19.

Illustrations

Dominion over nature (Gen. 1:26,28-30; Ps. 8:6-8); The ideal woman (Prov. 31:10-31); A little less than God (Ps. 8:5); Thirsting for God (Ps. 42:1-2); Grace restores grandeur (Luke 15:20-24; John 1:12); Seeing possibilities in people (John 1:42); God and we see persons differently (1 Sam. 16:1-13); Jealousy (1 Sam. 18:6-16); A prophet confronts a wicked king (2 Sam. 12:1-15); Contemplation of death (Isa. 38:9-16); Like grass and flowers (Isa. 40:6-8); Like a leopard and Ethiopian (Jer. 13:23); Humans as God's burden (Jer. 23:33); Brevity of life (Ps. 144:4; John 9:4; Jas. 4:14); Misery caused by strong drink (Prov. 23:29-35); Guilt makes cowards of us (Prov. 28:1); The misery caused by monotony (Eccl. 1:1-11); Old age and evil days (Eccl. 12:1-8); Fragility of human relations (Ps. 41:9); The desire to escape (Ps. 55:1-8); Our lostness (Luke 15:1-24); The sin of pride, the grace of humility (Luke 18:9-14); Loving darkness rather than light (John 3:19); A fierce conflict within (Rom. 7:13-20).

Notes

1. John Knox, *Life in Christ Jesus* (New York: The Seabury Press, 1966), p. 42.

2. Blaise Pascal, *Pensees* (New York: E. P. Dutton and Company, Inc. Last reprinted in 1948), p. 97.

3. Gerhard von Rad, *Genesis* (Philadelphia: The Westminster Press, 1961), p. 58.

4. Chevis F. Horne, *Crisis in the Pulpit* (Grand Rapids: Baker Book House, 1975), p. 140.

5. *The Christian Century,* December 19-26, 1984.

3
Sin:
Humanity's Blight

The two great tragedies of human life are sin and death. Men and women everywhere walk in the shadow of their guilt and into the night of their death. We are sinners, all of us; and we die, all of us.

We are concerned here with the first of these two tragedies. I am speaking of sin as humanity's blight. It is like a disease that has infected all of humankind, making all of us sick.

Reinhold Niebuhr once said that you can document sin more easily than any other theological truth. You don't have to have a Bible or a book on theology. The newspaper can tell you.

S. J. DeVries has written: "It might even be said that in the Bible man has only two theological concerns involving himself: his sin and his salvation. Man finds himself in sin and suffers its painful effects; God graciously offers salvation from it. This is, in essence, what the whole Bible is about."[1]

The Bible obviously takes sin seriously. As preachers we must. We can't speak of salvation unless we know how lost we are. We can't tell of healing unless we know how sick we are.

What Is Sin?

Sin is a theological term which has to do with our relationship with God. Sin is against God. I may break a moral law, injure a person, myself, or nature, and I may see these as being only remotely related to God. Yet, they are sin against Him.

Psalm 51 is one of the great penitential psalms. Many scholars believe it was written by David in one of the most an-

guished moments of his life after he had committed adultery
with Bathsheba and had sent Uriah, her husband, to the battle-
front where he was killed. Yet, he never said, "I have committed sin against Bathsheba," or, "I have committed sin against
Uriah." Rather he cried out, "Against thee, thee only, have I
sinned, and done that which is evil in thy sight" (v. 4).

I break a moral law, and God says: "That is My law. You
have sinned against Me." I hurt a person, and God says: "He
was My child. You have sinned against Me." I injure myself
and say to God: "I didn't hurt anybody else. I injured only
myself." His response is quick: "Your life belongs to Me, you
are My child. It is sin against Me." I make nature sick with
pollution, and God says to me: "You have sinned against Me.
Nature is My creation."

Now, let me be more specific. I want to mention four ways
of defining sin.

1. Sin is deviation from God's purpose for our lives. It is
missing the mark. We are like an arrow that has been deflected
from its course, missing its target. Sin is standing at the intersection of life and taking the wrong road. We get headed
wrong. We turn from God's objective. Our basic concern then
is not with sins, but sin—the wrong set of the face.

2. Sin is rebellion. We chafe under God's authority and want
to be free of it. We rebel against Him and set up our own
authority. In some basic sense we mutiny, taking up arms
against God. In our rebellion we become alienated from God.

3. Sin is transgression. We break God's laws which are not
only written in a holy book but are grounded in the universe.
God has built His ethical nature into the moral structure of the
universe. These moral and spiritual laws are just as demanding
and unrelenting as are the physical laws of nature.

If I live in the valley and along the slopes of a mountain, I
have to come to terms with nature's laws if I am to survive. If
I am careless, I can freeze in the blizzards and snow of winter,
and I can be washed away by floods in the spring when the
rains come and the snow melts. Just so with these moral laws.

They have a jagged and cutting edge and I can destroy myself on them.

These laws were built into our universe before they were written in our Bible. But because of God's revelation they are given a more urgent authority and they are seen in clearer light. God's disclosure of Himself gives these laws not a lessened but a heightened meaning.

4. Sin is disobedience. We flout God's authority and disobey Him. Our problem is not so much that of ignorance as it is of willful pride that drives us to take things into our own hands. We know better than we do. We knowingly and deliberately disobey God.

The Dynamics of Sin

Let us see first of all where the dynamics of sin do not lie.

The dynamics of sin do not lie in our bodies. Some philosophies and religions have located them there. They have seen a dualism between matter and spirit, between body and soul. Our bodies are evil by virtue of their being physical. The material is somehow tainted. This idea still clings to us. Many people are ashamed of having physical bodies. They feel there is something wrong with their drives of hunger, thirst, and sex. Yet, when God looked out upon His creation, which included our bodies, He said it was very good. Our bodies may be the occasion of sin but not the cause of it.

Others have seen the dynamics of sin in our finiteness. We don't like our creatureliness and the limitations it imposes on us. So we set about overcoming our finitude. We become pretentious and make claims for ourselves we cannot justify. Yet, our finitude and creatureliness were a part of God's creation when He pronounced it good. Our finitude may be the occasion of our sin, but it is not the reason for it. The dynamics lie elsewhere.

Where then do we locate the dynamics of sin? In our will with its freedom. We do not have as much freedom as we think we have, or as much as we want, but there is a core of freedom at the center of our life that is real and authentic. That core of freedom defies all mechanistic interpretation of life. When we come to some crucial intersection, while we have been goaded, pushed, and conditioned by many forces, we know that the decision we make is not like the turning of cogs in a wheel. We made it in freedom. We didn't make it because we had to, we made it because we wanted to. If we were robots, there would be no such thing as sin. But because in freedom we make wrong choices we know we are sinners.

If the center of the dynamics of sin is our will with its freedom, what then are those dynamics? Let me suggest three.

1. Pride

We have traditionally interpreted the fall in terms of pride. It was pride that drove our ancient forebears to disobey God. They wanted to usurp God's power, to become like God. They became dissatisfied with their low and creaturely state, and wanted something better. They were driven by overweening ambition. They were proud.

Yet, we have had to take another look at that. The behavioral sciences have forced us to. While the behavioral sciences can never be the source of our theology, they can be correctives. They are often able to point out weaknesses of our theology, as well as support its strengths.

Some psychology has been telling us that our problem is not our pride. It is not that we think too highly of ourselves but that we think too little of ourselves. We have a bad self-image, our self-esteem is too low, and we so often feel cheap, worthless, loveless, useless, empty, and guilty. Most people are better and more gifted than they will accept. "Don't condemn man for his pride," some say. "He needs more of it."

But the ideas of pride and low self-esteem are not necessarily contradictory. They may be two sides of the same coin. Were Adam and Eve driven by their poor self-concept to seek more power and a better status? Was it like an inferiority complex that causes one to pose as being superior?

Yet, the truth of the traditional position stands. For whatever reasons, pride was involved in the fall. Pride is a powerful dynamic in our sin.

2. The Appeal of Evil

In the story of the fall we read: "So when the woman saw that the tree was good for food, and that it was a delight to the eyes, and that the tree was to be desired to make one wise, she took of its fruit and ate; and she also gave some to her husband, and he ate" (Gen. 3:6). How tempting that fruit was! It appealed to her physical needs, her aesthetical appreciation, and her intellectual curiosity. How could it have been more powerful?

The plain truth is that we do find evil attractive. The devil is spoken of as appearing as light. He doesn't appear as shadows and darkness. We are lured by that false light. We like to walk toward it as if it were a sunrise.

There is about us a moral gravity that pulls us down. It may be more thrilling than a roller coaster in its downward movement. We give ourselves to those forces that do not love us or care for us, that intend to enslave us and someday to destroy us. Yet, we keep leaping into their arms. Jesus said that light has come and we love darkness better than light because our deeds are evil. Offered the ways of light we choose to walk in darkness. How strange!

3. The Desire and Lust for Power

This is probably the most powerful of the three.

The story of the Tower of Babel is very insightful. It understands the drive for power in men's lives. (See Gen. 11:1-9.) God came down in the midst of their vain striving, gave them different languages which divided them, and scattered them over the face of the earth. The desire for power was their undoing.

The temptations of Jesus are very revealing at this point. I would like to make four observations about them. First, they occurred when He was not with people. Usually temptation has a social setting. But He was away from the garish lights of the city, the tempting voices of the crowd, and the alluring ways of evil men who may be very suave and polite. Again, the temptations were not crude, vulgar, and obscene. They were very decent and do not shock the finest and most sensitive people. Further, there are idealistic possibilities in all three of them. That is very strange. We do not associate idealism with temptations to do evil. Finally, they were temptations to power. The fact they seemed so decent and innocent made them all the more dangerous.

You remember Jesus had been fasting for forty days and was very hungry. Lying at His feet were flat stones that may have reminded Him of the little loaves of bread His mother had baked in her oven in Nazareth. And Satan said: "If you are the Son of God, command these stones to become loaves of bread" (Matt. 4:3). It was the temptation of social and economic power. His body, with its pangs of hunger, must have been crying out for bread. And in His imagination did He see the poor and hungry, famished faces, and little children with bloated stomachs? If He should use this power He could feed, not only Himself, but them. You can see the possibilities of idealism in this power.

Then the devil took him to the holy city, and set Him on the pinnacle of the Temple, and said to Him, "If you are the Son of God, throw yourself down" (v. 6). This was the appeal of dramatic and spectacular power. Idealism could have been hidden in this. Could He not have used this power to confirm His being the Son of God? Would that not have been good?

Finally, the devil took Him to a high mountain and before Him lay the kingdoms of the world with their glory. The devil said to Him, "All these I will give you, if you will fall down and worship me" (v. 9). This was the appeal of political power. There could have been idealism in this. His little nation was a conquered country. Everywhere Jesus went He saw Roman soldiers who reminded Him of His people's servitude. His people groaned beneath heavy political and economic burdens. How Jesus must have wanted to see them freed with their honor and dignity restored. Why not organize an army of patriots and drive the hated Romans beyond the borders of His country? What could be more idealistic than that?

Yet, Jesus turned from all of them. They might be right for other men but they would be wrong for Him. The use of such power would not be in keeping with His mission. God had called Him to another kind of power—love, sacrifice, and a cross.

I have given considerable attention to the temptations of Jesus essentially to show that the appeal of power lay at their heart. I think that is true of our temptations. We are lured by power.

Paul wrote to Timothy: "For the love of money is the root of all evils" (1 Tim. 6:10). Obviously, we do not take that at face value since it is clear that there are other kinds of evil. But if by money Paul meant power—and it is possible that he did—then he is right in saying that the love of power is the root of all evil. I can't think of a sin that doesn't have the misuse of power in it.

Now abide the three dynamics of sin—pride, the lure of evil, and the appeal of power, but the greatest of these is power.

The Extent of Sin

How extensive is sin? How much of life has been affected by it?

1. Let us note that sin has affected the whole of personal life, the corporate life, humanity, and the cosmos.

The whole person has been affected. There is not an area of my life that has not been corrupted by sin.

The mind has been corrupted. Who escapes the lie? We cleverly use the truth to say what we want it to say. We turn truth into propaganda. We settle for a half-truth when the whole truth could be ours. We often twist the truth to justify some bias, prejudice, or selfish interest. How often we take truth that should be selflessly used and make it self-serving?

The heart has been corrupted. How often it seems easier to hate than to love. It frequently seems impossible to free the heart from the grip of bitterness and hatred. The mind is often pushed into the service of a resentful and prejudiced heart. A biased heart is frequently the basis of our clever rationalizations.

The will has been affected. Sin makes the will lazy, cowardly, or evil. We are often sluggish in a situation that is urgently demanding haste. We frequently run away from causes that are right but dangerous. We turn from good ways to walk in evil paths. Sin has made my will sick. My will is broken and the break is down the center.

Sin has corrupted my imagination. The imagination, like the will, has been made sick. How often the pictures on the screen of the imagination are lurid, lustful, and obscene. What is back of pornography except a sick imagination?

The whole personality has been made sick, we have capitulated to sin. In the struggle with evil, we have sacrificed not only a guard, an outpost, or a contingency of troops, we have surrendered the fort. The citadel has been taken. "The heart," wrote Jeremiah, "is deceitful above all things, and desperately corrupt; who can understand it?" (Jer. 17:9).

When the Bible uses the term "heart," it means more than the emotions. It means the center of thought, will, and feeling. How well Jeremiah knew that we had given up the fort, surrendered the citadel! The heart has capitulated.

2. Our corporate life has been infested by sin.

Sin is both personal and corporate. Isaiah knew that well. Standing near the altar in the Temple and being in the presence of a holy God, he became conscious of his own personal sin as well as the corporate sin of his people (see Isa. 6:5).

I not only sin alone, I sin with others. I am a part of the sin of my family, my community, my society, and my world. I am involved in the sinful structures of the world.

Often we limit sin to the personal and are scarcely aware of corporate guilt. But actually we are more sinful in our corporate life than we are in our personal living. In our corporate life we often do, without shame and blushing, what would be utterly distasteful and repugnant to us in our more personal relationships. Rienhold Niebuhr, over fifty years ago, was writing about moral man and immoral society. He believed man is more moral than his society.

I remember a young man I knew during World War II. He was artistic and a very fine musician. He often played the organ for our worship services. He had been very idealistic as a young man and was a pacifist during his college years. He had sworn never to kill. He became a captain, commanding an infantry company, and was noted for his fearlessness in combat. I remember where we found his dead body. It was a hot day in Sicily, and he had been leading his company in a direct assault on an enemy-held hill. He had thrown away his helmet, had pulled open his shirt, and had led his men to within a few hundred yards of the hill when he was shot down. His sister wrote me a letter in which she made inquiry about the circumstance of his death. In this letter she told me about her brother. She remembered him as an extremely gentle boy with great compassion who never even played with toy guns. He had never killed a bird. He had dreamed of a world at peace and had once sworn never to bear arms. But as a member of the corporate life of the Army he became a fierce killer, and did that which was utterly repugnant and disgusting to the person he essentially was.

Not only are we more sinful in our corporate life but we are slower to repent. When did you ever hear of a family, a corporation, a community, or a state repenting? Have you ever heard of a nation confessing its guilt except in defeat?

3. Humanity has been tarnished by sin. That is why I can speak of sin as the blight of our humanity. The Bible is perfectly clear here.

The classical statement of the corruption of our humanity by sin is found in Romans 3. "I have already charged that all men," Paul wrote, "both Jews and Greeks, are under the power of sin, as it is written: 'None is righteous, no, not one; no one understands, no one seeks for God. All have turned aside, together they have gone wrong; no one does good, not even one' " (vv. 9-12). (See Prov. 20:9; Eccl. 7:20; Isa. 53:6.)

There are many common denominators in the human race, and one of them is sin. We are all sinners. Sin, like a deadly pollution, has been poured into the stream of our humanity.

4. The cosmos has been affected by sin.

Brokenness and estrangement may be the primal reality of our existence. The human heart is divided. The human family has been split in many directions. Human history has frightening cleavages lying across its life. But that does not tell all the story about the dispoiling effect of sin. The universe, the cosmos, has not been spared. Paul spoke of how the creation is in bondage and subject to decay (Rom. 8:21). He saw the reconciliation of Christ in a cosmic dimension. He spoke of "a plan for the fulness of time, to unite all things in him, things in heaven and things on earth" (Eph. 1:10). Christ was not only bringing peace to human hearts, not only reconciling warring forces in history, he was healing brokenness and mending a rift that extended far beyond history into the cosmos.

The Answer to Our Sin

There is an answer to our sin. God has acted in such a way that we do not have to be destroyed by it. Sin can be forgiven, its wounds can be healed, and its estrangement overcome.

It is true that we are helpless in sin's grip. We cannot deliver ourselves. All efforts to save ourselves betray us into more subtle and destructive sin. We are like a fish trying to free itself from a net in which it has been caught, but all the while becoming more deeply entangled in it. That is the problem with legalism. The harder we seek to deliver ourselves by keeping rules, obeying laws, and practicing religious ritual, the more we are caught in less obvious, yet more damning sins. "Can the Ethiopian change his skin or the leopard his spots?" asked Jeremiah. "Then also you can do good who are accustomed to do evil" (Jer. 13:23).

Yet, we do not despair. We have hope. S. J. DeVries has

written: "The presence and the problem of sin are just as much a part of the New Testament as of the Old Testament, and yet one who reads it is immediately struck by an astounding difference. All the old terms and concepts are here in the New Testament, but deepened and strangely transformed. The one factor which makes this great difference is the work of Jesus Christ. He provides something which the saints of the Old Testament yearned for but could never find: real and certain victory over sin."[2]

Cicero once said that the thing that is wrong with humanity is that we are in a pit. Work as hard as we may we cannot scramble out of it. We try to scale its walls, and often almost reach the top, only to lose our grip and fall back into it again. So the arduous struggle begins over again, only to end in failure. We are never able to get out. What we need, he said, is for a hand to be let down into the pit which can lift us out. The good news of our gospel is that a hand has been let down. It is scarred and nail-pierced, but only that hand can lift us out. It is the hand of Christ.

Yes, someone has come who is more than a match for our sins. Jesus Christ has come. We do not forget why they named Him Jesus. The angel said to Joseph: "You shall call his name Jesus, for he will save his people from their sins" (Matt. 1:21).

Because we are sinful we are travelers of the night. We walk in shadows and darkness. Yet, we are always looking for the day. We believe morning will come, and morning does come because Christ has come. Matthew saw the coming of Jesus as a fulfillment of prophecy by Isaiah. "The people who sat in darkness/have seen a great light,/" he wrote, "and for those who sat in the region and shadow of death/light has dawned" (Matt. 4:16). It is true!

Thought Starters

A series of sermons: What Is Sin?
A series of sermons: Dynamics of Sin.
A series of sermons: The Temptations of Jesus.

A series of sermons: The Dimensions of Sin.

Other sermons: The Two Great Tragedies of Life; Sin—So Easily Documented; The Love of Power and Sin; Pulled Downward by a Moral Gravity; We Are in a Pit; Life's Estrangements; Travelers of the Night.

Scriptures

Genesis 3:1-24; 4:1-14; Psalms 14:1-4; 51:1-5; 53:1-6; 103:6-14; Isaiah 1:7-20; John 3:16-21; Romans 1:18-32; 5:1-11; 1 Timothy 1:12-17.

Texts

Genesis 6:5; Psalm 51:4,7; Ecclesiastes 9:3; Isaiah 1:18; Jeremiah 17:9; Hosea 8:5*b*; 8:7*a*; John 3:16; Romans 3:9,22*a*-23; 5:8; 6:23; 7:25; 1 Timothy 1:15.

Illustrations

Sin as jealousy (Gen. 16:1-6); Temptation of power (Deut. 8:17-20); Temptations of power; Jesus' three temptations (Matt. 4:1-11; Luke 4:1-13); When personal sin becomes corporate guilt (Josh. 7:10-26); Personal and corporate guilt (Isa. 6:5); Each must bear his own guilt (Jer. 31:29-30); Sin of pride (Obad. 1:3-4); Sin is against God (Ps. 51:4); The sin of deception (Ps. 55:20-21); Heightened by a vision of God (Isa. 6:5); Heightened by the presence of Jesus (Luke 5:8); The law of the harvest (Gal. 6:7-8); Hope (Isa. 43:25); What God demands (Ps. 51:17); The answer to our sin (Rom. 5:8); The answer to sin's death (Rom. 6:23).

Notes

1. *The Interpreter's Dictionary of the Bible,* R-Z (Nashville and New York: Abingdon Press, 1962), p. 361.
2. Ibid, pp. 370-71.

4
God:
Above but Within

In speaking of God, we are often driven to a paradox as I am in this chapter: God—Above, but Within. If I had used technical theological language, the chapter heading would have been: God—Transcendent, but Immanent. In using simple language, I give a clue to effective preaching: Keep it simple, use language people can understand.

We have a strong biblical basis for this concept of God. God is above and far away, God is near, within our world and our history.

God Above

God is above our world by virtue of His being creator. He stands above His world the way a craftsman stands above the thing he has made.

When God finished His creation, standing on some vantage point beyond it, He looked down on His creation and saw that it was good. He felt satisfied with His work: "And God saw that it was good" (Gen. 1:25b). Again we read: "And God saw everything that he had made, and behold it was very good" (v. 31). He was looking down upon it. We can't be sure where the farthest star is since our most powerful telescopes have not been able to find it. But wherever it is, God is beyond it. He made it. He, like a great cosmic craftsman, stands above the star which is the work of His hands.

There are many Scriptures that speak of the transcendence

of God. Two of the most prominent are Psalm 104 and Isaiah 40.

Psalm 104 is a hymn to God as creator. It is beautiful and rich in imagery. God is obviously above nature and the world. He clothes Himself with light as if it were a garment. He has stretched out the heavens like a curtain. He makes the clouds His chariots, and rides on the wings of the wind. The winds are His messengers, fire and flame His servants.

Isaiah pictures the transcendence of God even more magnificently.

God is above nature. "Who has measured the waters in the hollow of his hand and marked off the heavens with a span, enclosed the dust of the earth in a measure and weighed the mountains in scales and the hills in a balance?" (Isa. 40:12).

God is also above history. "Behold the nations are like a drop from a bucket, and are accounted as the dust on the scales" (v. 15).

He is above both nature and history. "Have you not known? Have you not heard? Has it not been told you from the beginning? Have you not understood from the foundations of the earth? It is he who sits above the circle of the earth, and its inhabitants are like grasshoppers; who stretches out the heavens like a curtain, and spreads them like a tent to dwell in; who brings princes to nought, and makes the rulers of the earth as nothing" (vv. 21-23).

There are many more Scriptures that speak of God's transcendence. Solomon in his prayer of dedication for the Temple said: "But will God indeed dwell on the earth? Behold, heaven and the highest heavens cannot contain thee; how much less this house which I have built!" (1 Kings 8:27).

Paul, in his sermon on Mars Hill, said: "The God who made the world and everything in it, being Lord of heaven and earth, does not live in shrines made by man" (Acts 17:24).

Isaiah had the same high, exalted concept of God. "Thus says the Lord: 'Heaven is my throne and the earth is my footstool' " (66:1b).

What is the significance of God's being above the world and history? I suggest four things:

1. There is wonder and mystery in life.

We quickly come upon frontiers of wonder and mystery beyond which our minds cannot pass. Our minds, brilliant and gifted as they are, cannot encompass God. Standing on those frontiers of mystery we worship best and we pray best. The human mind does not worship its explanations and formulas.

Augustine, once puzzled by the doctrine of the Trinity, fell asleep and dreamed he was walking along the seashore. He came upon a child who had made a hole in the sand and was running back and forth between the hole and the edge of the ocean, carrying water to the hole. "What are you trying to do?" Augustine asked. "Oh, nothing much," replied the child. "I'm only trying to empty the sea into the hole." Then a thought struck Augustine with the suddenness of lightning. What he had been trying to do was even more absurd. Standing on the shore of time, he had been trying to crowd the eternal and infinite God into his small and finite mind. There was a mystery about God that eluded all his intellectual effort to grasp it.

We need to recover wonder and mystery which can come only from a transcendent God. We are living when the ceilings of life are oppressively low. Many of the vaulted archways of other generations lie broken about our feet. So much mystery has fled our world in our time. We are stooped and bent beneath these low ceilings which are often no higher than our heads. We need something to get beneath those ceilings, lift them up, and keep on lifting them until we feel height, mystery, and wonder again. Only a God who is above us can do that.

2. God sees our world and time from a vantage point from which we can never observe them.

We walk the streets of a city. We can see only a few blocks away. We see streets and alleys but we cannot follow them to their end. God is not caught in such short and narrow vistas.

He is more like a pilot circling the city. He sees it in its wholeness, the pattern of its streets and boulevards, and its boundaries.

We are like mountain climbers with limited vistas. We can see some of the tall and stately trees, and we also see the underbrush, barren boulders, and deep ravines like gashes in the side of the mountain. We cannot see the whole unless we can stand on the summit. But we cannot stand there—only God does. We cannot see the trees, underbrush, barren boulders, and ravines as they form a pattern of wholeness. Only God sees that. We have to trust Him to tell us what He has seen, which He does in the revelation He has made to us.

Our problem is that we may judge the whole by its parts. We may judge the mountain by its tall and stately trees and thus be too visionary and idealistic. But we may judge it by the underbrush, naked boulders, and ravines, becoming cynical, and despair of beauty and meaning. Always our vision is partial, limited, and incomplete.

God has stood on the summit and beheld His creation in its wholeness. He originally declared it good. Then on another day from those heights He looked down upon it and declared it bad. Something had gone wrong, His creation had fallen. But He could not give it up. So He set about redeeming it, and His redemptive activity goes on to our day. He is seeking to reconcile the world unto Himself through Christ.

3. God is in control of our world and history. Even when history seems to be falling apart and things appear to be running awry, we can believe that God is in control of them.

A woman stood at the window one night when the winds were raging and when the gale was terrifying in its savage strength. "God," she said, "must have lost His grip on the winds tonight."

History is often like a terrible storm when the winds are running high. There seems to be a randomness and aimlessness about it. We may be tempted to feel that God has lost control, but that is only the way it seems. It is not that way at all.

When history is like a stallion running wild, God has the bit in its mouth and the reins are in His hands.

The passengers on a fast train headed for London were very nervous. There had been several tragic train wrecks only recently. But on board was a little girl who was perfectly relaxed. Someone asked her how she could be so calm, and the simple answer was: "My father is the engineer."

So we believe the transcendent God is our Father. We can trust Him.

We go on trusting Him when the facts seem often to argue against His being in control. We are living during such a time. Our history is like a stream at floodtime when its waters are overflowing its channel destructively. We believe God will pull the angry waters back into the channel, assuage them, and see the stream to its appointed sea.

Or, to use another metaphor, history may be like a giant ocean liner, driven many times off its course by fierce winds. The passengers often wonder if it will ever reach harbor. But Christian faith assures them that God is in charge, that He will see the liner safely into port at last. He will see that history is consummated, that it will end the way it should.

4. In order for us to get to know this transcendent God, He will have to reveal Himself.

His ways are not our ways, and His thoughts are not our thoughts. "For my thoughts are not your thoughts, neither are your ways my ways, says the Lord. For as the heavens are higher than the earth, so are my ways higher than your ways and my thoughts than your thoughts" (Isa. 55:8-9).

How shall we know this God Who walks in mystery and Whose dwelling is blinding light, Whose ways and thoughts are so high above us? How shall our finite minds grasp the infinite God? How shall we know Him? We can't unless He tells us who He is in language we can understand.

God Within

The God Who is above the world He has made is also within it. He makes Himself available. He is not a disinterested on-looker concerning the things of earth.

The fortieth chapter of Isaiah, the classical statement on the transcendence of God, brought hope to those in a concentration camp in ancient Babylon. The people were far away from home, their native soil, the setting of their history, and their Temple. They were homesick and dispirited and even the youth were giving up in despair. The transcendent God, Who measures the heavens with a span of His hand and stretches them out like a curtain, makes His strength available to those weak and despairing people. Isaiah says this God "gives power to the faint, and to him who has no might he increases strength" (v. 29).

What if this transcendent God remained a million light years above us? What if He were like a boy who spun his top and left it to spin itself down? What if He were like a skipper who abandons his ship, leaving the crew to fend for themselves the best they can on the high seas? He doesn't. He is with us.

Loneliness is one of the great problems of life. So many of us are jostled by the crowds on the sidewalks, but are lonely. We have neighbors just down the street, and yet we are lonely. We live with our family under the same roof and still remain lonely. It is not the journey we fear so much as having to make it alone. It is not the pain we fear so much as having to bear it alone.

Richard Spencer, in a devotional article on Christmas, re-minds us that Matthew framed his Gospel with the presence of God. Near the beginning of his Gospel, Matthew wrote: "Behold, a virgin shall conceive and bear a son, and his name shall be called Emmanual (which means, God with us)" (1:23). Matthew concludes his Gospel with the promise of the risen Christ to be with His disciples to the end of the age: "Lo, I am with you always, to the close of the age" (28:20*b*).

But what about the last journey, the journey of death? We lose our loved ones one by one. They turn from us and walk away alone into the solitary ways of death. We would go with them, but we can't. We turn back into the busy ways of life, bearing the pain of loss.

I remember reading a morality play, *Everyman*. Everyman was going on a journey and he invited his friends to go with him. All accepted the invitation and then one by one each declined it. Everyman told them he was going on the journey of death. He must make that painful journey alone.

Is there somebody who will go, is there somebody who can? The twenty-third Psalm gives us the answer: "Even though I walk through the valley of the shadow of death, I fear no evil; for thou art with me; thy rod and thy staff, they comfort me" (v. 4). God does not turn back as we begin that decent into the valley of the shadow of death. He doesn't have to turn back. He alone can go.

Families often request the twenty-third Psalm at the funerals for their loved ones. Why? Is it the beautiful imagery of quiet rest in green pastures beside still waters? As appealing as that imagery is, that is not the real reason. The reason is that God continued the journey with their loved ones when they had to turn back.

How is this great God present in His world? In three ways.

1. He is present in His world in His Spirit. One of the classical statements of this is Psalm 139. The psalmist is sure that he is known to God, that indeed God knows him better than anyone else. And there is no escaping God's presence.

> Whither shall I go from thy Spirit?
>   Or whither shall I flee from thy presence?
> If I ascend to heaven, thou art there!
>   If I make my bed in Sheol, thou art there!
> If I take the wings of the morning
>   and dwell in the uttermost parts of the sea,
> even there thy hand shall lead me,
>   and thy right hand shall hold me (vv. 7-10).

There is no escaping God's presence because there is no place in His creation where He is absent. There are no off limits to God anywhere in His universe. And there is no escaping His searching eyes. He pierces the darkest night. "For darkness is as light with thee" (Ps. 139:12b).

John Knox, in his autobiography, *Never Far from Home*, tells about experiencing the wonderful reality of God while a student at Emory University. He was walking from the home of a friend to the campus. "The air was clear of mist and cloud," he writes. "There was no moon, and the wide sky was brilliant with stars. Suddenly there broke in upon me the overwhelming power of a realization of the awful beauty and sheer immediacy of God. I felt at once an indescribable ecstasy and an almost incredible peace. The whole world became for a moment one vast delicious music. If I have ever had what could be called a single 'conversion' experience, it was this. I could never again doubt God's reality or feel that he could be made subject to question by anything that could happen to me or others or by anything I might discover or find true."[1]

One of the greatest devotional books ever written is *The Practice of the Presence of God* by Brother Lawrence. He knew he could practice the presence of God because God was always with him. "The time of business," he wrote, "does not differ from the time of prayer; and in the noise and clatter of my kitchen, while several persons are at the same time calling for different things, I possess God in as great tranquility as if I were upon my knees at the blessed sacrament."[2]

2. God is present because He speaks to us, discloses Himself, and tells us who He is in our history. We do not look to the heavens to see God's action but along the dusty ways of life. We do not listen to the celestial spheres but to the raucous noise of time. God speaks to us in persons, events, deeds, meetings, and encounters on the field of our history.

If I had been God, that is not the way I would have spoken. I would have been far more dramatic and spectacular. I would have jarred earth with my power, startled earth with my booming cosmic voice. I would have emblazoned my message in big letters across the sky so everybody could read it. But God chose more modest and inconspicuous ways of addressing us. There is a kind of everydayness about the way He speaks. Christmas tells us so. God revealed Himself in such simple things as a manger, a bed of hay, and swaddling clothes. He came to us in a thing as frail and fragile as a baby who may have whimpered intermittently through that first Christmas night.

The great event of the Old Testament was the Exodus which was a thoroughly historical event. It is dated and we know where it happened. God delivered Hebrew slaves from bondage into freedom. The fathers told their children about the deed.

When a Hebrew boy asked his father about the meaning of their history, the answer always was, "We were Pharaoh's slaves in Egypt; and the Lord brought us out of Egypt with a mighty hand" (Deut. 6:21).

Israel sang about her deliverance in her hymns. (See Ps. 44:1; 103:6-7; 114:1-2.)

Probably the oldest written part of the Bible is Miriam's song which celebrated the Exodus:

> Sing to the Lord, for he has triumphed gloriously;
> the horse and his rider he has thrown into the sea
> (Ex. 15:21).

Israel saw God more in the arena of history than in nature. And because they had met Him in history they could then trace His ways in nature.

Israel found three great nature (harvest) festivals in Caanan, but she did not leave them harvest festivals. She transformed them into historical festivals. If Israel had best seen God in nature, she would have left them harvest festivals. But since she saw God most clearly in history, she turned them into historical celebrations.

The Feast of Unleavened Bread, a spring festival at the beginning of the barley harvest, was merged with the Feast of Passover, commemorating God's mighty deliverance of His people from Egyptian bondage. The Feast of Harvest, a second spring festival at the end of the barley harvest and at the beginning of the wheat harvest, became the Feast of Pentecost, celebrating God's giving of the law at Mount Sinai. The Feast of Ingathering, a fall festival when the vintage was in, became the Feast of Tabernacles which called to remembrance the wanderings in the wilderness, that long trek made under the promise and judgment of God.

3. God was present in a historical person, Jesus of Nazareth. The Christmas angel sang at His birth: "Be not afraid; for behold, I bring you good news of a great joy which will come to all the people; for to you is born this day in the City of David a Savior, who is Christ the Lord" (Luke 2:10-11).

Where was He born? In some spiritual or ethereal realm? No, in the city of David, Bethlehem, which was an ancient city not far away. They would find the baby wrapped in swaddling clothes, lying in a manger. It could not have been more historical and mundane.

Paul wrote to the Galatian Christians: "But when the time had fully come, God sent forth his Son, born of woman, born under the law, to redeem those who were under the law, so that we might receive adoption as sons" (Gal. 4:4-5).

It would be a thoroughly historical event. Christ would be born when the situation was propitious, when time was like full clouds hanging low over earth ready to empty their rain on the dry and parched fields of history.

Jesus' life was historical. His was a dated life. We know His time in history. We know His place in history. We know where He was born, where He grew up, the setting of His ministry. We know where He died and we know where He was raised from the dead. We believe that in this historical person we have received the final revelation of God. There was a light in His eyes that had its source in God. In His words God was speaking, and in His deeds God was acting.

It is good to know that God is above our world with its change and decay, that He is above history with its flux and uncertainty. It is equally good to know that He is with us in our world, that He is in our history with its tumult and vicissitudes.

Thought Starters

A series of sermons on: The God Who Is Above Us
A series of sermons on: The God Who Is with Us
Other sermons: Beyond the Fartherest Star; It Was Very Good; The God Who Tells Us Who He Is; Riding the Wings of the Wind; No Off Limits to God; When Life Is Like a River at Floodtime; Like Full Clouds; God Is with Us; Framed by a Presence; Singing About Our Deliverance; When Nature Festivals Became Historical Ones; Who Will Go with Us on Our Last Journey?

Scripture

1. Above: 1 Kings 8:27-30; Job 26:7-14; Psalms 8:1-4; 19:1-6; 104:1-35; Isaiah 40:12-31.
2. Within: Psalms 139:1-18; Isaiah 57:14-21; Acts 17:24-28.

Texts

1. Above: Psalms 2:4; 113:5-6; Isaiah 6:1-3; 57:15; 66:1.
2. Within: Psalms 21:6; 23:4; 34:18; 38:21; 139:7; Isaiah 55:6; Matthew 1:23; Rom. 8:28; 8:38-39.

Illustrations

The God who is high above us (Isa. 55:8-9); Lord of all nations and history (Isa. 10:5; 44:28; 45:1; Jer. 27:1-7); Nature as God's servant (Ps. 104:1-4); God revealed in nature (Ps. 19:1-4; Rom. 1:20); God and time (Ps. 90:4); God in the secular: Jacob at Bethel (Gen. 28:10-22); Personal encounter with God (Ex. 3:1-8); Signs of God's presence (Ex. 13:21-22); Israel's creed: historical events (Deut. 26:5-11); God with us (Isa. 43:2); God's revelation in deeds (history) (Pss 44:1; 78:1-72; 103:7;

105:1-45; 114:1-8); The God who knows our innermost
thoughts (Ps. 139:1-6).

Notes

1. John Knox, *Never Far from Home: The Story of My Life* (Waco: Word Books,
1975), p. 43.

2. Brother Lawrence, *The Practice of the Presence of God* (Westwood: Fleming
H. Revell Company, 1958), p. 31.

公義와 仁愛의 하나님.

5
God:
Just but Loving

In the last chapter, we discussed God's relationship to His world and our human history. God is above both and He is within both, He is transcendent and He is immanent. The fact that He is above us gives us confidence in believing that our world is under His control and that history will ultimately fulfill His purpose. We are not at the mercy of blind randomness, we are under a strong but beneficient will. Because God is with us we are not like orphans alone in our world.

In this chapter we want to talk about the ethical nature of God. He is both just and loving. These two qualities do not put God in conflict with Himself, rather, they complement each other. God's love does not allow His justice to be heartless and too devastating, and His justice does not allow His love to be sentimental but helps give it firmness and sturdiness.

God Is Just

I once had a good friend who was a Jewish rabbi. One day I asked him: "What is the essence of Judaism?" He thought for a moment and replied: "Ethical monotheism. God is not only one, He is ethical. He is just and requires justice of those who believe in Him."

Let us make several observations about God's being just.

1. In addition to the word *just*, there are two other words that speak of His ethical nature—*holy* and *righteous*.

God is holy. It must be quickly said that before the term had ethical meaning it was heavily theological. Holiness is the distinctive thing about God. It is that, which, more than all things else, makes Him God. He is the Other. He is God and not man. He is that which man is not and never becomes. He is Creator. He is eternal and everlasting. His dwelling place is the heavens, He inhabits eternity. He lives in mystery and walks in unapproachable light.

Men, women, and things are not holy within themselves. They become holy because they are dedicated to God. Israel was a holy people, not because of any virtue, goodness, or gift within themselves, but because God had chosen them to be His people.

Yet the term *holy*, which was originally theological, was ethicized. The fact that this could happen tells a lot about Judaism and Christianity. It indicates the heavy stress both religions put on morality and how the theological and ethical are bound together. The theological and ethical belong together the way the back and palm of my hand are bound together. Try to separate the two and you get a mutilated hand. Attempt to separate ethics and theology and we get a broken, fragmented religion. We take theological terms and ethicize them, we take ethical terms and theologize them.

When we say that God is *holy* in an ethical sense, we say that he is *just* and *righteous*. The three words form a trilogy.

God is just. "The works of his hands are faithful and just, all his precepts are trustworthy" (Ps. 111:7). (See Ps. 145:7; Dan. 4:37.)

When we say that God is just, we mean that He is faithful, trustworthy, responsible. He wants life ordered with equity and fairness. He becomes angry when the strong take advantage of the weak and the rich exploit the poor.

God is righteous. "Thou hast fulfilled thy promise, for thou art righteous" (Neh. 9:8). While God's righteousness and justice mean essentially the same thing, He is spoken of much more frequently as being righteous than as being just. (See Ps. 7:9; Jer. 9:24.) The reason for this is likely that righteousness better expresses relationship than does justice.

God is holy, God is just, and God is righteous.

2. God exercises His just nature in judgment. God is judge. He is judge of peoples, nations, and the world. "Shall not the Judge of all the earth do right?" Abraham asked (Gen. 18:25).

In the first eleven chapters of Genesis where the theological setting of human life and history is vividly, yet profoundly described, the judgment of God is very prominent. Adam and Eve, after their sin, passed beneath the heavy judgment of God and were driven out of the Garden of Eden (Gen. 3:23). Cain, after he killed his brother Abel, experienced the fierce judgment of God and cried out, "My punishment is greater than I can bear" (Gen. 4:13). In the sixth chapter of Genesis, we read how wicked the race of men become (vv. 5-6). And God sent the flood which was His judgment upon them (vv. 11-22). Ambitious men in the land of Shinar began building the Tower of Babel which would reach into the heavens and God came down in judgment and threw up barriers of language among them, scattering them upon the face of the earth (Gen. 11:1-9).

There is a consistent picture of God's judgment running through the Bible. His judgment is impartial, falling on all alike. Israel, being the special people of God, felt that He would show partiality to them, but He didn't. Amos tells of God's judgment upon the surrounding nations, but He did not spare Israel. "You only have I known/of all the families of the earth," said God. "Therefore I will punish you/for all your iniquities" (Amos 3:2).

Let us be more specific and make the following observations about God's judgment.

There is nothing capricious, whimsical, or arbitrary about God's judgment. It is in keeping with who He is. His judgment flows from His righteous nature.

Again, the working of moral law and God's personal wrath are involved in His judgment.

God has built moral law into the structure of the universe, into the very warp and woof of it. While the moral laws have a kind of hiddenness that the physical laws do not, they are rock-ribbed, formidable, and powerful. Individuals, as well as nations, who willfully ignore and violate them, can be destroyed by them. These moral laws have their own kind of retribution and are a part of God's judgment. They may not draw blood or break legs the way physical laws do. Their judgment may be less obvious and it may seem to be delayed. But it eventually comes, often with shattering power.

But God's judgment has a more personal aspect than the impersonal working of moral laws. The Bible speaks of God as being a God of wrath: "As I swore in my wrath, 'They shall never enter my rest' " (Heb. 3:11). This is a reference to God's reaction to the wilderness generation who, because of their rebellion, were not allowed to enter the Promised Land, perishing on its borders.

When men in their arrogance flout moral laws which are God's ethical nature built into the universe, when people are heartless and ruthless, when the weak are trampled beneath the feet of the powerful, when men and women are shoved and pushed about as if they were things, God becomes angry. What kind of God would He be who could, with detachment, look upon such behavior through neutral eyes, being unmoved by it. Such a God would be immoral. The fact that God is wrathful in judgment does not indicate weakness. It is a sign of strength.

Further, there is love and mercy in God's judgment. His justice is a seeing justice; it is not blind. His justice is a feeling justice; it has heart in it.

I often think of a symbol of justice I see on a courthouse when I am driving to eastern North Carolina to visit my family. It is an arm holding a pair of perfectly balanced scales. It is cold and impersonal. There are no eyes that see the anguish of our world, no heart that feels its pain. God's justice is not like that. It is touched with mercy.

The Flood as an expression of God's judgment seems to be so heartless and ruthless. Yet, it has mercy in it. God said: "I will never again curse the ground because of man, for the imagination of man's heart is evil from his youth; neither will

I ever again destroy every living creature as I have done. While the earth remains, seedtime and harvest, cold and heat, summer and winter, day and night, shall not cease" (Gen. 8:21-22).

Also, the end of God's justice is salvation. His acts of judgment may be deeds of salvation. (See Ps. 36:6; Isa. 45:21*b*.)

God is like a surgeon who says: "You have a bad leg. It will have to come off, and it will be painful. But I shall amputate it so that you can live and be healthy."

God's judgment can be very severe like a surgeon's knife, but it cuts to save. It can be as devastating as the hot, scorching winds that sweep over us from the desert, but those winds are followed by refreshing showers.

3. God demands justice of those who believe in Him. Not only is God just, He calls us to be just and righteous (interchangeable terms).

The righteous person God calls us to be is a two-directional person who is right with God and right with one's neighbor. Therefore justice or righteousness is relational in nature. (Read the first Psalm where the righteous person is described as one right with God.)

The righteous person is also in right relations with his or her brother. Such a person is socially oriented. He seeks to preserve the peace and wholeness of the community, meeting the demands of communal living. He establishes peace. He cares for the poor, the fatherless, and the widow, and he does not allow the stranger to be turned away. He wants honesty in the marketplaces, honor in government, justice in the courts, parental respect and filial devotion in the home, and true piety at the altar. He seeks wholesome, supportive, and healing relations in the community.

God seeks righteous men and a just society. Justice gives stability to the community and righteousness wins the approval of God.

You remember Abraham's concern for Sodom and Gomorrah. He especially had a personal interest in the welfare of Sodom since his nephew, Lot, was living there. As he talked with God about that fated city, he wondered if the city would be spared if righteous people could be found in it. He made a wonderful discovery: ten righteous people could save the city. But ten could not be found, so the city went up in smoke. (See Gen. 18:16-33.)

The eighth-century Hebrew prophets heard God calling His people to justice. At the heart of their message was a just God who demanded justice of His people. Unless religion produced justice in the marketplace, community, and the courts, it was false.

Amos lived during a time when immorality and religion both flourished. Injustice and religious piety walked side by side without disturbing each other. Many of the people left their ill-gotten gain at the altar as tithes and offerings to God. They thought they could buy off God. But Amos told them that no matter how huge their crowds, or big their offerings, or moving their liturgy, or how lustily they sang their hymns, God would not accept their worship.

> Take away from me the noise of your songs;
>   to the melody of your harps I will not listen.
> But let justice roll down like waters,
>   and righteousness like an ever-flowing stream (Amos 5:23-24).

Micah's message was essentially the same:

> He has showed you, O man, what is good;
>   and what does the Lord require of you
> but to do justice, and to love kindness,
>   and to walk humbly with your God? (Mic. 6:8).

4. Let us look at righteousness that is of faith.

Paul strongly emphasized this. It makes a lot of sense if righteousness is, as I have claimed, essentially a relational term. By faith in Christ our lives are set right with God, and that relationship works itself out horizontally in faithful and loving relationships with the neighbor.

Paul spoke of "the righteousness of God through faith in Jesus Christ for all who believe" (Rom. 3:22). Or again, "For we hold that a man is justified by faith apart from works of law" (v. 28). Righteousness, then, was not so much keeping laws and rules which was legalism, as a relationship made possible by faith in Christ.

But this is not something new to Paul and the New Testament. The Old Testament knew about a righteousness that is of faith. (See the story about Abraham, Gen. 15:1-6.)

Paul wrote: "He who through faith is righteous shall live" (Rom. 1:17). Martin Luther, 1,500 years later, picked that up and made it the battle cry of the Protestant Reformation. But Habakkuk, who lived 600 years before Paul had said the same thing: "But the righteous shall live by his faith" (2:4).

God Is Love

We have heard people say that the God of the Old Testament is a God of justice, while the God of the New Testament is a God of love. That is highly inaccurate. The God of the Old Testament is also a God of love, and the God of the New Testament is also a God of justice although the love of God is accented in the New. We make a serious mistake when we break the continuity between the Old and New Testaments. The God of the Old Testament is also the God of the New. Yet, this is not to deny the uniqueness of the New Testament. It is indeed unique. The love of God is historized and personalized in Jesus of Nazareth as nowhere else. The best of the Old Testament is fulfilled in Him, and God is present redemptively in Jesus as in nobody else.

God's love was seen in His relationship with Israel. Why God chose Israel to be His special people was always a mystery. They were small and insignificant, living in the shadows of great nations. Frequently they were overrun by these powerful nations, their little country pillaged, and turned into a battlefield. Not only was their land despoiled, but often their citizens were taken away captive into a foreign country. And Israel could lay no claim to special virtue or gifts. She was often

morally blind and spiritually stupid. It is little wonder that
many times she asked: Why did God choose us?

Moses answered that question like this: "It was not because
you were more in number than any other people that the Lord
set his love upon you and chose you, for you were the fewest
of all peoples; but it is because the Lord loves you" (Deut. 7:7-8
a). They were elected to be God's people but not because they
could lay any claim on God. They did not merit God's choosing
them in any sense. Therefore, God had chosen them in grace.

After electing Israel as His chosen people, God entered into
covenant with them. The main motif of the covenant was love,
and the covenant love of God was steadfast. It was a love that
was loyal and lasting. They might fail God but He would not
fail them. He would be faithful to them amid all their fickleness and faithlessness.

The God of Mount Sinai, the giver of the law, is described
like this: "The Lord, the Lord, a God merciful and gracious,
slow to anger, and abounding in steadfast love and faithfulness, keeping steadfast love for thousands, forgiving iniquity
and transgression and sin, but who will by no means clear the
guilty, visiting the iniquity of the fathers upon the children
and the children's children, to the third and fourth generation"
(Ex. 34:6-7).

It is a strong, unfailing love, and is not weak and sentimental: "Who will by no means clear the guilty." God is not blind
to sin. He does not wink at it, saying, "It is not there." It is there
and God will judge it. As love is in His justice, so justice is in
His love.

The love of God in the Old Testament finds its most adequate expression in Hosea. Hosea, you will remember, was
married to a beautiful woman by the name of Gomer. Two
children were born to that marriage. One day he came home
to learn the awful truth that Gomer had left him and the
children. Any court in the land would have given him a divorce. But he didn't want a divorce. He could not give her up.
When he found her, she was a slave, being used and exploited

by other men. He took fifteen shekels of silver and a homer and a lethech of barley and bought her back, reinstating her in the family as his wife and the mother of his children. As Hosea reflected on his own anguish, he realized that God was like that, only in a much more wonderful way. Although Israel had forsaken Him, seeking other gods and therefore was guilty of spiritual harlotry, He could not give her up. God cries out: "How can I give you up, O Ephraim! How can I hand you over, O Israel!" (Hos. 11:8). Therefore, some of the tenderest passages of Scripture are found in Hosea. (See 11:1-4,8-9.)

I have spoken of God's love in his Judgment. There is no better example of this than Hosea.

When Israel looked back, she remembered that God had chosen her in love. When Israel looked upon her present life, she saw the steadfast love of God. Although she failed God many times, He never failed her. In all of her fickleness God had remained constant. As Israel faced her future she saw a new age of peace and justice which would be shaped and fashioned by God's strong love. Whether she looked into the past, present, or future, Israel saw God's love that had chosen her beyond her meriting.

As we come to the New Testament, we see God's love, in a more personal, concrete, and compelling way as expressed in His Son Jesus Christ.

There are few attempts to define God in the Bible. It is almost as if it says: "God is too wonderful to be expressed in our human definitions of Him." But there are three attempts at this in the New Testament and we are surprised by their simplicity: "God is spirit" (John 4:24), "God is light" (1 John 1:5), "God is love" (4:16). Three short words in each definition. Imagine it!

The greatest of these is "God is love." It is the most personal and comes closest to the heart of who God is.

God has caught up His whole creation in His great arms of love: "For God so loved the world that he gave his only Son, that whoever believes in him should not perish but have eternal life" (John 3:16). In spite of the brokenness, rebellion, and sin of His world, He cannot give it up.

We have seen God's love best in the face of His Son, Jesus Christ. God's love is embodied in Jesus.

Thomas a Kempis spoke of the love he had seen in Jesus: "O unspeakable grace! O wondrous condescension! O unmeasurable love bestowed on man!"

Karl Barth was once asked to give in a sentence the heart of his faith. He thought for a minute, and quoted from a song he had sung as a child:

> Jesus loves me! this I know,
> For the Bible tells me so.

Abbot Damascus was an old man when he died. He had suffered much and been betrayed, having been tested right down to the core. A few months before his death he wrote: "When I look back upon the seventy years of my own life, I see quite clearly that I owe my inner happiness, my peace, and my confidence, and my joy essentially to one fact: 'I am certain that I am infinitely loved by God.' "[1]

God has loved this whole world, but His love in Jesus became very personal. Paul could say: "The life I now live in the flesh I live by faith in the Son of God who loved me and gave himself for me" (Gal. 2:20*b*).

I, like Paul, am glad that God loves the whole world, but I want to know that He loves me. I rejoice that there is enough grace in Jesus Christ to cover the sins of the entire world, but I want to know that He has forgiven my sins. I am glad that God can identify His world, but I want to know that He can call me by name.

I remember one of the most meaningful communion services I was ever a part of. I was officiating and when a woman who was a deaconess in the church gave me the bread, she said: "Chevis, Christ's body was broken for you." And when she passed me the cup she said: "Chevis, Christ's blood was shed for you." I needed to hear that. I want to know that Christ loved me and gave Himself for me.

What kind of love is this we have seen in Jesus? The New Testament calls it *agape* love. It is a nonmanipulative, nonutilitarian, nonpossessive love. *Agape* does not depend in any sense on the object, but solely on the giver. It loves not only the healthy, beautiful, good, and virtuous, it loves the sick, broken, marred, and sinful. It loves those who do not love themselves, whom the world does not love, and those who do not love God. It loves the discards and the rejects of our world. There is no depth into which it will not descend to lift up the fallen, no distance it will not go to find the lost, and no pain it will not bear to heal the brokenness of our world.

It is God's love, *agape,* that came to us and our world in Jesus Christ. That makes our gospel exceedingly good news.

Karl Barth once said: "My experience has been that if I simply try to say, to repeat what the Bible says about God, the people understand. Many clergymen fail to do this. We must simply accept the fact that human beings are loved by God, even in their faults and hostilities. We must tell man that he is 'a loved one.' "

I have talked about the justice and love of God. They are inseparably bound up together in His life. His justice is in His love, and His love is in His justice. His justice keeps His love from being too soft and sentimental and His love keeps His justice from being too harsh and impersonal.

Thought Starters

A series of sermons: The Justice of God.

A series of sermons: The Love of God

A series of sermons: Three Definitions of God.

Other sermons: A Trilogy—Holy, Just, Righteous; Laws with a Jagged and Cutting Edge; God's Judgment Is Like a Surgeon's Knife; Justice Touched with Mercy; Called to Justice;

Ten Righteous Men Could Have Saved a City; Righteousness, Not Rules, but Relationships; Tenderness in Hosea; What Love Is This! Righteousness that Is of Faith.

Scripture

1. Just: Isaiah 1:16-17; Amos 5:14-15, 21-24; Micah 6:1-8.
2. Loving: Exodus 34:1-7; Deuteronomy 7:6-11; Psalms 51:1-17; 86:14-17; 103:8-14; Hosea 3:1-5; 11:1-4, 8-9; John 3:1-17; Romans 5:1-8.

Texts

1. Just: Proverbs 16:11; Isaiah 62:8; Amos 5:23-24; Micah 6:8; Matthew 23:23.
2. Loving: Psalms 27:8-9; 103:11; Isaiah 49:15-16; Hosea 6:1; 11:1; Habakkuk 3:2; John 3:16; Romans 1:7; 5:8; 1 John 4:19.

Illustrations

Adam and Eve driven from the Garden (Gen. 3:22-24); Story of Cain (Gen. 4:8-16); The Flood (Gen. 6—8); Tower of Babel (Gen. 11:1-9); Power of righteousness (Gen. 18:22-33); God's judgment (Deut. 28:58-68); God's judgment against social and religious evil (Amos 2:6-8; 3:13-15; 5:10-20); Privilege and justice (Amos 3:1-2); Plumb line (Amos 7:7-9); Religion that cannot stand the prophetic voice (Amos 7:12-17); Justice, not ritual (Amos 5:1-24); The wonder of justice (Isa. 32:1-2); God set against evil (Nah. 2:13; 3:5); Heart of prophetic and moral teaching (Isa. 1:16-17; 55:6-9; 58:6-12; Jer. 7:5-7; Amos 5:14-15, 21-24; Mic. 6:8); Story about social injustice (Luke 16:19-31); Story of Hosea and Gomer (Hos. 3:1-5); God like a shepherd (Isa. 40:11); God like a mother (Isa. 49:15-16); Thirsting for God (Ps. 42:1-2; 143:6); Waiting for the Lord (Ps. 130:6; Isa. 40:31); The God who hears, sees, chastens, knows (Ps. 94:8-11); A rent veil: God accessible (Luke 23:44-45); The whole world caught up in God's love (John 3:16); God is spirit (John 4:24); light (1 John 1:5); and love (1 John 4:16).

Note
1. Douglas V. Steere, *To God Be the Glory*, Edited by Theodore A. Gill (Nashville: Abingdon Press, 1973), p. 72.

6
Jesus Christ:
His Birth and Life

The birth of Jesus Christ was a powerful event. It divides history. From the Christian point of view, all that went before that event is BC; all that came after it is AD. We never write a letter, check a date on the calendar, observe a birthday, sign a legal document, or celebrate a national event without doing it in relation to that faraway event.

No life has had the impact on our world and history the way Jesus of Nazareth has. His shadow lies across the landscape of our modern world, to say nothing of His living presence among us. He is alive! That is the great exclamation of the Christian gospel.

In this chapter we want to talk about the birth and life of Jesus Christ.

His Birth

The earliest literary account of the birth of Jesus is not from the Gospels, but from Paul. That has always interested me. In Galatians, Paul wrote: "But when the time had fully come, God sent forth his Son, born of woman, born under the law, to redeem those who were under the law, so that we might receive adoption as sons" (Gal. 4:4-5).

Then there are the birth stories by Matthew and Luke. Both are beautiful, especially Luke's. Someone has said that Luke gave us Christmas. He was so human, so spiritually perceptive, and such a fine literary artist. His story is incomparably beautiful

While Matthew and Luke began their Gospels with the birth of Jesus, Mark skipped over His birth, bringing Him abruptly upon the stage of history when He was a grown man: "The beginning of the gospel of Jesus Christ, the Son of God" (Mark 1:1). John made a radical departure from the other Gospel writers, going back of history to eternity, where he pictured the preexistence of Christ.

In thinking about the birth of Jesus, I believe we should keep five things in mind.

1. His preexistence. John went back to eternity, to the beginning, to the preexistence of Christ. He existed before He became a historical person. "In the beginning was the Word, and the Word was with God, and the Word was God. He was in the beginning with God" (John 1:1-2).

Not only did Christ preexist but He was the agent of creation: "All things were made through him, and without him was not anything made that was made" (v. 3).

Paul developed the same idea in his Colossian letter: "He is the image of the invisible God, the first-born of all creation; for in him all things were created, in heaven and on earth, visible and invisible, whether thrones or dominions or principalities or authorities—all things were created through him and for him" (Col. 1:15-16).

Then this preexistent Word who was with God from the beginning, took a nose dive into our world and history: "And the Word became flesh and dwelt among us, full of grace and truth" (John 1:14). This is one of the most significant verses in the New Testament because it speaks of the incarnation.

In a preaching workshop in the early 1960s I wrote a sermon on "God Has Given His Answer in Christ," in which I quoted Jesus: "He who has seen me has seen the Father" (John 14:9). I have often thought of how shocking this must have been to those who first heard it. The man who spoke those radical words was a carpenter from Nazareth whose face had been tanned by the sun and whose hands had been calloused by carpenter's tools. He had sweated through many a hot summer day in His father's shop. Imagine His saying it! In that sermon I quoted Arthur John Gossip: "That is without exception, the most staggering saying to be found in human literature." And my old professor penciled in the margin: "Together with John 1:14."

Here is the doctrine of the incarnation. God came down to us and became enfleshed. He took upon Himself our frail and fragile form.

I heard a well-known theologian once say: "Christianity is a religion of Incarnation." That statement excited me and I've never forgotten it.

2. Jesus was conceived of the Holy Spirit and virgin born. Both Matthew and Luke speak of the divine conception.

"When his mother Mary had been betrothed to Joseph," Matthew wrote, "before they came together she was found to be with child of the Holy Spirit. . . . An angel of the Lord appeared to him in a dream, saying, 'Joseph, son of David, do not fear to take Mary your wife, for that which is conceived in her is of the Holy Spirit; she will bear a son, and you shall call his name Jesus, for he will save his people from their sins' " (Matt. 1:18,20-21). (See Luke 1:30-31,34-35.)

These accounts have been very important since their purpose was to affirm the divinity and uniqueness of Jesus. "Therefore the child to be born will be called holy, the Son of God" (Luke 1:35b). Yet, we should not claim more for the virgin birth than the New Testament does. Some people will tell you that belief in it is essential for salvation, but the New Testament makes no such claim. Neither Mark, John, Paul, nor even Jesus, mentions it. If they had felt that way you can be sure they would have emphasized it. Yet, this should not minimize its importance.

3. Jesus was born of a woman. This is the way Paul put it: "But when the time had fully come, God sent forth his Son, born of woman" (Gal. 4:4). Luke tells about Mary bringing forth her firstborn son.

It was a real birth. Mary knew the pain of childbirth. The

baby was no spiritual phantom. He was real and human. He needed to have shelter and clothing. So Mary wrapped Him in swaddling clothes and laid Him in a manger filled with hay. He likely cried off and on during that first night.

If conception of the Holy Spirit speaks of His divinity, then being born of a woman tells of His humanity.

On that first Christmas they were no doubt asking how they would know the child. Two signs were given: swaddling clothes and a manger (Luke 2:12), as well as the light of a star (Matt. 2:9). The swaddling clothes were coarsely woven wool. They were of earth most earthly. The child would be human, of which this would be a sign. But that was not all. He would be a baby with the light of a star in His face. He could only be fully known by a sign from heaven. He would be divine.

4. His birth was a historical event.

Jesus was born into our history. We know where and when He was born. The Christmas angels announced: "For to you is born this day in the city of David a Savior, who is Christ the Lord" (Luke 2:11). Where was He born? In heaven, in some ethereal realm? No, in Bethlehem, the city of David, which was not far away. This is very important since Christianity is a historical religion. God reveals Himself, speaks to us, and tells us who He is, not from the celestial realms, but along the common ways of life, in the Bethlehems of our world. He does not jar earth with His mighty power or address us with a cosmic voice. No, He speaks to us in much more modest ways. There is a kind of everydayness in the way He speaks.

5. His birth tells of God's radical action.

God entered our world in a strange new way in Christ. In some basic sense He clothed Himself in our flesh and came among us. That is what John says He did. Or to put it in a different way: He sent a Savior into the world. That is what the angel announced. God took the world seriously: He knew how sick, lost, and alienated it was. And God took Himself seriously —He knew that only He could redeem men and women and save the world.

His Life

Let us make six observations about the life of Jesus.

1. He was human.

Jesus was born the way other children are and we would expect His life to unfold in normal and natural ways. This it did.

Jesus grew normally. The years between His birth and the beginning of His public ministry are known as the silent years. Yet we know one very important thing about those years. In one sentence, Luke gives a summary of them: "And Jesus increased in wisdom and in stature, and in favor with God and man" (2:52). What Luke said in essence was that Jesus had a normal childhood, He grew the way other children do.

Jesus ate, became tired, slept, and arose refreshed in the morning the way we do. He became angry, was tempted, and wept.

You remember the story about Jesus and His disciples crossing the Sea of Galilee when strong winds arose and suddenly swept down upon the sea, turning it into a churning madness. The boat was about to sink, and the disciples, frantic with fear, began scurrying about, looking for Jesus. They found Him in the stern asleep on a cushion (Mark 4:38). He was tired and had dropped off to sleep. I heard a great Scottish preacher use that story as the basis for his sermon. I shall always remember his saying: "They found him asleep with his head on a seaman's pillow." A seaman's pillow. That has stayed with me. In its own way it speaks so forcefully of the humanity of Jesus.

One of the earliest heresies the church had to deal with was Docetism which denied the humanity of Jesus. He only appeared to be human, but He really wasn't. Jesus was too pure and spiritual to become corrupted by flesh which is evil. The church saw how much was at stake here so it vigorously defended the humanity of Jesus. You can hear the rumblings of that far-off battle which was fought and won, especially in the writings of John. In the prologue to his Gospel, John says:

"And the Word became flesh and dwelt among us" (1:14). It was our kind of flesh—flesh that gets tired, that bleeds, that dies. The blood that oozed from His wounds the day He died, under chemical analysis, would have proven to be our kind of blood.

John began his first letter like this: "That which was from the beginning, which we have heard, which we have seen with our eyes, which we have looked upon and touched with our hands, concerning the word of life—the life was made manifest, and we saw it, and testify to it, and proclaim to you the eternal life which was with the Father and was made manifest to us" (1 John 1:1-2). They had heard Jesus, seen Him, and touched Him, and didn't feel defiled.

2. Jesus was motivated by love.

Our hearts are muddled and our motives are rarely pure—they are often mixed. But not so with Jesus, His heart was pure, and His motives were crystal clear.

Jesus loved people with a pure and unsparing love. I sometimes think one of the most descriptive things ever said about Jesus came from John: "Having loved his own who were in the world, he loved them to the end" (John 13:1). Having begun to love them He never stopped loving them. John might have continued: "He will not only love them to the end, He will love them beyond the end, for we are His in life, and death, and far beyond death."

Jesus loved the socially ostracized and outcasts, He loved the rejects and discards of society. He loved those in whom nobody saw worth. He loved those who did not love themselves and whom the world did not love. He received publicans and sinners and ate with them. He loved His enemies and prayed for them while He was on the cross.

It was only after Jesus came that we dared define God as love. In Jesus we have seen that which is most ultimate in the universe. When the facelessness, the carelessness, the ruthlessness, the mercilessness, have been stripped away and we come to the heart of the universe, we find love—the kind of love we have seen in Jesus. God is love.

3. Jesus was a servant.

Jesus refused a crown, scepter, and throne. Once a plot was made to take Him and force a crown upon Him, and Jesus, learning of it, slipped through the crowd and went up into the hills to be alone. (See John 6:15-21.) Refusing a crown, He asked for a towel and basin of water and washed and dried the dirty feet of His disciples. (See John 13:1-20.) He would be a servant and His followers must also be servants.

Jesus would be more than a servant, He would be a Suffering Servant. There can be little doubt that He saw himself fulfilling Isaiah's image of the Suffering Servant. (See Isa. 53:1-12.)

The early church certainly saw Jesus as a servant. In Philippians 2, Paul pictures Christ as being on an equality with God. He didn't have to steal or filch it from God. The honor and glory were really His. Then He gave it all up. Down, down, down He came. He became a man, lower still a servant man, and lowest of all He died the shameful death of the cross (Phil. 2:5-11).

The most unique thing about the Christian faith may be that when God made ready to disclose Himself, to tell who He really is, He came as a servant who, refusing a crown, asked for a towel and basin of water.

4. Jesus spoke with a new kind of authority.

When Jesus had finished His Sermon on the Mount, Matthew says: "And when Jesus finished these sayings, the crowds were astonished at his teaching, for he taught them as one who had authority, and not as their scribes" (Matt. 7:28-29).

Jesus was not always quoting ancient authorities, as did the scribes. The scribes were like men who tried to draw water from dried-up wells, from springs that had failed, and from riverbeds where streams no longer flowed. Their words, which might have once been living, were now dry and lifeless. But Jesus—there was something firsthand, immediate, and spontaneous about His teaching. He was in touch with the reality about which He spoke. It was not so much quoting the truth as speaking it firsthand, as being and embodying the truth about which He spoke.

In Matthew 5, Jesus spoke of the authority of tradition as it related to five types of behavior—murder, adultery, divorce, oaths, and justice, and after each He said: "But I say to you." He was claiming a new and more binding kind of authority.

It was probably His authority that got Him into trouble more than anything else. Jesus came into the world not as a judge but as the Savior. "For God sent the Son into the world, not to condemn the world," He said, "but that the world might be saved through him" (John 3:17). While He was not an official judge, yet there was judgment in His life, not legal but moral. It was the kind of judgment that light exercises over darkness, truth over falsehood, and love over hatred.

There was a light in His eyes that exposed the darkness of people's minds, truth in Him that disclosed their falsehood, a breadth of sympathy that stood over against their narrow and provincial ways, a sacrificial spirit that laid bare their greed and lust for power, a generosity with people that showed how they used and manipulated others, a living faith that pointed to the formality and lifelessness of their religion, and a love that uncovered their jealousy, envy, and hatred. They couldn't stand Him, and therefore swore to do away with Him.

5. Jesus was sinless.

Jesus was without sin. There were no dark shadows beneath His eyes, no haunting memories, no wounds inflicted by an angry and outraged conscience. There were no shadows of guilt that dogged His footsteps across the years.

The author of the Letter to the Hebrews wrote: "For we have not a high priest who is unable to sympathize with our weaknesses, but one who in every respect has been tempted as we are, yet without sin" (Heb. 4:15).

Jesus was tempted. We read about those three temptations that assailed Him just after the great hour of His baptism. They were real. He was not shadowboxing out there in the wilderness. They were temptations to misuse power, the kind you and I have. Could He have sinned? Yes. If He could not have, the whole thing was a sham. To be tempted means you can sin. If you cannot, there is no temptation. But you ask: What if He had sinned? To try to answer that question would be to engage in idle speculation. The fact is: He did not sin! He won.

6. Jesus was divine.

He was human and He was divine. When His humanity has been under attack, the church has rushed to defend it. Also when Jesus' divinity has been attacked, the church has lost no time in moving to its defense.

The birth stories, as we have already seen, were told to stress both His humanity and His divinity. He was born of a woman. He was human. But He was conceived of the Holy Spirit and virgin born. He was divine.

Jesus combined the servant and Son of man motifs from the Old Testament. He was Isaiah's Suffering Servant, yet He referred to Himself as the Son of man. This was His favorite way of speaking about Himself. What does the term mean? Some see it as referring to His humanity. But Jesus probably used it in the sense in which it is used in Daniel. The Son of man was a divine figure. While the term is elusive, powerful, and mysterious, it likely means what the early church had in mind when it called Him the Son of God.

Recall the "I am's" of Jesus: "I am the bread of life" (John 6:35); "I am the light of the world" (John 8:12); "I am the door" (John 10:9); "I am the resurrection and the life" (John 11:25); "I am the way, and the truth, and the life" (John 14:6). The definite article is used. He was not one kind of bread among many, but the Bread of life; not one light among many, but the Light of the world; not one door among many, but the door; not one resurrection among many, but the resurrection; not one way among many, but the way; not one truth among many, but the truth; not one life among many, but the life.

Jesus did what only God could do: He forgave sins. Then

there was the resurrection. He broke the bonds of death and went free of our last and most formidable enemy.

The early church saw Him as the mighty Son of God. Thomas, a week after Easter, made this great confession: "My Lord and my God!" (John 20:28). He was now the exalted Lord, seated at the right hand of God, the place of sovereign power. Paul could say: "At the name of Jesus every knee should bow, in heaven and on earth and under the earth, and every tongue confess that Jesus Christ is Lord, to the glory of God the Father" (Phil. 2:10-11). Jesus as Lord would come from His place of power, consummate history, and bring in the new order.

Jesus Christ will be the main theme of your preaching. Do not neglect the great truths connected with His birth and life.

Thought Starters

A series of sermons on Encounters with Jesus.
A series on Conversations with Jesus.
A series on The Most Pertinent Sayings of Jesus.
A series on The Sermon on the Mount.
A series on The Lord's Prayer.
A series on Jesus' High Priestly Prayer.
A series on The I Am's of Jesus.
Christmas sermons: Incarnation—God Takes Our Fragile Form; A Manger—Where God Entered Through Lowly Doors; Bethlehem—Where Humanity Gets a New Start; A Savior Is Born; Where History Is Cleaved; When Time Was Full; How Shall We Know the Child? No Room for Christ; A Time to Be Generous; Mary Pondering—The Mystery of Christmas; Like the Coming of Morning (Luke 1:78-79).

Scripture

Matthew 1:18-25; 2:1-12; 3:1-17; 4:1-11; 4:18-22; 5:1-12,20-48; 6:1-15,19-34; 8:14-17; 12:46-50; 13:1-23; 14:22-33; 15:10-20; 16:13-20,21-28; 20:20-28.

Mark 2:1-12,23-28; 4:35-41; 6:30-44; 7:1-23; 9:1-8,14-29; 10:1-9; 11:1-11.

Luke 1:26-38,39-56,67-80; 2:1-20,22-38, 41-52; 4:16-30; 5:1-11,33-39; 6:6-11; 7:1-10,18-23,36-50; 10:25-37,38-42; 12:13-21; 14:25-31; 15:1-32; 16:19-31; 17:11-19; 18:9-14,35-43; 19:28-40.

John 1:1-14,29-42; 2:1-11; 3:1-16; 4:1-42; 6:41-59; 8:1-10,31-59; 9:1-41; 10:1-30; 11:1-44.

Texts

Matthew 1:21,23; 2:9,10-11; 3:2,17; 4:1,19; 5:13-14,20; 6:21,24,33; 7:11,21; 8:7; 9:36; 10:8*b*,31; 11:28-29; 12:50; 14:27; 15:18; 16:16,24; 18:22; 20:26-27; 23:23.

Mark 1:1,31,35,41; 2:5,27; 5:19; 7:20; 8:25; 9:8,23; 10:9,16,21.

Luke 1:31,37; 2:7,13-14,52; 3:22; 4:18,41; 5:8,36; 6:9; 7:9,16,22,50; 8:21; 10:29,37; 12:21; 14:28; 16:31; 17:17; 18:9,13,38; 19:41; 20:16.

John 1:4-5,12,14,29,39,41,42; 2:5,25; 3:7,14,16,17,19; 4:10,23,24,42; 5:39-40; 6:48,68; 8:11,32,36; 9:4,25; 10:10,15,28-29; 11:11,25-26,35,44.

Illustrations

God with us (Matt. 1:23); Tempted by social and economic power (4:3-4), by dramatic power (4:5-7), by political power (4:8-10); Those upon whom morning has come (4:16); Happiness is a by-product (5:3-12); A new authority (5:21-48; 7:28); A radically new life-style (5:39-48); The world's best-known and best-loved prayer (6:9-13); When the hour of crisis is upon us (7:24-27); The "how much more" in God (7:11); Radical demands of discipleship (8:19-22; 10:38; 16:24-26); A strange paradox (10:34-36); Games Jesus played as a boy (11:16-17); A family without boundaries (12:46-50); Great things from small beginnings (13:31-32); When similies are illustrations (13:31,33,44-45,47); Worth all of it (13:44-45); The tragedy of unbelief (13:58); Forgiveness must be interminable (18:21-22); Mastered by things (19:16-22); When values are turned upside down (20:20-28); The weightier matters (23:23).

From the solitary place to busy streets (Mark 1:35-39); The

calmer of stormy seas and human hearts (4:35-41); A story of mercy (5:1-20); When resources are multiplied (6:38-44); Torn between doubt and belief (9:23-24).

Touching the untouchables (Luke 5:13); Forgiveness and love (7:47); Jesus and women (8:2-3); When the kingdom of God is near (10:9,11); With no credentials except mercy (10:37); The value of human life (12:7); Something lost, something sought, and something found (15:1-24); Acceptance without reservation (15:1-20); A religion of grace versus a religion of legalism (15:1-32); When legalism dries up the springs of human compassion (15:25-32); A study in contrasts (16:19-31); A man who would not be silenced (18:35-43).

In the shadows of a city (John 3:2); Firsthand religion (4:42); One of the tenderest scenes from the life of Jesus (8:1-11); When metaphors are illustrations (10:9,11; 14:6); Death as sleep (11:11); When tears are louder than words (11:35); Being loosed from bondage (11:44).

7
Jesus Christ:
His Death and Resurrection

The death and resurrection of Jesus Christ are two of the most significant events of history, and they have given us two of the most revered and celebrated days of the church year. The death of Jesus gave us Good Friday and His resurrection gave us Easter. Our world looks with hope on both of these days.

The church from its earliest days has kept these two events before us, not only through its preaching, but in its ordinances and sacraments. Whenever celebrants of the Lord's Supper have gathered about the Lord's table across the centuries, they have heard these words: "This is my body which is [broken] for you," and "This cup is the new covenant in my blood" (1 Cor. 11:24-25). As believers have been baptized in streams, pools, and baptistries they have dramatically proclaimed the death and resurrection of Jesus. When the person is submerged beneath the water, that speaks of the death and burial of Jesus, and, as he or she is lifted up out of the water, that speaks of resurrection.

The church has been careful to remember and keep alive these two events because they form the heart of the Christian gospel.

The Heart of the Christian Gospel

One of the most important selections in the New Testament is 1 Corinthians 15:3-4. Here Paul tells us what the heart of the

Christian gospel was as the early church understood it—the
death and resurrection of Jesus Christ. This is what he said:
"For I delivered to you as of first importance what I also
received, that Christ died for our sins in accordance with the
scriptures, that he was buried, that he was raised on the third
day in accordance with the scriptures."

I still remember the day the meaning of this passage broke
in upon my mind. It was like a daybreak. The gospel, my faith,
and my preaching have not been the same since that day. I
realized that the Christian gospel is the answer to the two great
tragedies of human existence—sin and death. We are sinners,
all of us. Men and women everywhere are bent beneath a
heavy load of sin as they walk in the shadows of their guilt.
And men and women everywhere walk on limping feet into
the night of their death. The marks of mortality are heavy
upon us. And all our creations, like their human creators, perish at last.

What if the death of Jesus is the answer to our sin and the
resurrection of Jesus is the answer to our death? That is the
glad and confident claim we make. Our gospel is good news,
very good news.

The gospel preached by the early church was like an ellipse
with the death and resurrection of Jesus being the two focuses.
Which is the more important? We really can't say. Remove the
resurrection and the cross is tragedy. Without the cross we
could not have the resurrection.

I remember when we were building our sanctuary. Harold
Wagner, the architect, told me one day that he would like for
our architecture and symbolism to express basic tenets of the
Christian faith. Did I have any ideas? I didn't have to ponder
that question long. I suggested that our symbolism express the
heart of the Christian gospel as set forth in 1 Corinthians
15:3-4. This would be easy to achieve, he said. He would
suspend a large cross from the ceiling over our chancel and
then transcend the cross with a resurrection window.

The resurrection window was not to be to the side of the

cross or beneath it. It was to be above it, not because it is more important, but because, as already said, the resurrection saves the cross from being a tragedy.

In the resurrection window Jesus is emerging from the tomb, His right leg having cleared it. In His left hand He carries a banner of victory over death, and His right hand is raised in blessing. The combined message of the two is almost overpowering. That message is: "Jesus Christ, the strong one, who lived, died, and conquered death is now alive forever more, and is the reigning Lord of life and death. He loves and cares for you, and since He does, He wants to forgive your sins and give you life." That is the message the human heart cries out to hear above all things else. It is good news, exceedingly good news.

The Death of Jesus

Let us make five observations about the death of Jesus.

1. It was a free death. He chose to die.

If you casually read the life of Jesus, you can easily conclude that He was trapped, hemmed in, and caught by powerful forces over which He had no control. He was the victim of a pincer movement that closed in ruthlessly upon Him. But that is to misread and misunderstand His death. He made it perfectly clear that He freely chose to die, that He gave His life.

"For this reason the Father loves me," Jesus said, "because I lay down my life, that I may take it again. No one takes it from me, but I lay it down of my own accord. I have power to lay it down, and I have power to take it again" (John 10:17-18).

In the Garden of Gethsemane where Jesus was being arrested and after Peter had brandished his sword, Jesus said: "Put your sword back into its place, for all who take the sword will perish by the sword. Do you think that I cannot appeal to my Father, and he will at once send me more than twelve legions of angels?" (Matt. 26:52-53).

It was a free death. No one took His life from Him. If His death had not been freely chosen, it could not have been redemptive.

2. It was a death motivated by love.

Jesus loved our world despite the fact it had declared a false freedom from God, was alienated from God, was broken and ugly. He loved people like you and me and we know that often we are very unlovely. He loved the world with a pure, unbroken, and unsparing love. The love He gave the world depended in no way on the world's being lovely and attractive. It was not. The love He gave was solely dependent upon Him. It was His nature to love and His life was an open channel through which the love of God was poured for the healing of the brokenness of the world. Therefore, we see the love of God in the death of Jesus as we see it nowhere else in all the world and in all of human history.

In the Passion Play at Oberammergau, when the body of Jesus is being taken down from the cross and laid in the lap of His mother, the chorus sings a funeral hymn:

> All you who pass by here,
> Stand still, pay heed and watch.
> Where will you find a love
> Which can compare to this?

3. It was a shameful death.

Jesus died the most shameful death of the ancient world. He died on a Roman cross. It was so shameful that no Roman citizen was allowed to be put to death by crucifixion. The cross was reserved for slaves and insurrectionists. Cicero said that "the very name of the cross should never come near the body of a Roman citizen, nor even enter into his thoughts, his sight, his hearing."

Paul speaks of the radical descent of Christ from the glory of God to the lowest estate of human existence. The descent did not stop until it hit the lowest level of the human situation. "He humbled himself," Paul wrote, "and became obedient unto death, even death on a cross" (Phil. 2:8). There was nothing lower than that.

I often think of the transformations wrought by Christ. He

took unlikely things, sometimes even shameful things, and transformed them into power and beauty. He took a thing as shameful as a Roman cross and turned it into a mighty symbol of God's salvation. It would be a cross, more shameful in its day than the electric chair is in our own, that would become the sign of the religion that bears the name of Jesus.

His shameful death was so powerful and transforming that whatever the instrument of His death, that instrument would have become the symbol of His religion. If, like Socrates, He had drunk hemlock, the symbol would be a goblet. If He had been stabbed to death, the symbol would be a dagger. If stoned to death, the symbol would be a rock. If He had been electrocuted, the replica of an electric chair, not a cross, would crown our church steeples.

4. His death was vicarious.

The death of Jesus was vicarious. He died for others. He got beneath the terrible burden of our guilt and bore our sins far away. As the Suffering Servant, it could be said of Him: "He was wounded for our transgressions, he was bruised for our iniquities; upon him was the chastisement that made us whole, and with his stripes we are healed" (Isa. 53:5).

In the institution of the Lord's Supper, He said of the bread: "This is my body which is for you" (1 Cor. 11:24); of the wine, "This is my blood of the covenant, which is poured out for many" (Mark 14:24).

Paul speaks of Christ "who was put to death for our trespasses and raised for our justification" (Rom. 4:25). Or again, "Who gave himself for our sins to deliver us from the present evil age, according to the will of our God and Father" (Gal. 1:4); or once more, "For our sake he made him to be sin who knew no sin, so that in him we might become the righteousness of God" (2 Cor. 5:21).

The author of the Hebrews put it this way: "So Christ, having been offered once to bear the sins of many, will appear a second time, not to deal with sin but to save those who are eagerly waiting for him" (Heb. 9:28).

We are face to face with one of the great mysteries and realities of our faith: When the innocent freely takes into his or her life the sin and shame of another, not because one has to but because one wants to, and bears the guilt freely and uncomplainingly in love, something wonderful can happen. A person can be set free from some enslaving and destructive habit. This can happen on the human level. But it happens in a much more wonderful way on the divine level.

John Buchanan was a chaplain in World War I. While overseas he cultivated a friendship with a little redheaded Irishman who became the best friend he ever had.

One day as Buchanan and his friend were walking across a battlefield when the battle was subsiding, a sporadic artillery shell came screaming in and landed at their feet. Buchanan said he was frozen in his tracks, knowing that soon the shell would explode and both would be killed. But while he was immobile, his friend was not. The Irishman fell on the shell covering it with his frail body. When the shell had exploded, Buchanan saw lying at his feet the mangled form of a little man he could not have recognized had he not seen his friend plunge on the shell. As long as Buchanan lived a day never passed that he did not realize that he lived because a friend had died for him. He said that when he saw the little man at his feet he knew better than ever before what the New Testament means when it says that Christ died for our sins.

What if the great God of the universe, who made us and loves us, should get beneath the terrible burden of our shame and guilt, and bear it far away that He might give us a free forgiveness? That would be almost too good to be true. Yet it is true, nothing is so true. That lies at the heart of our gospel, it is the meaning of the cross.

When we were driving out of the little town of Oberammergau where we had seen the Passion Play, the oldest member of our tour, a woman in her eighties, said with considerable feeling: "I was greatly moved by the death of Jesus but the thing that moved me most was I knew He died for me."

5. His death is related to our sin.

Let me make several observations about this.

In the first place, sin is more severely judged in the death of Jesus than anywhere else.

Many strange events occurred in relation to the death of Jesus, but one of the strangest is that the most respectable forces united to put Jesus to death. Roman law and Jewish religion joined hands in the death of Jesus. The underworld did not put Jesus to death. Gangsters did not do away with Him. He was not stabbed to death by some hoodlum. No, the pillars of government and religion engineered the events that led to His death. It was not bad men but "good" men who were responsible for His death. At the cross of Jesus we see not how bad bad men are but how bad "good" men are. There the cloaks of self-righteousness and the robes of respectability are stripped away and we see ourselves in our moral nakedness. It is not a pretty sight. Nowhere is the light of judgment so merciless and searching as at the cross of Jesus. There is where we all know we are sinners and are in desperate need of mercy and grace.

Again, sin is forgiven, expiated, and cleansed at the cross of Jesus.

Paul, speaking of Christ, said "whom God put forward as an expiation by his blood, to be received by faith" (Rom. 3:25). John, in his first letter, wrote: "In this is love, not that we loved God but that he loved us and sent his Son to be the expiation for our sins" (1 John 4:10).

It is at the cross of Jesus where we lay down our arms of rebellion, where we hear the gracious words "Your sins are forgiven," where our soiled lives are made clean. It is there that sins like scarlet become white as snow, sin like crimson becomes as wool.

The city of Coventry, England, along with its beautiful cathedral, was destroyed by Nazi bombers in World War II. The city was rebuilt but the cathedral was not. Instead, within a stone's throw of the old, a new, contemporary cathedral was built. The old cathedral stands as a burned-out hulk, and in it is a charred cross, held together with metal bands, with these words written across its face: "Father forgive." Where better could these words be written?

Moreover, in the death of Jesus, despite our sins, we are justified.

No one ever tried harder than Paul to earn justification before a righteous God. He meticulously obeyed the law, studied diligently, gave time to prayer, kept vigils, buffeted his body, and did other things in a strenuous effort to stand before God as a just man. He was an ideal Pharisee, and blameless before righteousness that was of the law. Yet, peace eluded him and he felt guilty and alienated from God. But when he met the living Christ along the Damascus road, for the first time he found peace and knew that he stood as one justified before a just God. It was nothing in him that made it possible. It was all in Christ, especially in His death. Therefore Paul could write: "Since, therefore, we are now justified by his blood, much more shall we be saved by him from the wrath of God" (Rom. 5:9).

Further, it is at the cross of Jesus that we are reconciled.

Sin has brought estrangement, separation, and alienation between God and us. It is in the death of Jesus that we are reconciled to God. "For if while we were enemies," Paul wrote, "we were reconciled to God by the death of his Son, much more, now that we are reconciled, shall we be saved by his life" (Rom. 5:10).

History has not known more hostile and more separated people than Gentiles and Jews in the time of Jesus. Yet, Paul saw them being reconciled, not only with God, but with each other.

"For he is our peace," declared Paul, "who has made us both one, and has broken down the dividing wall of hostility, by abolishing in his flesh the law of commandments and ordinances, that he might create in himself one new man in place of the two, so making peace, and might reconcile us both to

God in one body through the cross, thereby bringing the hostility to an end" (Eph. 2:14-16).

Finally, the cross of Jesus is where we are redeemed.

Sin puts us in bondage, takes away our freedom, enslaves us. It delivers us into a servitude much worse than political enslavement. Sin turns us over to alien hands, and makes us the victims of dark, sinister powers. From such bondage the death of Jesus delivers us. "In him we have redemption through his blood," Paul affirms, "the forgiveness of our trespasses, according to the riches of his grace" (Eph. 1:7). And again, "He has delivered us from the dominion of darkness and transferred us to the kingdom of his beloved Son, in whom we have redemption, the forgiveness of sins" (Col. 1:13-14).

The Resurrection

Let us make five observations about the resurrection of Jesus.

1. It was an event that conquered death.

The young man at the tomb of Jesus on Easter morning said: "Do not be amazed; you seek Jesus of Nazareth, who was crucified. He has risen, he is not here; see the place where they laid him" (Mark 16:6).

Jesus did battle where death was king, in a tomb, and He won! He left His tomb empty against a breaking morning. Paul felt there was no event better documented than the resurrection of Jesus. (See 1 Cor. 15:5-8.)

2. The resurrection of Jesus changed attitudes about death.

The early Christians felt hope and confidence in the presence of death. Death was no longer the bleak reality it once had been. The light of Easter morning had driven away much of its darkness and despair. The followers of Jesus marked out the word *death* from their vocabulary, and spoke of their beloved dead, not as being dead, but as being asleep. (See John 11:11; Acts 7:60; 1 Cor. 15:6,18,20; 1 Thess. 4:13-15.) Paul said they no longer wept as those without hope (1 Thess. 4:13). They could even speak exuberantly about death.

> O death, where is thy victory?
> O death, where is thy sting? (1 Cor. 15:55).

Dr. Elizabeth Kübler-Ross is a psychiatrist who works with terminally ill patients. She observed a Negro woman who had a calming effect upon her patients. She would go to the bed of an agitated person, say a few words, and leave him or her calm and composed. This woman grew up in extreme poverty and was often hungry. Her family was too poor to go to the hospital, so they died in their own beds surrounded by their loved ones. One day Dr. Kübler-Ross, curious about the strange powers of the black woman, asked her what she said to the disturbed patients. "I say the simplest thing to them," she replied. "I tell them it's not so bad." There was something like that about the early Christians. In the light of Easter, death didn't seem to be so bad.

3. The resurrection validated Jesus Christ.

The evidence of the resurrection lay not so much in the empty tomb, although that was convincing, as in the appearances of Jesus. His appearances were proof that the man who came out of the tomb on the first day of the week was the same man who had been put to death on Friday.

John, in his account of Jesus' appearance to His disciples on Easter night, says that when He had greeted them, "he showed them his hands and his side" (John 20:20). The nail prints were in His hands and the wounds were in His side. He was Jesus their Lord whom they had seen die.

After the Easter experience, they could believe He was all He claimed to be. Those radical I am's! They could believe then. The resurrected Lord was able to make every one of them good.

4. The resurrection of Jesus validated the gospel.

Paul pictured the alternative to the resurrection in bleakest and starkest terms: "If Christ has not been raised, then our preaching is in vain and your faith is in vain" (1 Cor. 15:14). "For if the dead are not raised, then Christ has not been raised. If Christ has not been raised, your faith is futile and you are still in your sins. Then those also who have fallen asleep in

Christ have perished. If for this life only we have hoped in Christ, we are of all men most to be pitied" (vv. 16-19).

Paul didn't speculate seriously about the alternative to the resurrection. He didn't have to. He knew Christ was resurrected. "But in fact Christ has been raised from the dead," he wrote, "the first fruits of those who have fallen asleep" (1 Cor. 15:20).

Hans Küng has written how indispensable the resurrection is to the gospel and the life of the church: "Without Easter there is no Gospel, not a single narrative, not a letter in the New Testament. Without Easter there is no faith, no proclamation, no church, no worship, no mission in Christendom."[1]

5. The resurrection of Jesus tells us something about the form of our future life. — 예배 영제 내용기

Easter didn't find Jesus a disembodied spirit. He had a body that sustained a continuity with His earthly body, yet was different.

We are to be resurrected and given new bodies. The Christian hope is not in immortality but resurrection. We live again because God in power and love resurrects us to new life. The same power that brought Jesus Christ forth from the grave on Easter morning will give us new life.

We are to have bodies. Biblical faith never envisions persons without bodies. The final victory over death will be won when we are given new bodies:

"When the perishable puts on the imperishable, and the mortal puts on immortality, then shall come to pass the saying that is written:/'Death is swallowed up in victory'" (1 Cor. 15:54).

Then will our salvation have fully come.

When we preach on the death and resurrection of Jesus Christ, we should know that we are addressing men and women at the points of their deepest needs, and that our message is one of hope. That should keep our preaching fresh and exciting.

Thought Starters

A series of sermons on The Death of Jesus.

A series on The Resurrection of Jesus.

A series on The Transformations of Jesus—The Worth of Human Life, The Value of Women and Children, The Standard of Greatness, Love, A Cross, A Tomb, The First Day of the Week, The Nature of Religion.

Good Friday sermons: The Magnetism of the Cross (John 12:32); He Freely Chose to Die (John 10:18); The Most Shameful Death (Phil. 2:8); The Man Who Died for Others (1 Cor. 11:24); The Man Who Died for Me (Gal. 2:20*b*); The Cross and Forgiveness (Rom. 3:25); The Cross and Reconciliation (Rom. 5:10); Where We Are Set Free (Eph. 1:7); Where We Are Justified (Rom. 5:9); Where We Are All Judged; Humanity at Its Worst, God at His Best.

Easter sermons: Daybreak Over an Empty Tomb; Our World Bathed in Easter Light; The Easter Story; The Stones that Easter Rolls Away; The Witness of Easter Faith (Matt. 28:8); The Affirmation, Denial, and Evidence of Easter (Mark 16:6); How Shall We Know the Risen Lord? (John 20:20); The Keystone in the Arch (1 Cor. 15:14); Resurrection and Power (Phil. 3:10); Resurrection Now! (Rom. 6:4); The Invitation and Imperative of Easter (Matt. 28:6-7).

Scripture

Matthew 21:28-32,33-46; 22:34-46; 23:13-39; 25:14-30; 25:31-46; 26:17-30; 27:1-10,11-26,27-54; 28:1-10; 28:16-20.

Mark 12:41-44; 14:1-9, 32-34; 16:1-8.

Luke 20:9-18; 23:32-43; 24:13-35,44-53.

John 12:1-8,20-26; 13:1-17; 14:1-11,12-27; 15:1-11; 16:1-15; 17:1-26; 18:28-40; 20:1-18; 20:19-31; 21:1-17.

Texts

Matthew 21:10,43; 22:37-38; 23:23; 26:22; 27:42; 28:6, 19-20.

Mark 12:43; 14:9,36.

Luke 23:34,35,43,46; 24:27,30-31,32,46-47,48,49.

John 12:21,24,32; 13:1,15,34,35; 14:1,6,9,15,16,27; 15:1,13,15; 16:13; 17:3, 15; 18:36,37,38; 20:16,20,21,28-29,31; 21:15

Illustrations

A new kind of king (Matt. 21:1-17); Not words but deeds (Matt. 21:28-31); When appearances are deceptive (Matt. 23:27); The great betrayal (Matt. 26:48); The painful denial (Matt. 26:69-75); Repentance that led, not to life, but to death (Matt. 27:3-5); Pilate—a man afraid to be just (Matt. 27:22-26); A strange mockery (Matt. 27:29-31); The ultimate loneliness (Matt. 27:46); The veil that kept God in and people out (Matt. 27:51); The wall that kept some people in and others out (Eph. 2:14); Roman law and Jewish religion join hands: When the most respectable forces perform the foulest deed (Luke 23:1-56); At the cross: where you see, not how bad bad men are, but how bad "good" men are; When caring words lie (John 12:5-6); When night is more than physical darkness (John 13:30); Rolling dice near the cross (John 19:24).

Notes

1. Hans Küng, *On Being a Christian* (New York: Doubleday and Company, Inc., 1976), p. 396.

2. Ibid, p. 381.

8
The Holy Spirit:
God Present in His World

The basic meaning of the Holy Spirit is God present in His world, creating, giving life, sustaining, and guiding. The Holy Spirit is one of the persons in the Christian Trinity, and without Him the essential nature of Christianity would be changed. The Holy Spirit is many-faceted, both in terms of who He is and what He does. In the light of this an attempt will be made in this chapter to present a profile of the Holy Spirit.

The Holy Spirit and the Trinity

The Trinity is possibly the most difficult of our Christian doctrines. It seems to be elusive and hard to grasp. It escapes the power of our minds to understand it. Yet, it is helpful to realize that the doctrine of the Trinity originated in experience, not abstract thought. It was first experience, then doctrine. We have experienced God the Father above us, Jesus Christ the Son in our history, and the Holy Spirit as God in our world and present with us. When we attempted to articulate what we had experienced and put it into intelligible form, we got the doctrine of the Trinity.

All living theology begins with experience. The experience may have a setting as common as Jacob's vision of God while he slept in the wilderness with a stone for his pillow, as concrete as a burning coal from the altar laid on Isaiah's lips, or as personal as Paul's being addressed by the resurrected Lord along the Damascus road. Then we take the experience, put it into rational form so we can tell others what has happened to us, and theology is born.

Paul's encounter is a good example of theology being born of experience. He met the living Lord on the outskirts of Damascus. In that experience he felt morally bankrupt. He had no virtues with which to lay claim upon God. He brought only empty hands and discovered they were enough. God's salvation was of grace, it was a gift. Out of that experience came his doctrine of salvation by grace.

Paul had tried religious devotion and good works but they had not been effective. He still felt condemned and alienated from God. Along that Damascus road he made one of the greatest discoveries of his life: He believed in Jesus Christ and God accounted it to him as righteousness; he stood justified for the first time before God. Out of that experience came his doctrine of justification by faith.

While living theology is born of experience, it is worship, more than anything else that keeps it alive. Worship waters theology at its roots; that is, it keeps returning us to the experiences that gave birth to our theology. We have again those meetings and encounters which are the sources of our faith. We experience the transcendence and nearness of God, the mystery and holiness of God, judgment and mercy, guilt and forgiveness, despair and hope. The doctrine of the Trinity is kept alive more by worship than anything else. We worship God the Father, in the name of Jesus Christ the Son, in the illumination of the Holy Spirit.

You see the doctrine of the Trinity emerging in the New Testament. You find it in Paul's Trinitarian benediction: "The grace of the Lord Jesus Christ and the love of God and the fellowship of the Holy Spirit be with you all" (2 Cor. 13:14). You discover it again as a baptismal formula in the Great Commission: "baptizing them in the name of the Father and of the Son and of the Holy Spirit" (Matt. 28:19). You come upon it again in the twelfth chapter of 1 Corinthians where it appears in less sharply defined form, yet in reasonably clear outline: "Now there are the varieties of service, but the same Spirit; and there are varieties of working, but it is the same Lord; and there are varieties of working, but it is the same God who inspires them all in every one" (vv. 4-6).

It is interesting to observe where you find the Trinity along the theological spectrum in the New Testament. It lies somewhere between experience and a hard and exact theological formula. There is a vitality, freshness, and aliveness about it that reminds one of experience, yet there is sufficient form to remind us that it is taking shape as a doctrine.

As already suggested, the Holy Spirit is an indispensable person in the Trinity. Without Him Christianity could never be what it is. Without the Holy Spirit, God would be totally transcendent, faraway, and out of touch with us. He would not be present in our world. Without the Holy Spirit, Jesus Christ would be a dim figure far back in our history. It is the Holy Spirit that brings Him from a remote past, making Him our living contemporary.

A Profile of the Holy Spirit

In an attempt to present a profile of the Holy Spirit, let us make six observations.

1. The Holy Spirit as Presence.

The Holy Spirit more than anything else, as has been said, is God present in His world. God has not gone off and left His creation; He has not abandoned us. The psalmist, as earlier mentioned, discovered that he could not escape the presence of God, there was no place in the universe where God was not. There was no chance of fleeing God's presence. If he ascended into heaven, God was there; if he went into Sheol, God was there. If he took the wings of the morning and dwelt in the uttermost parts of the sea, there he would find the supportive presence of God. If he tried to hide from God in the darkest night, he could not escape God's searching eyes: "Even the darkness is not dark to thee, the night is bright as the day; for darkness is as light with thee" (Ps. 139:1-18).

John Knox has written: "The Spirit is God's own presence, his very being surrounding us and pervading us, his own love encompassing us and possessing us, and wanting to possess us utterly."[1]

Again, the Holy Spirit was a presence with Jesus.

John the Baptist, thronged by great masses as he baptized in the river Jordan, wondered how he would identify Jesus. "I myself did not know him," John confessed, but a sign of identification was given him: "but he who sent me to baptize with water said to me, 'He on whom you see the Spirit descend and remain, this is he who baptizes with the Holy Spirit' " (John 1:33). The sign was unfailing (vv. 32,34). Jesus all through His ministry knew the faithful companionship of the Holy Spirit. He was never alone.

Further, the Holy Spirit was a presence with the disciples of Jesus.

In one of the loneliest and most despairing moments in the life of the disciples, Jesus said to them: "I will pray the Father, and he will give you another Counselor, to be with you for ever, even the Spirit of truth, whom the world cannot receive, because it neither sees him nor knows him; you know him, for he dwells with you, and will be in you" (John 14:16-17).

The word translated "Counselor" ("Comforter," KJV) is Paraclete. It means one called to one's side. It can be translated *Counselor, Comforter, Strengthener, Helper, Advocate, Champion*. The Holy Spirit was like an unfailing friend by their sides, strengthening them in their weakness, comforting them in their sorrow, guiding them in their confusion, and giving them hope in their despair.

It must be further observed that the Holy Spirit was, and still is, a presence in the life of the church.

At Pentecost, the Holy Spirit was given to the church. It was given to the community of faith for the community of faith. The church was to be an instrument of the Holy Spirit. H. Wheeler Robinson has written: "As the orchestra offers opportunity to the composer which the single instrument could never afford, so the church becomes a larger organ for the Spirit of God."[2]

One of the most striking things about the Holy Spirit in the church was that it was as if Jesus had returned to the church He had loved and for which He had died. At times there was no attempt to differentiate between the Holy Spirit and the living Christ: "Now the Lord is the Spirit, and where the Spirit of the Lord is, there is freedom. And we all, with unveiled face, beholding the glory of the Lord, are being changed into his likeness from one degree of glory to another; for this comes from the Lord who is the Spirit" (2 Cor. 3:17-18). (See Acts 16:7.)

The Holy Spirit led and guided the church just as Jesus had. It was the Holy Spirit that led Philip to witness to the Ethiopian eunuch (Acts 8:29). It was in the church at Antioch, the first church established on Gentile soil, that the Holy Spirit said, "Set apart for me Barnabas and Saul for the work to which I have called them" (Acts 13:2). Thus the great missionary movement from Antioch was initiated and sustained by the Holy Spirit. (See Acts 16:6-7; 19:21; 20:22-23.)

There was a heightened sense of the worth of human life in the early church and this found its highest expression in their being the children of God. "Once you were no people," wrote Peter, "but now you are God's people" (1 Pet. 2:10). People who had been nobodies became somebodies. It was the Holy Spirit, more than anything else, that attested to this wonderful fact: "For all who are led by the Spirit of God are sons of God" (Rom. 8:14).

The Holy Spirit gave gifts to the early church. We call them *charismata* from which we get our words *charismatic* and *charisma*. (See 1 Cor. 1:7; 2:14; 7:7; 12:1-12; 14:1-19; 2 Cor. 3:6; Rom. 12:3-8.) Paul mentions nine of these gifts (1 Cor. 12:8-10). While these gifts were made to individuals, they were not individuals in isolation but members of the body of Christ, the church. These gifts were to be exercised, not for self-aggrandizement, but "for the common good" (1 Cor. 12:7). While they were spiritual gifts, they could be mundane and very practical, as, for example, the gift of administration (v. 28).

2. The Holy Spirit as Creator.

The Holy Spirit was active in the creation of the universe. While in the account of creation in the first chapter of Genesis, God created essentially by His Word, the Spirit of God is mentioned before the Word is. That obviously has significance. "The earth was without form and void, and darkness was upon the face of the deep; and the Spirit of God was moving over the face of the waters" (v. 2). The Holy Spirit was brooding over that primeval mass. One could wish for a clearer statement of the Spirit's role, yet it seems to have something to do with bringing order out of chaos. There are other places where the Holy Spirit is pictured as Creator. (See Job 33:4; Ps. 104:30.)

F. W. Dillistone has this to say about the importance of the Holy Spirit as Creator: "If the doctrine of the Holy Spirit be ignored, the doctrine of creation becomes merely the tale of a bit of carpentry, of a world knocked together by a craftsman out of material external to himself, and then left to run by itself."[3]

Again, the Holy Spirit as Creator is seen in the life of the early church. Once more He brought order out of chaos. He also brought unity out of diversity, wholeness out of fragmentation.

We call the fellowship of the early church *koinonia*. Paul twice designated the fellowship as the *koinonia* of the Spirit (2 Cor. 13:14; Phil. 2:1). The world had never seen anything like it. Into that fellowship came all kinds of people with no regard to race, nationality, culture, or religion, people who had once been separated, hostile, and warring. There they loved, accepted, and affirmed each other. They met around a common Lord, Jesus Christ, whom they served and in whose name they worshiped. Paul expressed it like this: "There is neither Jew nor Greek, there is neither slave nor free, there is neither male nor female; for you are all one in Christ Jesus" (Gal. 3:28).

H. Wheeler Robinson has written: "If we ask what is the

most characteristic and comprehensive work of the Holy Spirit, according to the New Testament, there can be little doubt that we should answer in the one word, 'fellowship.' "[4] This is the *koinonia* about which I have spoken.

Further, the Holy Spirit is creator of ethical values.

We may think of the Holy Spirit as being very ethereal, high above our common concerns. Some may even have eerie feelings about Him. But all of that is changed when we realize He is concerned with the practical and difficult question of lifestyle and ethical values.

Paul wrote about the fruit of the Spirit: "But the fruit of the Spirit is love, joy, peace, patience, kindness, goodness, faithfulness, gentleness, self-control; against such there is no law" (Gal. 5:22-23). It is little wonder that Schleiermacher once remarked that the fruits of the Spirit are the virtues of Christ.

The highest ethical creation of the Holy Spirit is love. Paul closed the twelfth chapter of 1 Corinthians with these words: "And I will show you a still more excellent way" (v. 31), and then gave us the thirteenth chapter which is his great poem on love. He began the next chapter like this: "Make love your aim" (14:1). Love is the great virtue without which all other virtues may become vices.

Not only does the Holy Spirit create ethical values but He also helps us realize them, especially the highest of them all: "God's love has been poured into our hearts through the Holy Spirit which has been given to us" (Rom. 5:5).

3. The Holy Spirit as Power.

Maybe the image of power better represents the Holy Spirit than any other. God gave His Spirit to the leaders of Israel, and often it was little more than power, as in the case of Samson (Judg. 15:14-15). But with the prophets of the eighth century the power of the Spirit was ethicized. The Spirit became a strong moral force in their lives. (See Mic. 3:8-12.)

The Holy Spirit was power in the life of Jesus. In Acts 10:38 we read: "How God anointed Jesus of Nazareth with the Holy Spirit and with power; how he went about doing good and healing all that were oppressed by the devil, for God was with him." F. W. Dillistone has reflected on the meaning of this: "It might well be claimed that the entire Gospel story is in the nature of a commentary on Acts 10:38."[5]

The Holy Spirit had been promised as power by Jesus in the life of the church. (See Luke 24:49; Acts 1:8.)

The Holy Spirit came upon the church at Pentecost like a tornado from heaven (Acts 2:2). It took men and women who were cringing behind locked doors like frightened children and gave them courage. It took people whose moral and spiritual knees were buckling beneath them and made them indomitable. This power was felt in the early preaching. Peter's sermon at Pentecost, possibly the most powerful sermon in the history of the church, is eloquent testimony as to how the Holy Spirit energized the spoken word. (See Acts 10:44; 11:15; 1 Cor. 2:4.)

The Holy Spirit is like the wind. You can't see it, but you can see its effect. Jesus said to Nicodemus: "The wind blows where it wills, and you hear the sound of it, but you do not know whence it comes or whither it goes, so it is with everyone who is born of the Spirit" (John 3:8). The wind may be very powerful. It can toss big ships about on the high seas. It can uproot huge trees and hurtle large boulders down the side of a mountain. But it can be very gentle, a soft breeze in the summer or a puff of fresh air in your face on a hot day. Just so with the Spirit.

4. The Holy Spirit as Life.

The Hebrew *ruah* and the Greek *pneuma* can mean breath or wind. They are both translated *spirit* which reminds us how similar are wind and spirit. Both are unseen and intangible, yet you can see the signs of their presence.

Primitive people associated breath with life. As long as a person lived he breathed. When he no longer breathed he was dead. The life was in the breath. So life was early associated with breath or spirit. We should not forget that the primitive mind often grasps rudimentary truth the more sophisticated mind may overlook.

In the creation story recorded in the second chapter of Genesis, God formed man from the dust of the earth "and breathed into his nostrils the breath of life; and man became a living being" (v. 7).

Ezekiel, in his marvelous vision of dry bones, finally sees perfectly formed human bodies lying upon the desert sand but they did not live. There was form without life. And God said: "Come from the four winds, O breath, and breathe upon these slain, that they may live. . . . And the breath came into them, and they lived, and stood upon their feet, an exceedingly great host" (Ezek. 37:9-10).

You remember Jesus' meeting Nicodemus, a member of the supreme court of Israel, who was the finest flowering of his culture and religion. You are shocked at what Jesus said to him: "You must be born anew" (John 3:7). You would not have been surprised if Nicodemus had been a bum or some kind of criminal, but he was not. He was a cultured, polished gentleman with great integrity. Jesus made it perfectly clear that the new life was a gift of the Spirit (John 3:6,8).

The early church, so aware of the new life in its midst, traced it to its source which was the Holy Spirit. (See Rom. 8:6, 10-11; Gal. 6:7-8.)

Then there was the supreme and unique life, Jesus Christ. He was conceived of the Holy Spirit and born of the virgin Mary. (See Matt. 1:18-25; Luke 1:26-35.)

The gift of new life is so wonderful. Yet, one of the questions that persists is: How shall I know that I possess it? The New Testament gives two tests. The first is spiritual: "It is the Spirit himself bearing witness with our spirit that we are children of God" (Rom. 8:16). The second is social: "We know that we have passed out of death into life, because we love the brethren" (1 John 3:14). Therefore, the new, made possible by the Holy Spirit, keeps before us the two dimensions of great religion—the spiritual and the social. We are to be right with God and we are to be right with our brother and sister.

5. The Holy Spirit as Revealer.

Christianity is a religion of revelation; that is to say, God discloses Himself. We could never know who God is unless He tells us. This He has graciously done and the Holy Spirit has played an important role in the revelation. It is the Spirit of God who knows the mind of God and therefore tells us who God is and how He thinks. Paul wrote: "God has revealed to us through the Spirit. For the Spirit searches everything, even the depths of God. For what person knows a man's thoughts except the spirit of the man which is in him? So also no one comprehends the thoughts of God except the Spirit of God" (1 Cor. 2:10-11).

We should not be surprised at the necessity of revelation. That is how we know each other, to say nothing of God. A small child says to you: "I've got a secret." You cannot know the secret unless the child tells you. That is revelation in its simplest and most basic sense. If you cannot know the secret of a child unless he tells you, how can you know the mystery and secret in the mind of God unless His Spirit reveals it?

There is another sense in which the Holy Spirit is revealer. He is like a flare dropped across the shadowed and darkened landscape, enabling us to see where God is acting and what He is doing. God could not reveal Himself in history unless the Holy Spirit illumines His ways for us.

Imagine the day Jesus said to His disciples: "He who has seen me has seen the Father" (John 14:9). How shocked they must have been! Here was a carpenter from Nazareth whose face had been tanned by the sun and wind. How could they see God in the face of a carpenter? They couldn't unless the light of the Holy Spirit should fall upon it. Then they could.

6. The Holy Spirit as Promise.

We understand the Holy Spirit as promise in two senses: As promise fulfilled, and as guarantee of promise yet to be fulfilled.

We have talked about the strategic place in which the early church found itself. It stood where the shadows of an old age were being lost in the dawn of a new one. It faced the early morning of a most exciting new age. This was the age of the kingdom of God, the resurrected Lord, and the church as the new Israel with its new covenant of the Spirit. But maybe the early church thought of the new age as the age of the Spirit more than in any other way. The presence of the Spirit as promise fulfilled was a sign that the new age had come. This was the way Peter saw it. The prophecy of Joel was being fulfilled which said in part: "And in the last days it shall be, God declares, /that I will pour out my Spirit upon all flesh" (Acts 2:17a).

The Holy Spirit was also promise fulfilled when the risen Christ sent the Paraclete, the "Spirit of truth" (John 14:17) on the Day of Pentecost. The Paraclete was indeed like one called to their sides to be their counselor, guide, and strengthener.

But you will discover that the Holy Spirit is a guarantee of promise yet to be fulfilled—the promise of full and ultimate salvation. Paul speaks three times of the guarantee (earnest) of the Spirit. (See 2 Cor. 1:22; 5:5; Eph. 1:18.) "Guarantee" was a translation of *arrabon* which was a Greek word lifted from business and trade. *Arrabon* was the first installment of the price that was the guarantee that in due time the full payment would be made. It bound the purchaser to complete the payment of the full price agreed upon.

God, in the gift of the Holy Spirit, has given us a foretaste of our final salvation, and the gift is a pledge that He will at last bring us to full redemption. If frail men honor their commitments, how much more can we expect God to be faithful. He will at last bring us into a future more wonderful than we can imagine.

We are still in the age of the Spirit. We should let Him give us hope, quicken the lives of our churches, and make our pulpits powerful.

Thought Starters

A series of sermons on The Holy Spirit and the Trinity.
A series on A Profile of the Holy Spirit.

Other sermons: When Theology Is Born of Experience; The Basic Meaning of the Holy Spirit; Worship and the Nurture of Our Faith; The Trinity in the New Testament; The Holy Spirit as Indispensable for Christianity; Called to Your Side; Order Out of Chaos; The Fruits of the Spirit and the Virtues of Christ; New Life as the Gift of the Holy Spirit; How Shall We Know the Mind of God? The Holy Spirit Like a Flare on Our Darkened Landscapes; The First Installment.

Scripture

Genesis 1:1-31; Psalm 139:7-12; Ezekiel 37:1-14; Luke 1:26-35; John 14:15-17,25-26; 15:26-27; 16:5-11; Acts 2:1-13; Romans 8:1-17; 1 Corinthians 12:1-31; Galatians 5:16-25.

Texts

Genesis 1:2; Zechariah 4:6; Luke 24:49; John 14:16; Acts 1:8; 2:2; 4:31; Romans 5:5; 7:6; 8:2; Galatians 5:22; Revelation 22:17.

Illustrations

Valley of dry bones (Ezek. 37:1-14); The better gift (Luke 11:13); Paraclete passages (John 14:15-17; 25-26; 15:26-27; 16:5-11); Pentecost as power (Acts 2:1-4); The Holy Spirit and the new age (Acts 2:16-21); The Holy Spirit pouring God's love into our hearts (Rom. 5:5); The Holy Spirit helps us in our praying (Rom. 8:26-27); The Holy Spirit and the new life (Rom. 8:2, 13); The Holy Spirit and our being sons of God (Rom. 8:14-17); Our body as the temple of the Holy Spirit (1 Cor. 6:19); The Spirit as unity in diversity (1 Cor. 12:1-13); The Holy Spirit as first installment (guarantee) of better things (2 Cor. 1:22; 5:5; Eph. 1:13); Near identification of the Holy Spirit with the risen Lord (2 Cor. 3:17); The Holy Spirit and the new covenant (2 Cor. 3:4-6); The ethics of the Spirit (Gal. 5:22); The law of the harvest (Gal. 6:7-8); The Spirit authenticates the new life in Christ (Eph. 1:13).

Notes

1. Knox, *Life in Christ Jesus,* p. 75.

2. H. Wheeler Robinson, *The Christian Experience of the Holy Spirit* (London: Nisbet and Company, Ltd., 1928), p. 44.

3. F. W. Dillistone, *The Holy Spirit in the Life of Today* (Philadelphia: The Westminster Press, 1947), p. 18.

4. Robinson, p. 141.

5. Dillistone, p. 55.

9
Israel and the Church:
The People of God

There are over one hundred metaphors in the New Testament that refer to the church. Obviously, the church is a many-faceted and versatile reality. But more than all the others I like the metaphor that speaks of the church as the people of God.

I am impressed with this metaphor for four reasons. First of all, the church is under divine authority and, for that reason, is unique. Here is our basic identification: We are God's people. Right here the church finds its great weakness: We often don't know who we are, and therefore do not know what we are to do in the world. We can't belong to everybody and everything.

Again, there is something warm and human about this identification. We are people, not angels or semidivinities. We are sinners who have been forgiven by God and called into His service. We are plain, ordinary, everyday people who have been touched by a grace that is not ordinary.

Further, there is a mobility in the idea. People are on the move. It is easy to become tethered too closely to sacred places, times, and buildings. We may be caught within institutional structures and lose our mobility.

Finally, there is a world orientation in the identification which I like very much. People live in the world. They do the work and carry on the commerce of the world. The church is to fulfill its mission in the world. The concept helps the church to look beyond its own life, to turn outward rather than inward, to be world-serving rather than self-serving.

Let us look at Israel as the people of God, then at the church as the new people of God, and finally at the modern church in the light of this concept.

Israel as the People of God

There is no more obvious truth in the Old Testament than that Israel was God's special people. Scriptures making this declaration abound.

The classical statement is found in the nineteenth chapter of Exodus: "You have seen what I did to the Egyptians, and how I bore you on eagles' wings and brought you to myself. Now therefore, if you will obey my voice and keep my covenant, you shall be my own possession among all peoples; for all the earth is mine, and you shall be to me a kingdom of priests and a holy nation. These are the words which you shall speak to the children of Israel" (vv. 4-6). (See also Deut. 4:20; 7:6; Mal. 3:17.)

We should observe four things which God did in making these insignificant people His special people.

1. He loved them. We have earlier mentioned how the fact that God chose Israel was always a puzzle to them. Why? That was a question she often asked. God had not called her because she was powerful and strong. She was the smallest of nations. Nor was she particularly gifted. She was often spiritually obtuse, morally insensitive, and faithless in her commitments to God. She was willful, stiff-necked, and rebellious. There was only one thing that made any sense out of the puzzle: God loved her and had called her in grace.

2. God had redeemed them. They were helpless slaves in Egypt under the merciless hand of a powerful and ruthless king. Humanly speaking, there was no way of escape. Any kind of rebellion would have been suicide. But God delivered them at the Red Sea. Israel remembered how He delivered them with "the mighty hand and the outstretched arm."

3. God had bound these free people to Him in covenant. Before anything else, this covenant was a relationship. But

Israel must exercise her freedom responsibly. Therefore, God gave her laws which set limits and boundaries beyond which she could not go. It was inside these boundaries that Israel was to find freedom.

4. God then declared them a special people, His very own. They were to be His people, doing His work, in His world. They were to let the whole world know that there is only one God, powerful and mighty, a God of justice and mercy, to whom the world belongs and to whom all people are to offer praise and give service. That was their task.

Israel made serious mistakes. They turned from the God who had redeemed them and claimed them. They went after false gods. They violated God's laws and broke His covenant. They mistook God's election of them as privilege rather than a call to service. They thought of themselves as the aristocrats of God rather than His servants. They became arrogant, proud, and condescending in their relationship with the other people of the world. God had to ask finally: Can I continue to use Israel or must I turn to another people?

The Church as the New People of God

Israel forgot who she was, to whom she belonged, and what she was to do. She became so proud and blind that she did not recognize her Messiah when He came. She was greatly offended by His cross.

Jesus in His parable of the vineyard told about a householder who lived in another country, sending his servants at harvesttime to collect his share of the crop. The tenants beat and abused the servants, sending them back empty-handed. Finally the householder sent his own son whom they killed. What would the householder do when he returned? "He will put those wretches to a miserable death, and let out the vineyard to other tenants who will give him the fruits in their seasons." Then said Jesus: "Therefore I tell you, the kingdom of God will be taken away from you and given to a nation producing the fruits of it" (see Matt. 21:33-44).

So God turned from Israel to the church which is seen as the new Israel or the new people of God. This is very obvious.

The classical statement of this is from Peter: "But you are a chosen race, a royal priesthood, a holy nation, God's own people, that you may declare the wonderful deeds of him who called you out of darkness into his marvelous light. Once you were no people but now you are God's people; once you had not received mercy but now you have received mercy" (1 Pet. 2:9-10). (See Rom. 9:25-26; Gal. 6:16; Titus 2:14.) Note the similarity of language in Exodus 19 and 1 Peter 2.

We can't remember all the Scriptures where great truths are found, but we should remember cardinal or classical passages such as Exodus 19:4-6 and 1 Peter 2:9-10.

I have mentioned that God did four things in calling Israel as the people of God into being. It is interesting and important to note that He did four things—the same four—to bring into being the new Israel as the new people of God, which would be the church.

1. God loved the church. No one states this more emphatically or more beautifully than Paul in the fifth chapter of Ephesians: "Husbands, love your wives, as Christ loved the church and gave himself up for her, that he might sanctify her, having cleansed her by the washing of water with the word, that he might present the church to himself in splendor, without spot or wrinkle or any such thing, that she might be holy and without blemish" (vv. 25-27).

These new people were aware they had been called, not because of their goodness and virtue, but by the grace of Christ. The truth is they were a pretty motley group. You have only to look in upon the life of the church at Corinth to see this. Many of them had brought the low standards of the world into that church. There was immorality among them, with members suing each other in the pagan courts. They were factious and immature, bickering and quarreling as if they were children. Only the grace of Christ could have seen anything good in them and made anything out of them.

2. Christ had redeemed them, setting them free, so they could be His new people.

It is true that they were not held in political bondage the way old Israel had been in Egypt. But they had been held captive by dark and sinister powers. They had been imprisoned by the two ultimately enslaving powers—sin and death. But Christ, through His death and resurrection, had set them free from both. Paul could write: "For the law of the Spirit of life in Christ Jesus has set me free from the law of sin and death" (Rom. 8:2).

3. A new covenant was given.

Jeremiah had envisioned a new covenant. The old one had been external and too easily broken. In the new covenant, God would write His law, not upon tablets of stone, but upon their hearts. It would be inward, touching the deepest springs of their life. Jesus enacted this new covenant when He instituted the Lord's Supper. With a goblet of wine in His hands, He said: "This cup is the new covenant in my blood" (1 Cor. 11:25).

4. God declared the church His new people. We remember that Peter had said: "Once you were no people, but now you are God's people; once you had not received mercy, but now you have received mercy" (1 Pet. 2:10).

But what really happened between the old Israel and the new? Was there continuity or was there a complete break, discontinuity? There was both continuity and discontinuity.

Note the continuity.

There was no change of God. The God of the Old Testament is the same God in the New. He is the Father of our Lord and Savior Jesus Christ.

The new Israel kept the Holy Scriptures of the old Israel. The Old Testament is a part of our Bible and we read from it just the way we do the New Testament which is uniquely our own.

There is continuity in the concept of Israel. It is carried over. We are not something else. We are still Israel, the new one.

We are still the people of God; albeit, the new people of God. Paul spoke about how the church was not a completely new tree. It was like a wild olive branch grafted into an old, living tree. The new tree is supported by the old roots. (See Rom. 11:17-18.)

We are also the spiritual descendants of Abraham. We are not his biological descendants, but, like him, we believe God and it is reckoned unto us as righteousness. (See Gal. 3:6-18.)

As already noted, God did the same four things to bring about the new people of God as He had done to make possible the old.

Yet, there is also discontinuity. There is a break. It is more than a continuation of the old. There is a new turning, a new beginning. Something radically different has happened. The redemption of Christ is a new redemption. The covenant given by Christ is new. The church is the new people of God. Christ is still a promise in the Old Testament but in the New Testament He is no longer a promise. He has really come. The boundaries of the new Israel are greatly enlarged. The old Israel was hemmed in by national boundaries. But in the new Israel, the church, there are no national, cultural, or geographical boundaries. In the seventh chapter of Revelation there is a magnificent picture of the new people of God:

"After this I looked, and behold, a great multitude which no man could number, from every nation, from all tribes and peoples and tongues, standing before the throne and before the Lamb, clothed in white robes, with palm branches in their hands, and crying out with a loud voice, 'Salvation belongs to our God who sits upon the throne, and to the Lamb!' " (vv. 9-10).

There is more than continuity. There is something radically new.

The Contemporary Church

The contemporary church needs to recover the sense of being the people of God. I don't know of anything it needs more. It would help us in four basic ways.

1. It would help us to recover our identity. We are God's

people, at least we should be. The church can so easily belong to somebody else—to the community, or the culture, or the world.

Imagine your own church. Envision your congregation on Sunday morning as you stand before them. They have come from every segment of the community's life. In some sense they are the community's people, and they come to church bringing with them the values where they live. Many of them take pride in their community, remembering that for many generations their family has lived there. They would not live anywhere else. This of itself is not bad. At least it keeps the hour of worship in touch with where they live.

But they belong to somebody else. As the church, they belong to Christ. They are God's people, but this is often dimly perceived and poorly understood. It is so much easier to establish their identity as being the community's people than being God's people. And while it should be clearly understood that the two are not mutually exclusive, the most difficult thing a church ever does is to step across the line that demarcates them and truly become the people of God.

We still feel the threat of civil religion. In this religion, we are tempted to equate the Christian gospel with our American values. It is God, country, and flag. We get them all mixed up. We talk about faith in God but what we are really saying is that we believe in democracy, the free enterprise system, and the American way of life. Whenever civil religion prevails, the church becomes America's people, not God's. We become our culture's people. For example, when the church doesn't want black people, it is more the people of a segregated culture than the people of God.

I often think of Theodore O. Wedel's parable of the lifesaving station![1]

On a dangerous seacoast where shipwrecks often occurred, there was once a crude, little lifesaving station. The building was just a hut, and there was only one boat, but the few devoted members kept a constant watch over the sea, and, with no thought for themselves, went out day and night tirelessly searching for the lost. Many lives were saved, and the little station became known far and near. Many wanted to become associated with the station and gave their time, money, and effort for the support of the work. New boats were bought and new crews trained. The little lifesaving station grew.

Some of the members became restless because the building was so crude and poorly equipped. They felt a more comfortable place should be provided as the first refuge of those saved from the sea. They replaced the emergency cots with beds and put better furniture in the building that had now been enlarged. They decorated it beautifully and furnished it exquisitely, and the station became a popular gathering place, all the while taking upon itself more and more the atmosphere of a club. Few members were now interested in going to sea on lifesaving missions, so they hired professionals to do their work. The lifesaving motif still continued in the club's decoration, and there was a liturgical lifeboat in the room where the club initiations were held. As the life of the station was becoming more comfortable, a large ship was wrecked off the coast, and the hired crew brought in a boatload of cold, wet, and half-drowned people. They were filthy and sick, some of them had black skin and some had yellow skin. The beautiful new club didn't know how to handle the situation. Everything was in chaos. So the property committee took quick action, having a shower house built outside the club where victims of shipwrecks could be cleaned up before coming inside.

At the next meeting, there was a dropping off of attendance. The members felt anxious and insecure. What was happening to them? Most of the members wanted to stop their lifesaving activities since obviously they were a hindrance to the social life of the club. Some of the members insisted that lifesaving was their primary business and that they were still called a lifesaving station. But they were voted down, and told that they could build their lifesaving station farther down the coast. This they did.

They began their new venture with enthusiasm, but soon the same corroding forces that worked on the original lifesaving station began to work on them. The pleasure of comfort became more appealing than the discipline and danger of the sea. It evolved into a club, the same vote was taken, and a new lifesaving station was founded farther on down the coast. History continued to repeat itself, and, if you visit that seacoast today, you will find exclusive clubs lining its shore. Shipwrecks are frequent in those waters, but most of the people drown!

The same thing happens to the church.

2. It would keep the church from turning in on its own life.

How often the church is more concerned about saving its own life than saving the world. It becomes introverted.

There is something extrovertish about the church as the people of God. People are mobile, on the move, and in the world.

Gordon Cosby tells of an incident that occured a few years ago when he and his wife were traveling in the Highlands of Scotland. A flock of sheep crossed the road, and while waiting for them to cross, their friend asked: "What do you know about sheep?" "I don't know anything about sheep," came the reply. Then Gordon turned the question: "What do you know?" "Well," began the friend, "I discovered something very interesting. Sometimes in the winter when the snow comes, the sheep get hemmed in against the walls. It is a very interesting thing that a sheep can live for seven to ten days in such a blizzard by eating its own wool. But, the problem is that it dies from exposure."

Just so with the church. When it turns in upon its own life, its vitality ebbs and its spiritual life diminishes. It may maintain impressive forms but they will be more like a mausoleum than a living organism.

3. It will help the church to live by two great imperatives—come and go.

Jesus called His disciples to a kind of double action. He called them to Himself and then sent them out: "And he called to him the twelve, and began to send them out two by two, and gave them authority over the unclean spirits" (Mark 6:7).

In authentic worship we have the same kind of experience Isaiah had, as recorded in the sixth chapter of Isaiah, although our experience will seldom be so dramatic and life rending. He had a clear vision of the greatness and glory of God, felt guilt, and had his sins forgiven. He was given a pure heart and clean lips. But the experience didn't end there. Beyond the quiet and beauty of the Temple, lay a big world in upheaval, pain, sin, and death. And Isaiah heard the voice of God calling him to go into that world with a word from God.

The imperative to come is important. We need our church with its worship, gospel, and fellowship. It is there we get a clearer vision of God, and we have our hearts infused with the love and compassion of Christ. It is there also that we get a clearer vision of our world, and we are touched by its hurt and pain. This is God's world and we see it in the light that comes from Him.

But we can't linger too long in our sanctuary. God sends us back into the world to be ministers of Christ. We leave it knowing that the church must fulfill its mission in the world.

When we are hesitant to be the church in the world, we need to listen to George MacLeod: "I am recovering the claim that Jesus was not crucified in a cathedral between two candles, but on a cross between two thieves; on the town garbage-heap; at a crossroad so cosmopolitan that they had to write His title in Hebrew and in Latin and in Greek; at the kind of place where cynics talk smut, and thieves curse, and soldiers gamble. Because that is where He died. And that is what He died about. And there is where churchmen should be and that is what churchmanship should be about."[2]

4. It will create tension between its own life and the life of culture. The church is God's people but it must fulfill its mission in the world.

The church cannot, nor should it want to, escape this tension. It must be willing to keep one foot in its own authentic life and one in the world. It must live with one hand gripping its own life and the other touching its culture. It is called on to walk a tightrope. It must not fall off into the secularity of the world or fall into a kind of ethereal spiritual existence.

This tension is very painful, and the church is constantly tempted to relax it. It may relax it by capitulating to the world and becoming an extension of its culture. Or it may relax it by retreating into its own life. But in either case it cannot be itself and fulfill its mission. The price it must pay for its authenticity is tension.

Philippi was a Roman colony. It was an outpost of Roman culture and the citizens had a missionary zeal for transplanting Roman culture where they were. They took pride in a double citizenship. Their names were on the citizenship rolls of Philippi and of Rome. Paul saw an analogy that pointed up the genius of the Christian church there: "But our commonwealth is in heaven" (3:20). They belonged to two commonwealths—one political and one spiritual. The light from heaven revealed the shadows, darkness, and sin of the city. But they must live in it. They must be salt, saving it from decay, and they must be light, driving away its shadows and darkness. They could not escape the tension of the two commonwealths.

Thought Starters

A series of four sermons: Advantages in Being the People of God.

A series of sermons: God's Four Steps in Making Israel His People.

A series of sermons: God's Four Steps in Making the New Israel His People.

Other sermons: The Church Versatile and Many-Faceted; A Chosen People; Redemption as Being Set Free; Once No People, Now God's People; From Darkness into His Marvelous Light; Set Free from Life's Two Ultimately Enslaving Powers; The People of the Community, The People of God;

How Much Is Old, How Much New? The Threat of Civil Religion; Getting the Flag and Cross Confused; Story of a Lifesaving Station; The Danger of the Church Losing Its Identity; There Is Something Extravertish About the Church; The Church Turning In Upon Its Own Life; Living by Two Imperatives; Isaiah's Experience as a Model for Our Worship; Citizens of Two Worlds; A Tension We Cannot Escape.

Scripture

Exodus 19:1-6; Acts 2:37-42; Ephesians 2:11-22; 4:1-16; Colossians 3:12-17; 1 Peter 2:1-10; Revelation 7:9-17.[3]

Texts

Matthew 20:28; John 13:14; Acts 2:41; 2 Corinthians 5:18-19; Galatians 3:28; Ephesians 2:14; 5:25-27; 1 Peter 1:18-19; 2:9-10; Revelation 5:10; 7:9-10.

Illustrations

No barriers in the church (Acts 10:9-48; Gal. 3:28; Col. 3:11; Eph. 2:14-16); The church as a temple (1 Cor. 3:16-17; Eph. 2:21); As the people of God (Ex. 19:3-6; 1 Pet. 2:9-10); The church as the body of Christ (Rom. 12:4-5; 1 Cor. 12:12-31; Eph. 4:14-16; Col. 3:15); The church as a reconciled and reconciling fellowship (2 Cor. 5:16-21); The church as a new humanity (Gal. 3:28; Eph. 2:11-16); The church as a redeemed and redeeming fellowship (1 Pet. 1:18; Rev. 1:5-6; 5:9-10); The church as a servant (Matt. 20:25-28; John 13:1-16); The church as a commonwealth (Eph. 2:19); The church as the family of God (Eph. 2:19); The unity of the church (Eph. 4:1-6); Citizens of two worlds (Phil. 3:20); More like the city than a church (Rev. 3:14-19); The church without boundaries (Rev. 5:9-10; 7:9); The church as the bride of Christ (Eph. 5:22-32; Rev. 19:7); The church as God intends it (Eph. 5:23-32; Rev. 7:9-12).

Notes

1. Chevis F. Horne, *Crisis in the Pulpit* (Grand Rapids: Baker Book House, 1975), pp. 73-74.

2. Foy Valentine, *The Cross in the Market Place* (Waco: Word Books, 1966), p. 17.

3. It should be observed that the Scripture, texts, and illustrations represent a wider range of meaning than the church being only the people of God.

10
Covenant:
Relationship, Boundary,
Responsibility

Covenant is without doubt one of the overarching themes of the Bible. It is so important that unless we understand covenant, we cannot understand our Bible.

The Hebrew word translated *covenant* is *berith,* and its root meaning seems to be "fetter." Therefore a covenant is a relationship that binds two parties to mutual commitments. The word *covenant* occurs 286 times in the Old Testament, which gives some indication of how extensively it is used.

The Greek word translated *covenant* is *diatheke* which can mean either last will and testament or covenant. The term is used in the New Testament to mean covenant with the exception of Hebrews 9:16-17 where it means last will and testament.

In the light of this it becomes clear that our Bible is misnamed. It should be the Old and New Covenant rather than the Old and New Testament. If this is so, how did we go wrong? We went wrong through the Latin. The Greek word was translated *testamentum* in the Latin, and passed on to us.

When I learned that our Bible is really the Old and New Covenants, my heart leaped up. It took on an immeasurably greater meaning, becoming alive as never before.

The Old Covenant

There are several covenants spoken of in the Old Testament. For example, there was a covenant between God and Abraham, as well as one between God and Noah. And there were others, also. But we are concerned with the basic covenant of the Old

Testament, known as the Mosaic Covenant which had Moses as its mediator and was enacted at Mount Sinai or Mount Horeb while the Israelites were en route from their bondage in Egypt to their free life in the Land of Promise.

Covenants were very common in the ancient world. There were covenants between individuals, tribes, and nations. For example, the suzerainty treaties of the Hittite Empire have been preserved in abundance. The Hittite Empire was vast, existing in the late Bronze Age (ca. 1400-1200 BC), and these treaties or covenants were the formal basis by which the king bound vassal states to his rule. We call them suzerainty treaties because they existed between unequals, between the king as suzerain and vassal states. It is interesting and significant to note that the covenant between Yahweh and His people follows the pattern of these Hittite commands. That fact tells us something extremely important about us and our religion: we are a historical people whom God meets in our history, and in expressing our faith we use historical tools and models. That is a clue that helps us understand our Bible better.

There are three basic elements in that covenant we want to look at—relationship, boundary, and responsibility.

We cannot know the importance of relationship unless we know how basic it is. The truth is we cannot live without relationship. It is the essence of life which is fulfilled in terms of this basic reality. The tragedy of life is found in broken basic relationships, and salvation is experienced in terms of having those basic relationships mended and healed.

I remember how John Knox spoke about the crucial importance of relationship: "Our malady is not our ignorance or even our weakness but our homesickness. What we all most deeply need is not an answer to the ultimate question about our existence, but an environment of relationships which will enable us to bear the unanswered and [in our present life] unanswerable question."[1]

The basic formula of the covenant was: "I will be your God, and you shall be my people" (Jer. 7:23). It is a formula of relationship. Note that with the coming of the new Jerusalem when God will come down to dwell with His people, the formula is announced again. A voice is heard saying:

"Behold, the dwelling of God is with men. He will dwell with them, and they shall be his people, and God himself will be with them" (Rev. 21:3).

That is what the covenant was all about and that is what the church is all about.

It should be remembered that God took the initiative and that the covenant was not between equals but unequals. It was between the creator and the creature, between almighty God and weak people, between eternal God and men and women caught in fleeting years.

The covenant was an intimate relationship. The prophets likened the covenant to marriage which is the most intimate of all human relations. Ezekiel wrote: "Yea, I plighted my troth to you and entered into a covenant with you, says the Lord God, and you became mine" (16:8). (See Isa. 54:5; Hos. 2:19.)

2. Also, the idea of boundary is very important in the covenant.

The basic theological background of the covenant is redemption or freedom. God had freed His people from slavery. But freedom often brings problems. Freedom, when so suddenly and radically given, may go to excess, expressing itself in lawless and disorderly ways. The liberated may become libertines, freedom can become license. The people must use their freedom responsibly. Therefore it was necessary to set their lives within boundaries, to establish limits beyond which they could not go. So, as a part of the covenant, God gave them laws which set boundaries for them.

The laws given initially with the covenant were the Ten Commandments or Decalogue and what is called the Covenant Code. The Ten Commandments are recorded in the twentieth chapter of Exodus as well as in the fifth chapter of Deuteronomy, the Code of the Covenant in Exodus 20:22—23:33. The reason we call it the Code of the Covenant is that in the story of the enactment of the covenant, after Moses had thrown blood on the altar which bound God to the covenant, it is written that Moses "took the book of the covenant, and read it in the hearing of the people" (Ex. 24:7). It is generally believed that this book of the covenant was the code that now bears the name of the Code of the Covenant.

Both codes, the Decalogue and the Code of the Covenant, set limits beyond which they could not go. The Decalogue defined boundaries which they could not cross in their relationships with God and their fellow Israelites. The Code of the Covenant is essentially an elaboration of the last six Commandments of the Decalogue.

These codes defined boundaries for their lives, but within them they were free.

3. Finally, responsibility was involved in the covenant.

The covenant was enacted in freedom. No one was coerced. God took the iniative in freedom and the people responded in freedom. Therefore, both God and the people were responsible for fulfilling the provisions of the covenant.

When Moses read the book of the covenant to the people, their response was: "All that the Lord has spoken we will do, and we will be obedient" (Ex. 24:7). There was no threat or intimidation.

God had promised to be their God, and they had promised to be His obedient people. That lay at the very heart of the covenant.

God brought to the covenant what is called steadfast love. "All the paths of the Lord are steadfast love and faithfulness," wrote the psalmist, "for those who keep his covenant and his testimonies" (25:10). (See Jer. 31:3.)

There was nothing fickle, moody, or temperamental about the love God brought to the covenant. It was faithful, steadfast, abiding.

The thing that made the covenant so poignant was Israel's unfaithfulness. If the relationship of the covenant was like a marriage, then Israel's faithlessness was like adultery. They turned from the God who loved them with steadfastness to gods who had no capacity for love. Therefore God spoke of Israel as an adulteress. (See Deut. 31:16; Jer. 3:6.)

Yet, through all of Israel's faithlessness, Yahweh remained faithful; amid all her broken loyalties, He remained loyal; despite Israel's fickleness, God remained steadfast. God was like Hosea who could not give up his faithless wife. (See Hos. 3:1-5; Isa. 54:7; Jer. 31:34; Zech. 8:7-8.)

A New Covenant Envisioned

While laws played such an important role in the covenant, they tended to become a god. Israel was tempted to worship her laws rather than the Lawgiver. These laws became too sacred. They had about them an aura of mystery. Listen to the record. (See Ex. 31:18; Deut. 4:13.) Imagine their believing their laws were written by the finger of God.

God might be far above the earth, but His will was on earth in something as concrete and objective as a code cut in stone. There was a concentration on law, and they lost sight of God's grace that gave it and the relationship into which God had called them. Their covenant became law and their religion legalism. They forgot the great dimensions of moral and spiritual religion. It was all too external.

It was Jeremiah, more than anyone else, who envisioned a new covenant that would correct the externality of the old. God would write His law on the hearts of His people, not on tablets of stone. Jeremiah's vision of the new covenant is one of the finest things in the Old Testament. (Read Jer. 31:31-34.)

Jeremiah wrote in the best of the covenant tradition. He remembered the great event that lay back of the covenant, that of redemption: "When I took them by the hand to bring them out of . . . Egypt." He used the metaphor of marriage to indicate the intimate relationship of the covenant: "though I was their husband" (v. 32). He remembered the covenant formula: "I will be their God, and they shall be my people" (v. 33). And he recalled the faithfulness of God in forgiveness: "For I will forgive their iniquity, and I will remember their sin no more" (v. 34*b*).

In spite of their sin and faithlessness, God was not willing to abrogate the old covenant, leaving them with no covenant at all. Yet it seemed futile to continue with the old covenant which they would keep on breaking.

What was the answer to the dilemma? A new covenant which would have two unique features: the new law would be written on their hearts, and the accent would be, not on knowing the law, but on knowing God. "They shall all know me, from the least of them to the greatest" (v. 34*a*).

The New Covenant

Jeremiah's vision of the new covenant became a reality in the New Testament.

Now, before we go further, while the spirit of the covenant permeates the New Testament, we must observe that not much is said about it. What we have are sketchy accounts of the new covenant, isolated references, and allusions to it. It becomes our task to take these sketchy references and fill out the picture of the new covenant.

Why there is not more said about the new covenant in the New Testament puzzles scholars. No one can be sure, but some scholars believe it can be explained by the fact that while covenant, for the Jew, meant the Mosaic law, for the Roman it was an illegal secret society. Christianity early got into trouble with the Roman government, and constant references to the covenant by the church would have put it in further jeopardy. That may explain why the term is used with such restraint.

What do we know about the new covenant? Let me suggest five things.

1. It was enacted by Jesus at His last supper with His disciples before His crucifixion. The earliest account of this is not to be found in the Synoptic Gospels but in Paul's First Letter to the Corinthians as recorded in the eleventh chapter. That

night, after having blessed and passed the bread, Jesus took a cup of wine, blessed it, and gave it to His disciples, saying: "This cup is the new covenant in my blood. Do this, as often as you drink it, in remembrance of me" (1 Cor. 11:25).

Just as the old covenant was sealed in blood, so was the new. You remember how Moses sprinkled blood on the altar which represented God and then on the people, binding both of them in deep commitment to the covenant. (See Ex. 24:3-8.) The fact that covenants were signed in blood gives some indication of the solemnity upon which they were entered. But at this point there was one great difference between the old and new covenant: While the first was sealed with the blood of animals, the second was sealed with the blood of the Son of God.

2. The new covenant enacted by Jesus was, as already indicated, a fulfillment of Jeremiah's vision of a new covenant. The author of Hebrews makes that very clear in the eighth chapter of his book. He speaks about the covenant mediated by Jesus and then quotes that magnificent passage from Jeremiah 31 as the promise fulfilled in the new covenant.

3. The law of the covenant is love.

Now this is not said explicitly anywhere. But what other law could be written on the human heart? This is an example where we have to fill in the picture.

Jesus said the law and the prophets were fulfilled in the commandment of love. Jesus gave a new commandment: "A new commandment I give to you, that you love one another; even as I have loved you, that you also love one another. By this all men will know that you are my disciples, if you have love for one another" (John 13:34-35). His new law befitted the new covenant which He made possible.

Paul wrote: "Owe no one anything, except to love one another; for he who loves his neighbor has fulfilled the law" (Rom. 13:8). And James called love the royal law: "If you really fulfil the royal law, according to the scripture, 'You shall love your neighbor as yourself,' you do well" (Jas. 2:8).

4. It is a covenant written, not in code, but in the Spirit.

God "has made us competent to be ministers of a new covenant," Paul wrote, "not in a written code but in the Spirit; for the written code kills, but the Spirit gives life" (2 Cor. 3:6).

When Paul says the written code kills, he is speaking about the destructive power of legalism. Laws create guilt but cannot forgive. Therefore legalism drives us deeper and deeper into guilt and despair and finally to death. "The written code kills."

"But the Spirit gives life." The Spirit, like love, is inward. The Spirit is vital, powerful, and life-giving. The Spirit puts the grace of Christ into hearts and they are transformed. The Spirit makes possible forgiveness and life, while the law condemned, but could not offer forgiveness. The law was like a heavy, clammy hand over the spirits of men and women, while the Spirit is a life-giving power.

5. The new covenant is superior to the old.

Paul asked: "Now if the dispensation of death, carved in letters on stone, came with such splendor that the Israelites could not look at Moses' face because of its brightness, fading as this was, will not the dispensation of the Spirit be attended with greater splendor?" (2 Cor. 3:7).

It is true the old covenant with its law was given in splendor and glory. Moses' face shone brightly as he came down the mountain with the tablets of stone on which were cut the law. But like all things, it was a passing glory and a fading splendor. The Spirit with its gift of the new covenant comes in a glory that is more lasting and a splendor that is more enduring. The new is superior to the old.

The writer of Hebrews says: "But as it is, Christ has obtained a ministry which is as much more excellent than the old as the covenant he mediates is better, since it is enacted on better promises" (8:6). "In speaking of a new covenant he treats the first as obsolete. And what is becoming obsolete and growing old is ready to vanish away" (v. 13).

It was as if the old covenant was tentative and provisional, and with the passing of its time became obsolete.

A New Covenant for the Contemporary Church

While we are people of a covenant, we often do not use as we should covenants which have played such a vital role in the historic life of the church. The covenant in many places has fallen into disuse. That is certainly true of many Baptist churches which I know best. It is a tragedy!

I think of the Baptist churches in eastern North Carolina I knew as a boy. My father was a Baptist minister serving rural and village churches, and I visited many of those churches with him. I still remember those covenant banners that hung on their walls. When I go back to those churches, I find that those banners have been taken down, and many of the churches never use their covenant.

I feel the time is here when churches should take seriously their covenants, writing new ones that have meaning for our time. The new covenant should have a solid theological basis, keep continuity with historical ones, be in touch with the great issues of our time, and lay down guidelines for faith and behavior within the life of the church as well as outside the church, where the people of God are called to live out their lives in the world.

With those things in mind I would like to try my hand writing a new covenant for churches of our time:

We are people whom Christ has set free. We belong, not to ourselves, but to our Liberator. We are God's people. We praise Him "who loves us and has freed us from our sins by His blood."

Being led, as we believe by the Holy Spirit, and in order to use our freedom responsibly, we do most solemnly enter into covenant with one another under God. We shall make over and over again the earliest confession of Christian faith: Jesus Christ is Lord. We shall be faithful in proclaiming the good news of Jesus Christ, in prayer, in the study of God's Word, the practice of Christian stewardship, and the nurturing of the

Christian fellowship. We shall love, accept, affirm, and pray for one another. There will be no worthless person among us and no friendless person in our midst. We want the doors of our church to be as wide as the love of Christ.

We shall be especially concerned about our families that they be Christian, that a faithful love exist between husband and wife, and that our children be wanted, loved, and cared for.

Knowing that we are dependent on the church which is the body of Christ the way the hand depends on the physical body, we promise to be vitally connected with our church here and wherever we may live.

With the benediction on Sunday, we shall not leave the church within these sacred walls. We shall be the church in the world! We shall go, all of us, into the world as ministers of Christ. We shall speak the reconciling word and do the reconciling deed.

We shall reach across barriers, keep open communication, and care for people the way Christ has cared for us. We shall seek economic justice so that the good life will be within the reach of everyone. We shall try to overcome racial prejudice and all conditions that demean and cheapen human life.

We shall abstain from the use of drugs while being concerned about those who are victims of drugs.

We who have been so richly blessed will share our affluence with the poor, hungry, and starving of our world.

We shall be the careful keepers of the good earth, passing it unspoiled to those who will come after us.

We shall say and do those things that make for peace in a world where the threat of nuclear war falls like an ominous shadow.

We would live in such a way that people can see Jesus Christ in us, recognizing Him as the one who loves them, would save them, and cannot give them up. Amen.

Thought Starters

A series of sermons: Elements in a Covenant.

A series of sermons: The New Covenant.

A series of sermons: A New Covenant for the Modern Church.

Other sermons: Relationship—the Essence of Life; A Covenant Formula; Hosea, in Whom We See God's Love; Jeremiah's Vision of a New Covenant; On Breaking God's Covenant; The Royal Law; "The Written Code Kills"; "The Spirit Gives Life"; The Glory that Fades, The Splendor that Abides; When the New Is Superior to the Old; That Which Becomes Obsolescent; Being the People of God Inside and Outside the Church; Where in the World Is the Church? Chaining the Church Behind Sacred Walls.

Scripture

Exodus 24:1-8; Jeremiah 11:6-13; 31:31-34; Matthew 26:20-29; Mark 14:22-25; 1 Corinthians 11:23-26; 2 Corinthians 3:4-18; Hebrews 8:1-13; 9:15-22.

Texts

Jeremiah 31:31; Matthew 26:27-28; Luke 22:20; 1 Corinthians 11:25; 2 Corinthians 3:6; Hebrews 8:6

Illustrations

The great covenant with Israel (Ex. 24:1-8); Most serious violation (Jer. 34:8-22); Covenant love (Ps. 25:10); The height of covenant love (Ps. 57:10; 108:4); Covenant love like a fortress (Ps. 59:16); The quality of covenant love (Ps. 63:3; 69:16); The quantity of covenant love (Ps. 69:13); The extent of covenant love (Ps. 33:5; 119:64); The timelessness of covenant love (Ps. 103:17); The durability of covenant love (Ps. 118:2-4; 136:1-26); Covenants in blood (Ex. 24:6-8; 1 Cor. 11:25); A covenant around a table (1 Cor. 11:23-26); When the useful becomes obsolete (Heb. 8:13).

Note

1. Knox, *Life in Christ Jesus,* p. 96

11
Grace:
Love Beyond Meriting

I often think of the beautiful and rich words in our Christian vocabulary. They not only stimulate our minds, they move our hearts. We use such words as *light, love,* and *life.* But I sometimes think that grace is the most beautiful of them all. It sets our hearts singing.

Grace is love beyond meriting. It cannot be earned, achieved, or merited. It has no price tags on it. It cannot be bought. It is a gift.

Grace pierces the heart of our faith. It is very comprehensive, gathering many other truths around it, and it reaches out in various directions. If, for some strange reason, we should be denied the use of all our theological words except six, grace would certainly be one of the six we would keep. It is that important.

The Centrality of Grace

Grace is central in our faith and the gospel we preach. Let me say five things about its centrality.

1. God is a God of grace who acts graciously. Both the Old and New Testaments bear witness to this. We sing "God of grace and God of glory."

God created in grace. To whom was He under obligation to create? No one. God sustains His creation in grace. God called Israel in grace. God established His covenant and gave His law in grace. God sent Jesus Christ, His Son, in grace. That was His supreme act of grace. In grace God called His church, the new

Israel, and in grace He sustains it. God saves in grace, and redeems in unmerited love.

This is no sentimental view of God. As we have already seen, God is just, executing His justice in judgment. His judgment can be fierce like the hot, blasting winds from the desert. There is a rough, jagged, cutting side to God's moral law. We can wound and destroy ourselves on those sharp edges. This must be said, however: His justice is in His hands of love, His judgment is in His hands of grace. His judgment is bent toward our salvation. He wounds to save, He cuts to heal.

2. Grace is central in Jesus Christ. The birth, life, death, and resurrection of Jesus are supreme expressions of God's grace. "For God sent the Son into the world," John wrote, "not to condemn the world, but that the world might be saved through him" (3:17).

Jesus was the embodiment of perfect love, the expression of pure grace.

Paul spoke of the grace of Jesus in a very interesting and imaginative way: "For you know the grace of our Lord Jesus Christ, that though he was rich, yet for your sake he became poor, so that by his poverty you might become rich" (2 Cor. 8:9).

Many stories about heroes are from rags to riches. We love to remember and tell about some poor immigrant boy who hitched his wagon to a star and scaled the heights of success. American lore abounds in stories like that and we are richer for them. But the story of the grace of Jesus is the very opposite: It was from riches to rags. He was rich, yet for our sakes He became poor that we through His poverty might be rich.

Paul stood amazed before the grace of Jesus Christ. One of his favorite greetings to those early churches was: "Grace to you and peace from God our Father and the Lord Jesus Christ" (1 Cor. 1:3).

Paul's blessings to those early churches were essentially benedictions of grace. He gave one threefold (Trinitarian) benediction: "The grace of the Lord Jesus Christ and the love of God and the fellowship of the Holy Spirit be with you all" (2 Cor. 13:14). The grace of Jesus Christ comes first. Usually grace was sufficient within itself. He says it simply: "The grace of our Lord Jesus Christ be with you" (Rom. 16:20). He gave this simple blessing six different times.

3. Grace is central in the life of the church.

Not only does God save us by grace, but He calls us together as His people by grace. The church must be a fellowship of grace. We are to live our lives in grace, we are to be a gracious people.

We are to forgive as we have been forgiven by Christ: "Be kind to one another, tenderhearted, forgiving one another, as God in Christ forgave you" (Eph. 4:32). But not even that is enough. We are to love one another as Christ has loved us: "And walk in love, as Christ loved us and gave himself up for us, a fragrant offering and sacrifice to God" (Eph. 5:2). In these two admonitions we are at the ethical heart of our faith.

The church should be one of those points of our world where the love of God is poured forth for the healing of our brokenness, where the grace of Christ overcomes our estrangement and alienation.

4. Grace is a great reality, linking the Old and New Testaments together. The God of grace is active in both, but He expresses His grace most savingly in Jesus of Nazareth.

I am always looking for clues that will help me understand the Bible better. I often think of the Bible as a story in three episodes with a prologue and epilogue. The prologue is Genesis 1:1 to 11:32 which contains a theological interpretation of our human existence. We find the promise of grace there. The first episode is a special people, Israel, called not because of their goodness, giftedness, or power but because God loved them. The second episode is a special person, Jesus Christ, whom God sent into the world because He loved it, although the world did not deserve it. The third episode is about another special people, the church, whom God called to be His people in grace. The epilogue is the Book of Revelation which tells of the consummation of history with the new heaven, the new earth, and the new city. As the epilogue comes to an end a great invitation of grace is given: "The Spirit and the Bride say, 'Come.' And let him who hears say, 'Come.' And let him who is thirsty come, let him who desires take the water of life without price" (Rev. 22:17).

5. Paul is primarily responsible for making grace so central in our faith and in our vocabulary. He perceived it more clearly and spoke of it more forcefully than any other person.

The word is not used at all in Matthew, Mark, 1 John, 3 John, and Jude. In 2 John it occurs only once, and in James, 2 Peter, and Revelation twice each; only three times in John and that in the Prologue, six times in Luke, eight in Hebrews, ten in 1 Peter, and seventeen in Acts. Out of the 152 references to grace in the New Testament, 101 occur in the Pauline letters.

Why this intense concern about and clear articulation of grace by Paul? It grew out of a dramatic and radical deliverance from the bondage of the law. He knew that on the day of his deliverance he brought nothing that could have caused it. He brought nothing but empty hands to God, about which he might have said: "I wish I had something to bring you—some virtue or moral achievement, but I do not. I bring only empty hands." And God, moved by pity, could have said: "Your empty hands are enough. If you had all the moral wealth of the universe, you could not buy My salvation. It is a gift, it is of grace." For the first time Paul experienced the peace for which he had long sought but which had always eluded him. For the first time he felt forgiven and accepted by God. He was no longer caught in the meshes of law, he was free. What else could he do but talk about grace, and, as he did, he put it right at the center of the Christian vocabulary.

Grace and the Human Situation

It is a grace that is not aloof and detached. It gets involved. It gets hurt and wounded. It is not cheap grace, it pays a price. It is grace that speaks to the human situation and addresses us in our need. Let me speak of three of these needs—frailty, sin, and death.

1. As human beings we are very weak and fragile. How often we are overcome by weakness, fatigue, or pain. We are frequently taxed beyond our strength and our resources are often no match for life's demands. Grace is a source of strength and renewal.

Paul talked about some weakness or handicap he had. He called it a thorn in the flesh. We can't be sure what it was. It may have been bad eyes, but in any case, it was limiting and crippling. He said he asked Christ three times to remove it, but rather than removing it Christ gave him strength to accept it and live with it. Out of this weakness strength was born. He turned the handicap into creativity. But what was the enabling strength Christ gave? Grace. Christ said to him: "My grace is sufficient for you, for my power is made perfect in weakness" (2 Cor. 12:9a).

In the light of this, Paul assumed an entirely new attitude toward his weakness, whatever it was. He said a thing that may sound strange to us: "I will all the more gladly boast of my weaknesses that the power of Christ may rest on me. For the sake of Christ, then, I am content with weaknesses, insults, hardships, persecutions, and calamities; for when I am weak, then I am strong" (2 Cor. 12:9b-10). Imagine it!

Grace was power, and it helped Paul accept his weakness. But it did more: Grace turned his weakness into strength.

2. Not only are we weak but we are sinful. Sin separates, alienates, and destroys. Sin cuts us off from the primary spring of life which is God, and from the secondary one, which is our brother. Sin creates guilt, shame, fear, and anxiety, and finally brings death. What is the answer to our sin? Grace.

One of the most wonderful verses of Scripture is Romans 5:20: "But where sin increased, grace abounded all the more." Let us hear it in two more versions. *The New English Bible:* "But where sin was thus multiplied, grace immeasurably exceeded it." "Yet, though sin is shown to be wide and deep, thank God his grace is wider and deeper still!" (J.B. Phillips).

There is more grace than there is guilt. There is enough grace in Jesus Christ to cover all the sin in the world. There is more forgiveness than there is condemnation. That is good news!

Imagine God holding in His hand a giant pair of scales. On one side He puts all the sin of the world, and the scales are brought to a sharp vertical position. More grace is added, and the end of the scales with grace is pulled down farther. Finally there is a balance. Still grace is poured on, and now the scales are tilted radically in favor of grace. There is more grace than sin.

3. Not only are we weak and sinful but we are mortal. We die. And all things we create are like us. We build our mortality into everything we touch. Is there any answer to our mortality? Yes, grace is the answer.

"God so loved the world," John tells us, "that he gave his only Son, that whoever believes in him should not perish, but have eternal life" (3:16). God didn't love the world because it was lovely. It was very unlovely and was terribly marred and scarred. It could never be worthy of God's love, yet He loved it anyway. That love was grace. And those who responded to that grace did not have to perish. They could have everlasting life. (See John 4:14; 11:28-29.)

Paul makes the same claim for grace: It gives life. "As sin reigned in death grace also might reign through righteousness to eternal life through Jesus Christ, our Lord" (Rom. 5:21).

I remember as a young boy slipping into my uncle's house early one morning before the day's work on the farm began. My uncle and aunt were the first people in our community to own a radio and I was endlessly fascinated by it. There was a miracle before my eyes! That morning I got a sermon and the preacher was using as his text Romans 6:23: "For the wages of sin is death, but the free gift of God is eternal life in Christ Jesus our Lord." He was not a good preacher but he had a great text, which he repeated over and over again. That great truth cast a spell over me from which I have never gone free. Indeed, I don't want to be free of it. I can still feel its power. It spoke of eternal life as the free gift of God. It is of grace.

There is a mystery that hangs over the New Testament idea of eternal life. It seems so elusive, so hard to grasp and understand. But maybe it is more simple than it seems. What if grace restores a broken relationship with God who is the primary source of life? That is what grace does. It puts us in touch with the spring of life from which sin has cut us off, and nothing can ever break that relationship again. That is to have eternal life.

Grace When It Is not Called Grace

The reality of grace occurs often without the term. Grace is often found in the Bible without the word. While a concordance is indeed a helpful tool, here is one of its great weaknesses: It depends on key words to find the truth. But where the truth occurs without a pivotal word, the concordance is helpless.

As we have seen, the word *grace* does not occur in Matthew, Mark, 1 John, 2 John, and Jude. But that does not mean that there is not grace in these five books. There is plenty of it. Grace occurs only three times in the Gospel of John and those in the Prologue. Does that mean that the reality of grace does not occur in the main body of that Gospel? No, not at all. The reality of grace runs throughout that Gospel.

Let us look at some of those passages where grace is present but the term is missing. (See Isa. 1:18; 55:1.)

Consider the parable of the workers in the vineyard (Matt. 20:1-16). Jesus began the parable like this. "For the kingdom of heaven is like a householder who went out early in the morning to hire laborers for his vineyard" (v. 1). He agreed to pay a denarius for a day's work. He hired the workers at 9:00 in the morning, then at noon, then at 3:00. Then he hired some at 5:00, just an hour before quitting time. In paying the laborers that evening, two strange things happened: The householder paid the last first, and, stranger still, he paid the same to those who worked only one hour as he did to those who worked the full day. There was discontent, as would be expected, among the workers. Those who had worked all day began grumbling: "These last worked only one hour, and you have made them equal to us who have borne the burden of the day and the · scorching heat" (v. 12). The householder in reply said three important things. First, I have been just: "Did you not agree with me for a denarius?" (v. 13). Again, I have authority over my possessions to do with them as I please: "Am I not allowed to do what I choose with what belongs to me?" And finally the bottom line was: "Or do you begrudge my generosity?" (v. 15). The meaning is grace.

There is a strangeness about grace. The story sounds odd to us, and doesn't seem quite right. We feel that those who worked all day got cheated. And by common standards they did. No economic system could survive with such a haphazard system of paying. But what we forget is that grace is not common, it is uncommon. The order of grace lies beyond the order of justice, yet is constantly intersecting it. On those levels of life which matter most, we live by grace. When it comes to love, forgiveness, reconciliation, and salvation, we are like those men who worked for only one hour in the cool of the day. We are recipients of grace.

Another example is the prodigal son. He was a bad boy. He had squandered his wealth, had been reckless and immoral, besmirched his name, and brought disgrace to his family. He came home friendless, penniless, barefoot, and in tattered rags. The expensive ring he had once worn was perhaps in a pawn shop in the country he had left. When at last he stood before his father he was a pitiable and tragic figure. The father didn't put him on probation and tell him that after six months he would review his case. He didn't send him to live in the servants' quarters as the boy had planned to request. Nothing like that. A banquet was quickly prepared. And who was the guest of honor? That rascally boy. The father began by saying: "This is Joseph. He has been away from home for a long time and I thought he was dead. But he has returned home. Rejoice with me." And a long, loud applause went up. It was all of grace, yet the word *grace* does not occur.

If you preach only from those passages where grace is mentioned, your preaching will be greatly impoverished. There is grace, plenty of it, without the word.

Grace and Legalism

The Christian religion is a religion of grace, although we are shocked to see how often we Christians keep slipping back into legalism.

Jesus grew up in a legalistic religion. It was a religion of legalism that rejected Him and finally put Him to death. It was His religion of grace that set Him in such sharp tension with the religious leaders of His day.

Paul's great escape was from a religion of law into a religion of grace. But it was only as he escaped that he found freedom, life, and peace with God. The gospel he preached was the good news of grace. And what good news it was!

Let us look at a religion of law versus a religion of grace as seen in Jesus. We will look at one of His stories.

Let us return to the prodigal son. In the father we see a religion of grace, in the elder brother a religion of law. The father accepted the prodigal boy back into the family freely, spontaneously, and lovingly. He laid down no laws, insisted on no restitution, and did not put his son on probation.

But how different with the elder son. The story ends with him, who had stayed home and had been so dutiful, a slinking, sulking character standing in the shadows of the banquet hall within the sound of the music and dancing. He said to his father: "Lo, these many years I have served you, and I never disobeyed your command" (Luke 15:29). And the father did not dispute his word. It was all true. Yet, he did not know the meaning of grace. Therefore, he refused the entreaty of grace made by his father: "Son, you are always with me, and all that is mine is yours. It was fitting to make merry and be glad, for this your brother was dead, and is alive; he was lost, and is found" (vv. 31-32). His legalism had made the elder brother proud, censorious, and judgmental, drying up the milk of human compassion in his heart.

The story comes to such a strange end. The bad boy is saved, the "good" boy is lost. And the difference was grace. The bad boy was humble enough to accept it, and the "good" boy was too proud to receive it.

We are constantly being tempted by legalism. That will be one of your greatest temptations as well as that of your people. One of your most important tasks will be to prevent yourself from slipping into it and help keep your people from falling into it.

We have to ask: What makes legalism so appealing? It is tangible. We long for handles to our religion and legalism gives them to us. Laws and rules can be very concrete and specific. It is easy. It is easier to keep rules than to be loving and forgiving. And since it is easy, we can be successful with it. Who doesn't want to be successful, even in one's religion? Yet, legalism can be very devastating and enslaving. It heaps guilt upon guilt but cannot forgive the smallest bit of it. It makes us harsh, proud, and judgmental, drying up our compassion. We get caught in its meshes of requirements like a fly in a spider's web and the more we struggle to go free the more entangled we become. It enslaves us and then it destroys us.

There is only one answer to legalism and that is grace. Jesus knew this and Paul found it out. Every generation has to learn that answer again.

Yet, a religion of grace is not without its dangers, as Paul learned. He had said: "But where sin increased, grace abounded all the more" (Rom. 5:20). Yet there were those who said, "Let us continue in sin that grace may abound. The more we sin the more grace." (See Rom. 6:1.) It is easy for us to turn freedom into license, for the liberated to become libertines. It is easy to become antinomians, those who are against the law.

What is the answer? We should know that law still has a valid function as guidelines and as a setter of boundaries beyond which we cannot go. We should know further that love is the law of a religion of grace, and love creates its own restraints and sets its own perimeters.

Grace is such a wonderful and surprising thing. Maybe preaching, more than anything else, is announcing the surprises of grace.

Thought Starters

A series of sermons on grace: The God of Grace; Jesus Christ, the Person of Grace; The Church, the People of Grace; The Bible as the Book of Grace; Paul, the Apostle of Grace.

A series of sermons on the Bible: Prologue; A Special People; A Special Person; Another Special People; Epilogue.

A series of sermons on grace meeting our human needs: Frailty, Sin, Death.

Other sermons: The Centrality of Grace; No Price Tags; God of Grace; From Riches to Rags; A Trinitarian Benediction; Grace and Peace; Forgive as Christ Has Forgiven Us; Love as Christ Has Loved Us; Grace Without the Word *Grace;* Bringing Empty Hands; Salvation as a Gift; No Cheap Grace; When Weakness Is Strength; More Grace Than Guilt; Scales in God's Hands; What Is Eternal Life? Connected to the Springs of Life Again; No Probation; When the Dead Comes Back to Life; The Deadly Religion of Legalism; A Religion of Grace; The Surprise of Grace.

Scriptures

Deuteronomy 7:6-11; Isaiah 55:1-5; Matthew 20:1-16; Luke 15:11-32; John 8:1-11; 2 Corinthians 8:8-15; 12:1-10; Ephesians 2:1-10.

Texts

Deuteronomy 7:7-8; Isaiah 55:1; John 1:17; Acts 11:23; Romans 1:7; 5:2; 5:20; 6:23; 1 Corinthians 15:10; 2 Corinthians 8:9; 9:15; 12:9; Ephesians 1:6,7-8; 2:8-9; 4:32; 5:2; Revelation 22:17

Illustrations

The strangeness of grace (Matt. 20:1-16); Grace's greatest gift—to become children of God (John 1:12-13); Grace versus legalism (Luke 15:20-32; John 8:1-11); The prodigal son (Luke 15:11-24); The elder brother (Luke 15:25-32); A Pharisee and tax collector (Luke 18:9-14); Eternal life as a gift of grace (John 4:14; 10:28); Grace abounding (Rom. 5:20); Eternal life as a free gift (Rom. 6:23); From riches to rags (2 Cor. 8:9); Grace turns weakness into strength (2 Cor. 12:7-10); Grace, love, and a presence (2 Cor. 13:14); An invitation of grace (Rev. 22:17).

12
Faith:
The Saving Response

In the last chapter we were concerned with grace. We are saved by grace. Paul, writing out of his own experience could say: "For by grace you have been saved through faith; and this is not your own doing, it is the gift of God—not because of works, lest any man should boast" (Eph. 2:8-9). While it is grace that saves us, we can speak of faith as the saving response.

God does not overwhelm us, we make a free response. We are not passive, not like a cup into which God pours His grace. We sing of God's being the potter and our being the clay, of His molding us and shaping us after His will. While the imagery tells an important truth, being very concrete and vivid, it is quite inadequate. We are not like inert clay in the hands of God. We have the power to respond to God or reject the shaping power of His grace.

Grace is the divine side of our salvation, the objective side, while faith is the subjective, human dimension. Yet, we have to be very careful here. Faith is something more than our own doing. In some basic sense, faith is the gift of God made possible by His grace. It is not purely subjective. If it is the gift of God's grace, it has an objective side.

I am like a man with both legs broken. I cannot get up and run to God. He has to come to me, stoop to me, and lift me up. God, in grace, enables me to believe. Yet, His grace is not irresistible. I am not an automaton. I am free. I can make a response.

Exploring the Meaning of Faith

John Knox says there are at least five different meanings of faith in the New Testament.[1]

First, faith may be used in an objective sense to mean something like the Christian religion. In verse 3 of Jude we find this use: "I found it necessary to write appealing to you to contend for the faith which was once for all delivered to the saints." He was obviously talking about the Christian religion. Second, faith can roughly be equivalent to our word *loyalty,* or faithfulness. That is what it normally means when applied to God. God's faith is His reliability, His steadfastness. Third, occasionally, although not often, faith means an intellectual acceptance of a statement as true. This is likely what James meant when he asked: "What does it profit, my brethren, if a man says he has faith but has not works? Can his faith save him?" (2:14). Fourth, there is the meaning of faith as used by the writer of Hebrews. It is seen as "the assurance of things hoped for, the conviction of things not seen" (11:1). Fifth, there is the basic use of the term—reliance upon the goodness and grace of Christ. It is trust. It is receptivity.

We find the same basic meaning of faith in the Old Testament. It is reliance on the goodness of God. It is response to the gracious, saving action of God.

Faith in the Old Testament is never subscribing to formal dogmas and beliefs. It is not giving intellectual assent to propositional truth. It is trust in God.

The psalmist could say: "Commit your way to the Lord; trust in him, and he will act" (37:5). (See Ps. 62:8.)

You feel the sure trust of Israel put in her God, even when the word *trust* is not used. (See Deut. 33:7; Ps. 23:1; 46:1; 90:1-2.)

You trust God when the securities of life have been swept from beneath you, when you are in a crisis you cannot manage, when the earth seems to be disintegrating. "Therefore we will not fear," the psalmist exclaimed, "though the earth should

change, though the mountains shake in the heart of the sea"
(46:2).

John Knox felt this inalterable faith of the Old Testament.
He closes his autobiography like this: "But if the worst should
come and we destroy ourselves, whether in swift stages or in
some total fiery debacle—even so, God's being does not depend upon man's fate on this planet. We know that, either late
or soon, eventually this fate is death, as surely as death is the
earthly fate of every man. But our faith and hope in God are
not confined within this 'bourne of time and place'. Not merely
from generation to generation, but from everlasting, to everlasting, he is God; and in ways beyond our understanding and
in worlds beyond our imagining he will fulfill the loving purpose of his creative work."[2]

We have talked about the covenant that bound Israel to God
and God to Israel. God loved Israel, as we have seen, with a
wonderful love which they called steadfast love. We can trust
a love like that. The psalmist spoke eloquently and movingly
of that love. (See Pss. 57:10; 59:16; 63:3; 119:64.)

In Deuteronomy 26:5-11 we find what is sometimes referred
to as Israel's creed. It was given as part of the liturgy of the
presentation of the firstfruits at the central sanctuary.

"And you shall make response before the Lord your God, 'A
wandering Aramean was my father; and he went down into
Egypt and sojourned there, few in number; and there he
became a nation, great, mighty, and populous. And the Egyptians treated us harshly, and afflicted us, and laid upon us hard
bondage. Then we cried to the Lord the God of our fathers, and
the Lord heard our voice, and saw our affliction, our toil, and
our oppression; and the Lord brought us out of Egypt with a
mighty hand and an outstretched arm, with great terror, with
signs and wonders; and he brought us into this place and gave
us this land, a land flowing with milk and honey. And behold,
now I bring the first of the fruit of the ground, which thou, O
Lord, has given me.' And you shall set it down before the Lord
your God; . . . and you shall rejoice in all the good which the

Lord your God has given to you and to your house, you, and
the Levite, and the sojourner who is among you."

It would be helpful in understanding Israel's faith to look
more closely at this "creed." Let us make five observations.

First, it is not a typical creed. Its ideas and language are not
abstract. It is vivid, concrete, historical. It speaks of God's
mighty, saving action. Second, it has worship as its setting for
the recital of God's saving acts. Those Israelites knew an important secret: When a creed is isolated from worship, it
becomes cold, formal, lifeless. A creed has to be infused with
the vitality of worship if it is to live. Third, the creed is historical in its setting: "A wandering Aramean was my father." That
statement plunges the creed into history where God discloses
Himself and saves us. Fourth, the basic theme of this statement
of faith is about freedom, liberation, redemption: "The Lord
brought us out of Egypt with a mighty hand and an outstretched arm." Fifth, the creed has a contemporary, existential
quality about it. It soon ceases to speak of Israel's ancestor and
begins to speak about the generation of worshipers. It is no
longer He but us: "And the Egyptians treated us harshly, and
afflicted us, and laid upon us hard bondage." There was a
solidarity that bound them to those who went down into
Egypt. It was as if they were being redeemed. The God who
had acted, acts again; the God who saved, saves again.

When we come to the New Testament, God's mighty act of
deliverance is in a person, Jesus Christ, His Son. Here is God's
mighty deed of love and grace. Through the life, death, and
resurrection of Jesus, God delivers us from the bondage of sin
and death. We see that faith in the New Testament is essentially what it is in the Old, except with a different focus which is
Jesus Christ. It is trust in God and response to His mighty
action in Jesus Christ.

There can be no doubt that God's gracious deed has been
performed in Jesus Christ, that He is the Savior of our world.
(See Luke 2:10-11; John 1:14, 29; 3:16, 20:31; Acts 4:12; Rom.
8:37-39; 1 Cor. 1:18,24; 2:2.)

There is something radical in the faith that responds to God's gracious action in Jesus. Kierkegaard spoke of the leap of faith. It is like a pilot bailing out of his plane that has been shot from beneath him and trusting his parachute alone, like a sailor leaving his torpedoed ship and relying completely on his lifeboat. It is almost like saying: "Open your arms, Jesus, I am jumping!" It is casting our whole life, weary, anxious, and sinful on the mercy of Christ, believing that He alone is able to save.

When my son, Chip, was a small boy, he would look through the windows of the parsonage which was next to the church to see when the Sunday morning worship was over. When he had determined the people had gone, he would slip out of the parsonage and enter a side door of the church. Near the front of the sanctuary near the pulpit were some swinging doors through which he would burst and take me by surprise. He would come full speed ahead and leap into my arms. Do you think I ever closed my arms to him? If I, weak as I am, held open arms to my little son, how much more will Christ receive with open arms all who seek Him?

The Importance of Faith

If faith is what I have said it is—reliance upon the goodness of God, trusting His steadfast love, and responding to His saving grace in Christ, then faith is important. That is what the New Testament says about it.

Jesus, on coming down from the Mount of Transfiguration, found His disciples at the base with an epileptic boy whom they could not heal. After rebuking them, He said: "For truly, I say to you, if you have faith as a grain of mustard seed, you will say to this mountain, 'Move from here to there,' and it will move; and nothing will be impossible to you" (Matt. 17:20-21).

The father of this epileptic boy, came to Jesus half doubting and half believing, imploring Him: "If you can do anything, have pity on us and help us." And Jesus said to him: "If you can! All things are possible to him who believes" (Mark 9: 22b-23).

Jesus was always disappointed by little faith and always exulted in great faith. (See Matt. 8:10,26; Luke 24:25.)

When the author of Hebrews looked back over the history of his nation, the real heroes were men and women of faith. In the eleventh chapter of his book, he gives a roll call of the faithful. They had done impossible things because of their faith, and they had suffered much because of it. The world was not worthy of them. He spoke of how Moses "endured as seeing him who is invisible" (v. 27a). But that was true of all of them. They trusted unseen reality and lived as if the things hoped for were real. These stalwart men and women of faith inspired one of the most unique definitions of faith in the New Testament: "Now faith is the assurance of things hoped for, the conviction of things not seen" (v. 1).

John, writing possibly near the end of the first Christian century, marveled at how far the Christians had come and the victories they had won. What was the secret of it all? "This is the victory that overcomes the world, our faith" (1 John 5:4).

Faith in an Inhospitable Climate

As you study your Bible you will discover that faith often flourishes in an inhospitable climate. It is not a fair-weather faith, it often walks in shadows and darkness. It is a faith that originates, not in quiet and sequestered harbors, but on the high seas where the winds are high and the storms are fierce. Often life seems to argue against justice, goodness, and God. Yet men and women, while sometimes doubting, go on believing. It is a tenacious faith. It keeps on holding on.

The God of biblical faith does not accommodate Himself to our little categories, does not satisfy our childish and immature ways. He does not come at every beck and call. He refuses to be a cosmic valet carrying our luggage for us. The psalmists would argue with God. Why are you so far away? Why are you silent? Why don't you speak?

You remember the Babylonian captivity. The Israelites were captives in a strange land. Back home their land was despoiled, their sacred places desecrated, and their Temple, where they made their sacrifices and where God was present as nowhere else, lay in shambles. You feel their anguish in one of their psalms.

> How shall we sing the Lord's song
>   in a foreign land?
> If I forget you, O Jerusalem,
>   let my right hand wither!
> Let my tongue cleave to the roof of my mouth,
>   if I do not remember you,
> if I do not set Jerusalem
>   above my highest joy! (Ps. 137:4-6).

And yet here emerges one of the most significant things about Israel's history: It was in that strange land that they came to their best understanding of God. In that inhospitable climate, their finest flower of faith grew.

One of the things that helped biblical people to go on believing when the situation was not conducive to faith was the feeling that God was present, although hidden, in the tragedy of life; that while He Himself was not evil, He was often in the midst of evil bringing forth good out of it.

Israel had been a nomad people of the desert where they learned the ways of eagles. One of the seemingly most ruthless things was to see an eagle claw away the nest from beneath her eaglets. God is likened to an eagle stirring up its nest: "Like an eagle that stirs up its nest, that flutters over its young, spreading out its wings, catching them, bearing them on its pinions" (Deut. 32:11).

The imagery is vivid and meaningful. High up on some craggy rock an eagle has built her nest. The time comes when the eaglets must learn to fly. There will be danger and risk in this adventure. Then one day the nest is ruthlessly torn from beneath the eaglets, and what is so completely mystifying is that it is not an enemy but the mother that destroys the nest.

The eaglets find themselves falling to the rocky earth beneath. They spread their wings and flutter, but still they continue to fall. And just before they hit the earth, the mother swoops down, spreading her great pinions beneath them upon which they are gently and strongly borne upward. Then they understand that there was love in the ruthlessness, that it was a caring act. So God was often like an eagle that stirs up her nest.

H. H. Farmer remembered the Sunday morning, when as a young man, he was preaching on the love of God. There was in the congregation an old Polish Jew who had been converted to the Christian faith. At the close of the service he came up to Farmer and said: "You have no right to speak of the love of God until you have seen, as I have seen, the blood of your dearest friends running in the gutters on a gray, winter morning." Farmer later asked him how it was that, having seen such a massacre, he had come to believe in the love of God. The answer the man gave, in effect, was that the Christian gospel first began to lay hold on him because it bade him see God in those bloodstained streets on that gray morning. It pointed him to the love of God—not somewhere else, but in the midst of that sort of thing, in the blood and agony of Calvary. He did at least know that this was a message that grappled with the facts. Then he went on to relate something, the sense of which Farmer said he would always remember although he had forgotten the exact words. It was, in effect, "As I looked at that man upon the cross I knew I must make up my mind once and for all and either take my stand beside him and share in his undefeated faith in God or else fall finally into a bottomless pit of bitterness, hatred, and unutterable despair." The old Jew had seen God in the worst, bringing out of it hope and salvation. The situation that was calculated to cause doubt became the source of faith. How often that kind of thing happens. People go on believing in the face of the greatest suffering and tragedy.

A young Jewish girl in the Warsaw ghetto managed to escape over the wall and hide in a cave. She died there shortly before the allied army came, but before her death, she had scratched on the wall three things: First, "I believe in the sun, even though it is not shining." Second: "I believe in love, even when feeling it not." Third: "I believe in God, even when He is silent."

We should give attention to faith. There is no joy, vitality, or hope without it. It opens up life to God in whom are the springs of life. And while it does not save us, it is the saving response.

Thought Starters

A series of sermons on The Meaning of Faith.
A series on An Ancient Creed.
Other sermons: What Is Faith? Faith as the Saving Response; When the Past Becomes Present; When the God Who Saved Saves Again; Casting the Whole Life on Christ; Like a Pilot Bailing Out of His Plane; Like a Grain of Mustard Seed; The Victory that Overcomes the World; No Fair-Weather Faith; Like an Eagle Stirring Up Her Nest.

Scripture

Matthew 8:5-13; 15:21-28; 17:14-21; Mark 4:35-41; 5:24-34; Romans 10:5-13; Galatians 2:11-21; 3:1-9; Philippians 3:1-11; Hebrews 11:1-39.

Texts

Habakkuk 2:4; Mark 11:22; Luke 17:5; John 20:31; Romans 1:17; 3:26, 28; 5:1; 10:10; 16:26; 2 Corinthians 5:7; Galatians 3:9; Ephesians 1:15; 1 Peter 1:8; Hebrews 11:1.

Illustrations

Abraham justified by faith (Gen. 15:1-6; Rom. 4:1-25); Like Everlasting Arms (Deut. 33:27); Pilgrimage from cynicism to faith (Book of Eccl.); The tragedy of unbelief (Matt. 13:53-58; Mark 6:1-6); Little faith (Mark 4:35-41); Between faith and doubt (Mark 9:21-29); Great faith (Luke 7:1-10); Faith that does not give up (Luke 18:35-43); Faith as reception (John 1:12-13); Faith and eternal life (John 3:16,36; 5:24); Door of faith (Acts 14:27); A new kind of righteousness (Rom. 3:21-22); Justification by faith (Rom. 3:26,28,30); Two poles of great religion: faith and love, personal and social (Eph. 1:15).

Notes

1. *The Interpreter's Bible,* volume 9 (New York: Abingdon Press, 1954), pp. 391-92.

2. Knox, *Never Far from Home,* p. 170.

13
Forgiveness:
Guilt Is Lifted

Sin is our undoing. It estranges us from God, our brother, the authentic self, and nature. It destroys those relationships without which we cannot live. It is the great burden we bear, and, if it cannot be lifted, it will destroy us. Sin brings death.

Our gospel is good news, and one of the reasons is that it promises the forgiveness of sin; that guilt can be lifted.

The Reality of Forgiveness

The Bible thinks hopefully about the solution of our problem of sin. Certain ways of speaking about the solution emerge. Sin has been covered, sent away, removed, wiped out. God has cast it behind His back (Isa. 38:17); He has thrown it into the depths of the sea (Mic. 7:19).

There are four theological terms we need to look at which speak of the solution of this great problem. The words are *propitiation, expiation, atonement,* and *forgiveness*.

Propitiation speaks of the effect sin has had on God and what must be done to change the mind of God from wrath to favor and acceptance. The term comes to us through the King James Version where it appears three times—Romans 3:25; 1 John 2:2; 4:10. (In Rom. 3:25 the Greek word translated propitiation is *hilasterion* which means mercy seat, expiation, or propitiation; in 1 John 2:2 and 4:10 the word is *hilasmos* which means expiation, propitiation, or sin offering.) The Revised Standard Version translates both terms "expiation," which is likely more correct, since God who makes the sacrifice would not be propitiating Himself. Paul tells us that "in Christ God was reconciling the world to himself" (2 Cor. 5:19). It wasn't God who needed to be reconciled, it was the world. It wasn't God whose attitude needed to be changed, but the world's mentality that needed to be radically altered.

In Jesus' parable of the prodigal son, the boy at the end of a bitter day when he was so hungry he was tempted to feed on the pods the swine ate, decided he would go home. He felt he must appease an angry father so he carefully prepared a prayer: "Father, I have sinned against heaven and before you; I am no longer worthy to be called your son; treat me as one of your hired servants" (Luke 15:18-19). But he was not given the opportunity to say the prayer. When he met his father, he started to repeat the carefully rehearsed prayer, but when he got ready to ask his father to treat him as one of his hired servants the father broke in: "Bring quickly the best robe, and put it on him; and put a ring on his hand, and shoes on his feet" (v. 22). Here was a prayer never delivered. The boy made the happy discovery that the father didn't need to change his mind toward his son. The father had loved him all the while and was glad to accept him back anytime. It was not the father who needed to be reconciled to his son. It was the boy who needed to be reconciled to his father.

The next term, *expiation,* speaks of its effect, not on God, but on sin itself. It may have the meaning of covering or blotting out of sin. It does not occur at all in the King James Version of the New Testament but in the Revised Standard Version it appears four times (Rom. 3:25; Heb. 2:17; 1 John 2:2; 4:10).

The term *atonement* focused not so much on God and the sinner as on the relationship between the two. It means the removing of sin so that man and God can be brought together in peace and harmony. It is at-onement. The word appears eighty-seven times in the Old Testament. It occurs only once in the King James Version of the New Testament, in Romans 5:11, where *katallagen,* which means reconciliation, is translated "atonement." It doesn't occur in the Revised Standard Version.

The Greek term is translated "reconciliation." This really means that atonement and reconciliation are interchangeable terms.

It is important to note that the Day of Atonement was one of the most important days, if not the most important, in the Jewish religious calendar. It came in the fall and was the only fast day prescribed by the Mosaic law. It was concerned, as the title suggests, with the removal of sin so that God and the people could be brought together in harmony and peace.

On that day, the only day in the year, the High Priest entered the holy of holies and made a sacrifice for himself, the priests, and the sacred places and vessels in the Temple. Also, on that day two goats were chosen by lot. One was sacrificed as a sin offering for the people, and the other became the scapegoat sent into the wilderness, symbolically bearing away the sins of the people. The religious and the secular, the priests, Temple, and the people, were cleansed from their sin so their relationship with God could be right. It is not strange then that the Day of Atonement has been called the Good Friday of the Old Testament.

Finally there is the term *forgiveness.* We are much more familiar with it than we are the other three. Forgiveness is the removal of the barrier of sin, the canceling of it, the lifting of its penalty, and the restoration of the sinner to the favor of God. It is where our guilt is lifted. This is our basic concern in this chapter.

What God Does

In a sense God does it all when it comes to the solution of our sin. It is not our doing, it is what He does. He loves us before we love Him. He seeks us before we seek Him. He finds us before we find Him. It is He who expiates our sin, who covers it, purges it, blots it out. It is He who spans the wide chasm between Himself and us, who overcomes our estrangement, who makes atonement for us. It is He who forgives us, lifts our guilt, and bears our sin far away.

But more specifically, what is it that God does? Let me suggest three things.

1. God judges sin.

God is holy and cannot take our sin lightly. He sets Himself against sin, He abhors it. Therefore, He judges it.

The fact that God judges sin indicates not only that He takes it seriously but that we must take our own sin seriously. You remember Isaiah's response in the Temple when He realized he was in the presence of a holy God. "Woe is me!" he cried. "For I am lost; for I am a man of unclean lips, and I dwell in the midst of a people of unclean lips; for my eyes have seen the King, the Lord of hosts!" (Isa. 6:5).

Yet, as I have said earlier, God's judgment envisions our salvation. His judgment is like a surgeon's knife. He cuts that He may save and heal.

2. God exercises grace and mercy.

God's grace follows His judgment. His grace heals the wounds His judgment has inflicted. He is a gracious and merciful God.

> The Lord is merciful and gracious,
>   slow to anger and abounding in steadfast love,
> He will not always chide,
>   nor will he keep his anger for ever.
> He does not deal with us according to our sins,
>   nor requite us according to our iniquities.
> For as the heavens are high above the earth,
>   so great is his steadfast love toward those who
>   fear him;
> As far as the east is from the west,
>   so far does he remove our transgressions
>   from us (Ps. 103:8-12).

This is a beautiful picture of God's grace and mercy. The heavens were the highest point the psalmist could imagine. Just so high and great was God's steadfast love. The two most distant points were east and west. Just so far had God removed their transgressions.

No one in the Old Testament understood better the mercy of God than Hosea.

> How can I give you up, O Ephraim!
>   How can I hand you over, O Israel!
> How can I make you like Admah!
>   How can I treat you like Zeboiim!
> My heart recoils within me,
>   my compassion grows warm and tender.
> I will not execute my fierce anger,
>   I will not again destroy Ephraim;
> For I am God and not man,
>   the Holy One in your midst,
>   and I will not come to destroy (Hos. 11:8-9).

It is this reality of grace and mercy in God that holds out hope for the sinner.

Martin Luther faced the same religious problem that Paul had: How does an unjust man stand justified before a just God? And 1,500 years later Luther found the same answer. The answer was *solo gratia!* Grace alone! That became the slogan of the Protestant Reformation. It was born, not of speculation, but of experience.

Luther was no ordinary monk. He was a scrupulous monk, keeping all the rules and obeying all the Commandments. "I kept the rule of my order so strictly," he said, "that if ever a monk got to heaven by his monkery, it was I. If I had kept on any longer, I think I should have killed myself with vigils and prayers and reading others' works." He fasted until he was weak and famished. He would sleep without any cover until he was chilled to the bone. He was always asking himself: "Am I hungry enough? Am I cold enough? Am I deprived enough? Is there ever enough that will satisfy a holy and righteous God, and will constitute a claim upon God?" Then one day he learned with great joy the meaning of Paul's words: "For in it the righteousness of God is revealed through faith for faith; as it is written, 'He who through faith is righteous shall live'" (Rom. 1:17). Salvation was of grace, not of works; it was not to be achieved, but accepted by faith as a gift. His night of despair was turned into a morning of hope.[1]

Paul Tillich in one of his greatest sermons, "You Are Accepted," talks about the same thing: "Sometimes at that moment a wave of light breaks into our darkness, and it is as though a voice were saying: 'You are accepted. You are accepted, accepted by that which is greater than you, and the name of which you do not know. Do not ask for the name now; perhaps you will find it later. Do not try to do anything now; perhaps later you will do much. Do not seek for anything; do not perform anything; do not intend anything. Simply accept the fact that you are accepted! If that happens to us, we experience grace. . . . In that moment, grace conquers sin, and reconciliation bridges the gulf of estrangement. And nothing is demanded of this experience, no religious or moral or intellectual presupposition, nothing but acceptance."[2]

On the original manuscript of this sermon are these words written by his own hand: "For myself! 20 August, 1946." It was his sixtieth birthday. Like Paul, Luther, and many who had gone before him, as well as many who would come after him, Tillich knew that he had been accepted by a wonderful grace.

3. God sent his Son, Jesus Christ, as His supreme act in solving our problem of sin.

Jesus Christ was the historical, concrete, personal expression of God's grace and mercy. He was the aggressive, seeking love of God. He ferreted out men and women in their dens of iniquity, found them in their places of hiding, walked with them in shadows and darkness where they were seeking to escape the light, and overtook them as they were running away from God.

Francis Thompson in his poem, "The Hound of Heaven," tells how he fled Christ "down the nights, and down the days," and "down the arches of the years." Yet, he heard behind him those pursuing feet and a voice that called.

But with unhurrying chase

And unperturbed pace,
Deliberate speed, majestic instancy,
They beat—and a Voice beat
More instant than the Feet—
"All things betray thee, who betrayest Me."

When Christ had finally overtaken him He said to him:

Ah, fondest, blindest, weakest
I am He whom thou seekest!
Thou dravest love from thee, who dravest me.

We are the sought ones. Jesus made that emphatically clear in two of His parables, the lost sheep and the lost coin.

The sheep didn't find his way back to the fold. He could not have done that. When a sheep is lost, he is lost. He has no sense of direction. He doesn't know in which direction home is. So the shepherd left the ninety-nine, and went after the one lost one. When he found him, he put him on his shoulders and brought him back to the flock. There was great rejoicing.

The lost coin didn't leap back into the purse. The woman lighted a lamp and swept her house carefully, not giving up until she had found it. Once more there was great rejoicing.

Some animals have a fine sense of direction. The pigeon, for example, has a homing instinct. You cannot lose a pigeon.

At the beginning of this century some experiments were being done in animal psychology. In a northern state some pigeons were blindfolded, put in cages, and brought to the town in Virginia where I live. Some of the old-timers who saw the experiment said they took the pigeons out of their cages, removed their blinds, and released them. They flew to a certain height, circled several times as if getting their bearing, and then flew back home. A pigeon can do that but a sheep can't. The Bible tells us that we are like sheep, not pigeons. Somebody has to find us.

When Christ finds us He, in great love, breaks down our resistance, overcomes our estrangement, and forgives our sins. Jesus so often exercised the power and authority of forgiveness.

One of the loveliest stories of the New Testament is found in the second chapter of Mark. Jesus was in Capernaum and a large crowd had gathered at the house to hear Him preach. The rooms were filled and the doors were blocked by eager people straining to hear what He said. Four men, bearing a paralytic on a stretcher, appeared on the scene. They had brought him, hoping Jesus would heal him. The men saw the impossible situation. But being imaginative and indefatigable, they climbed to the roof, tore away some tile, and let the paralytic down at the feet of Jesus. They explained that they had brought him to be healed, but Jesus said to the sick man: "My son, your sins are forgiven" (v. 5). It was only after Jesus had forgiven the man that He healed him. Jesus knew how sin separates people from God, how guilt could make them sick. The most important thing was that the man be forgiven. That is still true of us.

When we seek forgiveness, we do not look to some ethereal grace, but to Jesus Christ, the man of grace. He is our Savior. We turn to Him for forgiveness.

Rodney (Gipsy) Smith became one of the greatest preachers of the Christian church, claiming five continents as his parish. He was born in a Gypsy's tent in England. His family made a living by peddling tinware, clothes pegs, and baskets. When Rodney was a small boy his mother died from smallpox. He had no chance for a formal education. He could never forget his conversion, which was an experience of grace. It happened in a little primitive Methodist Church in Cambridge.

He knelt at the communion rail and an old man with great flowing locks, whose name he never knew, knelt beside him and put his arm around him. "You must believe that [Jesus] has saved you," he told the lad: " 'To as many as received Him, to them gave He power to be the sons of God; even to them who believed on His name.' "

"Well," I said to my dear old friend, "I cannot trust myself, for I am nothing; and I cannot trust in what I have, for I have nothing; and I cannot trust in what I know, for I know nothing; and so far as I can see my friends are as badly off as I am."

"So there and then I placed myself by simple trust and committal to Jesus Christ. I knew He died for me; I knew He was able to save me, and I just believed Him to be as good as His word. And thus the light broke and assurance came. I knew that if I was not what I ought to be, I never should be again what I had been. I went home and told my father that his prayers were answered, and he wept tears of joy with me."[3]

Here was one of the secrets of Gipsy Smith's powerful preaching. He knew where grace was, where forgiveness could be had. He never tired of telling that. It was all in Jesus Christ.

We should not forget how badly we need corporate forgiveness. We are usually more sinful in what we do together than what we do individually and personally. We can learn much from ancient Israel. She not only sought forgiveness for the individual, she sought forgiveness for the nation. How badly the family, the community, the corporation, business, industry, education, the nation, and the world need forgiveness. Since we are so dimly aware of our corporate guilt, we are so slow to seek it and ask for it. Yet, Christ is eager to grant it.

Human Forgiveness

There is, of course, some basic sense in which only God can forgive, since sin is ultimately against Him. If I break a moral law, it is God's law I violate. If I injure another human being, it is God's child I hurt. If I inflict pain on myself, it is still God's child I am harming. Sin is against God and forgiveness is with Him.

Across a long ministry I have done a lot of counseling. I have been endlessly amazed at how people get their lives messed up. They often get trapped with no obvious way out. I have heard so many stories of anguish and pain. Often the basic problem is guilt and there is no hope unless there can be forgiveness. I have often wished I could speak the word of forgiveness, but I have been unable to do so. Only God can forgive.

Yet, forgiveness is not only theological, it is also social, and since it is there is a place for human forgiveness. I need to forgive the brother.

Peter asked Jesus one day, "Lord, how often shall my brother sin against me, and I forgive him? As many as seven times?" Jesus replied, "I do not say to you seven times, but seventy times seven" (Matt. 18:21). Forgiveness must go on and on. It must be interminable. It must have no end.

Paul could write: "As the Lord has forgiven you, so you also must forgive" (Col. 3:13).

Jesus completed the Model Prayer, and then lifted out one of the six petitions to stress it. This was the petition concerning forgiveness: "For if you forgive men their trespasses, your heavenly Father also will forgive you; but if you do not forgive men their trespasses, neither will your Father forgive your trespasses" (Matt. 6:14-15).

Did Jesus consider this the most important part of the prayer? Yes, maybe in a practical sort of way. He knew how hard forgiveness is and how destructive hatred can be.

Did you note? Jesus said that unless we forgive others their trespasses, God would not forgive us. He certainly didn't mean that our forgiveness earns His. He likely meant that hatred so clutters up the channels of our lives that we are unable to accept His forgiveness which is of grace.

While war is a horrible thing, some beautiful stories come out of it.

A little Belgian girl went into her bombed-out church during World War II to pray. The roof was fallen in, the walls were damaged, the beautiful stained glass lay in shattered pieces on the floor, and the altar was broken in the middle. She knelt before the altar to say the Lord's prayer. She got along well until she came to "as we also have forgiven our debtors." She choked on the word *forgiven*. How could she forgive those hated Nazis who had bombed her city, killed some of her friends, and destroyed her church? She tried again and again but to no avail. She could not say that word. She would try once more, and as she came to that difficult place a gentle voice from behind led her on: "As we also have forgiven our debtors. And lead us not into temptation, but deliver us from evil. For thine is the kingdom, and the power and the glory forever and ever, Amen." She turned to see who had led her on. He was the Belgian king. Sometimes *forgiveness* is the hardest word to say, but we need to say it.

General Oglethorpe once said to John Wesley: "I never forgive." And Wesley answered wisely: "Well sir, I hope you never sin."

Hatred is such a terrible thing. It can be like an inward volcano that someday will erupt to destroy you. I had rather be the hated than the hater.

Booker T. Washington once said: "I will allow no man to drag me so low as to make me hate him."

If any man ever had a right to hate it must have been Martin Luther King, Sr. His distinguished son, Martin Luther King, Jr., had been assasinated, and he had seen his wife murdered at the organ while she was playing for a Sunday worship service. Yet, once he said: "Hate is too heavy a burden for any man to carry."

There is theological forgiveness and there is social forgiveness. Finally there is personal forgiveness—I need to forgive myself.

Jesus said I am to love my neighbor as I love myself. There is a kind of self-love that is necessary if we are to be happy, creative, and productive. Self-hate can be so crippling. It really is demonic and destructive. I cannot love myself if I hate myself. It is only as I forgive myself that I can love myself. Unfortunately, too many of us hate ourselves. We feel guilty, empty, useless, and loveless.

In a counseling session, a woman who was very lonely and depressed, said: "I hate myself and at night I dread to see the morning come, I don't want to begin the day." I explained to her that hatred that turns in upon oneself is likely the most common cause of depression. As long as she hated herself she would be depressed. It was only as she learned to love herself that the shadow would be lifted.

I have written of how Tillich insisted that we accept the fact that we have been accepted. If Christ has accepted me, then I should be willing to accept myself, and by His grace I can.

There is theological, social, and personal forgiveness. But the greatest of the three is the forgiveness of God which is essential for the other two.

Thought Starters

A series of sermons on the Answer to Our Sin: Expiation, Atonement, and Forgiveness.

A series on What God Does to Make Forgiveness Possible.

A series on Forgiveness: Divine, Social, Personal.

Other sermons: Sin Is Our Undoing; Sin Brings Death; Sin Has Been Covered; At-onement; A Prayer Never Delivered; Who Needs to Be Reconciled? What About the Day of Atonement? How Does an Unjust Man Stand Before a Just God! Grace Alone! Accept Your Acceptance! We Are the Sought Ones! Like a Hound of Heaven; Lost Like a Sheep; Borne by Four; The Man of Grace; Where Can Forgiveness Be Had? How Often Shall I Forgive? On Loving God, Neighbor, and Self; I Had Rather Be Hated than to Hate.

Scripture

Psalm 103:8-12; Hosea 11:8-9; Isaiah 6:1-8; 55:1-7; Jeremiah 31:31-34; Matthew 6:5-15; 18:15-22; Mark 2:1-12; 11:20-26; Luke 23:32-38; Ephesians 4:25-32; Colossians 3:12-17.

Texts

Psalm 103:12; Hosea 11:8*b*; Isaiah 1:18; 6:5; 38:17*b*; 43:25; 55:7; Jeremiah 31:34; Matthew 6:14-15; 9:2; 18:21; Mark 2:5; Luke 15:18-19; Acts 2:38; Romans 3:25; Ephesians 4:32; Colossians 3:13; Hebrews 2:17; 1 John 1:9; 2:2; 4:10

Illustrations

The weight of guilt (Ps. 38:4); Isaiah's forgiveness (Isa. 6:1-8); The prodigal son is forgiven (Luke 15:11-24); Paul's forgiveness (Acts 9:1-9); We must forgive if we are to be forgiven (Matt. 6:14-15; Col. 3:13); Forgiving others as Christ has forgiven us (Eph. 4:32); Forgiving the brother (Matt. 18:21-22; Luke 17:3-4); Forgiven much (Luke 17:3-4).

Notes

1. Timothy George, "Luther's Last Words: 'Wir Sien Pettler, Hoc Est Verum'" in *Pulpit Digest,* September-October, 1983, pp. 29-30.

2. Paul Tillich, *The Shaking of the Foundations* (New York: Charles Scribner's Sons, 1948), p. 162.

3. Cited in Clyde E. Fant, Jr. and William M. Pinson, Jr., *20 Centuries of Great Preaching,* Volume VII (Waco: Word Books, 1971), p. 91. Based on Gipsy Smith, *Gipsy Smith: His Life and Work,* rev. ed. (New York: Flemming H. Revell, 1902), pp. 79-81.

14
Reconciliation:
Our Separation Is Overcome

I have already said that if I could use only one word to tell of our human tragedy, it would be *separation*. No other word can tell our sad story so well. We are caught in conflict and rebellion. We are cut off from the sources of life. The relationships that support us, relationships without which we cannot live, have been broken, and we are lonely, estranged, and hostile. In our best moments we want to be reunited, but we do not know how to go about it. Our best efforts seem to fail. The barriers that separate us are too high, we cannot get over them.

Yet, we do not despair. There is hope. Our gospel promises that our estrangement can be overcome, that reconciliation can take place, that our brokenness can be healed.

Separation as Our Tragedy

Our separation is no simple matter. It is inside us, outside us, and above us. We shy away from simplistic answers, overly optimistic solutions, and easy panaceas.

Let us note our separation in five dimensions.

1. We are separated from God.

This is our basic separation, our primal break. When we are estranged from God, we are separated from His creation. We can't be right with anything else.

Just after the creation stories, the Bible tells about man's sin and separation from God. The story is told in the third chapter of Genesis. Adam and Eve sin and are driven from the presence of God and from the Garden of Eden which was their home. They became the wandering, homeless ones.

I was in Bone, Algeria in 1944. As I was leaving the modern city for the ruins of the old Roman city, my guide said to me: "Bone is a corruption of Hippone which was the Roman city. You remember that the great Augustine lived and preached here." I did remember. Then he continued: "We should soon uncover his church. Augustine said the city reservoir was only a stone's throw from his church." Just back of us was the reservoir which had been excavated. "And Augustine told us that the amphitheater was not too far away, that the games often disturbed his preaching." To our left only several hundred yards away was the amphitheater. "It is just a matter of time," he continued, "before we shall unearth Augustine's pulpit." It became one of the great moments of my life when I stood so near the pulpit of the great preacher and the great theologian who, more than anyone since Paul, has shaped Christian theology. And standing there I remembered the loveliest thing he ever said: "Thou hast made us for thyself, O God, and our souls are restless until they find their rest in thee."

What if we are cut off from Him for whom we were made? We are, the Bible tells us. That is our real tragedy.

There is a break in the spiritual fabric of life.

2. We are separated from our brother.

The ultimate anguish in life is to be separated from God. What if someone should tell you that you are doomed to be separated from God forever, that you could never know again His presence, love, acceptance, and forgiveness? Can you imagine the despair into which you would be plunged? That would be life's final pain.

But the next most painful thing is to be separated from fellow human beings. I am socially incurable. I can't get along without my brother. If I were in a hall of mirrors, looking at my face from every conceivable angle, I could never know who I am. I can only know who I am as I look into another human face. I need, indeed must have, those who will reach out and touch me, call me by name, strike cadence, and walk with me, who will descend with me and walk with me in the valley of deep shadows and darkness, who will not leave me but will stay with me until the night has gone and the morning is come.

We are separated from God. And hard upon that is another tragic announcement: We are separated from our brother.

The first tragedy is told in the third chapter of Genesis. The second tragedy is found in the fourth chapter of Genesis. There you see a slain man lying in his own blood, killed by the hands of his brother. Cain has slain Abel.

I have seen, as you have, so much pain in broken human relations.

I remember a father who was estranged from his teenage son. It was so painful. He wanted desperately to be loved and accepted by his son. Indeed, he couldn't be happy again until he was in the good graces of his son. When asked if he ever complimented his boy, he said he did not. But why? "I was afraid," he said, "it would make him proud." How foolish. There was the boy wanting some word of praise from his father, desiring to hear his father say: "Son, I am proud of you. You are all I could hope for in a boy." But he never heard it. The boy took the silence as rejection, and, in turn, rejected his father. That story can be repeated many, many times.

I recently heard of a gifted seventeen-year-old boy who committed suicide. Why? He felt he was not understood, that his excellence was not appreciated. He felt lonely, isolated, cut off, rejected. The pain became unbearable. How many of these people are among us!

I have been talking about interpersonal relations, but what about destructive human relations on larger and vaster social dimensions—race against race, class against class, nation against nation? We have always had these conflicts, but there is a new and tragic element in the modern situation. For the first time in history we have power to destroy ourselves, to make life on our planet extinct. Our old hands of hostility hold a new weapon—nuclear power.

There is a break in the social fabric of life.

3. We are separated from the authentic self.

There is an authentic self that is free and spontaneous, that finds laughter easy, and is full of surprises. That self is responsible, having integrity, and is loving and generous, humble and reverent. It lives by the acceptance of others and the grace of God.

Then there is a false self that is selfish and grasping, stiff and formal, exploits situations and uses people, loves power and seeks a false independence. It is irreverent and it is sinful.

Paul knew well the struggle between the true and false selves, and he knew how painful it was for the man he wanted to be to go down in defeat at the hand of the self he didn't want to become. He confessed: "I do not understand my own actions. For I do not do what I want, but I do the very thing I hate. . . . I can will what is right, but I cannot do it. Wretched man that I am!" he cried, "Who will deliver me from this body of death?" (Rom. 7:15,18,24).

There is a break in the personal fabric of life.

4. We are separated from nature.

Our relation with nature is not what it should be as the ecological crisis of our time is telling us. Rather than being the guardian, keeper, and protector of nature as God intended it, we have become her exploiter. We have been profligate with her, wasting her wealth, and turning her into easy profit. We have marred her beauty, polluted her air, made unclean her soil, and contaminated her water. And now, as if in wrath, nature lifts her hand to strike down those who should have been her keepers.

There is a break in the natural fabric of life.

5. There is a cosmic separation.

The cosmic separation is much more difficult to grasp and understand than the reality of spiritual, social, personal, and natural separation. It is very elusive. Yet, biblical faith makes it clear that the break that lies across the human heart and human history is projected beyond space and time. (See Rom. 8:19-21; Col. 1:19-20; Eph. 1:10.) Brokenness, splitness, and riftness seem to be one of the basic, elemental facts of cosmic existence as it is in our historical situation.

There is a break in the cosmic fabric of the universe.

Reconciliation as the Answer to Our Separation

The good news of the gospel is that God has acted in such a way that we can be reconciled, that our separation can be overcome. God does for us in Christ what we, even in our best efforts, cannot do.

The person of reconciliation is Jesus Christ, the place of reconciliation is His cross. "For if while we were enemies," Paul wrote, "we were reconciled to God by the death of his Son, much more, now that we are reconciled, shall we be saved by his life" (Rom. 5:10). We stack our arms of rebellion at His cross and ask for peace. And peace is given!

As indicated, separation has occurred in five dimensions and reconciliation takes place in all of them. Yet, the two areas most crucial for reconciliation to occur are with God and other human beings. We often speak of this as a double reconciliation. We are reconciled to God and to our brother.

Reconciliation with God is the primary reconciliation. Until this takes place with Him, separation can't be overcome anywhere else. Here was the thrust of God's mighty action in Jesus Christ. Paul tells us that "in Christ God was reconciling the world to himself" (2 Cor. 5:19). (See Rom. 5:6-11; Eph. 2:11-22.)

The death of Jesus was a powerful event. Matthew tells us that when Jesus died, "the curtain of the temple was torn in two, from top to bottom" (27:51). That curtain was a beautifully woven tapestry that hung over the entrance into the holy of holies in the Temple. No one except the high priest ever went behind that curtain and he was allowed that privilege only once a year, on the Day of Atonement. In some basic sense that curtain kept God in and people out. But now that the curtain was rent the most ordinary could go before God. The death of Jesus had blazed a path in which the most common feet could walk into the presence of God. The distance between God and people was not so great nor so forbidding. God had been brought close to men and women and they could now lay hold of His grace by faith.

Not only did Jesus Christ reconcile men and women to God but He reconciled them to each other.

As earlier observed, never have people been more hostile and separated than Jews and Gentiles in the time of Jesus. The Jew was often proud, condescending, and exclusive, and the Gentile, feeling the rejection, was very angry and hostile. It was beyond the farthest reaches of human imagination to see them united in love, peace, and forgiveness. Yet, their separation was overcome and many were reconciled in the church which was the body of Christ.

Peter, after his transforming vision, stepped across the threshold of a Gentile home, Cornelius's, to preach to a small Gentile church gathered there. It was the longest step Peter had ever taken. He had been forbidden by his religious laws to enter a Gentile home. And the first thing he said to them was "Truly I perceive that God shows no partiality" (Acts 10:34).

Not only had Christ's death rent the veil in the Temple but it had broken down a very formidable wall. "For he is our peace, who has made us both one, and has broken down the dividing wall of hostility" (Eph. 2:14).

Paul probably was making reference to the wall which divided the inner court of the Temple, open only to Jews, from the outer court to which Gentile visitors were admitted. Written on that wall, in Greek and Latin, were these words: "No man of another race is to proceed within the partition and enclosing wall about the sanctuary; and anyone arrested there will have himself to blame for the penalty of death which will be imposed as a consequence." With the great wall separating them now broken down, Jews and Gentiles could be brought together.

Paul spoke of how Christ in His death made it possible to "create in himself one new man in place of the two, so making peace" (Eph. 2:15). The reference was to Jew and Gentile. Christ brought the two old warring humanities together, making out of them one new humanity. The impossible had been done!

As Paul looked out across his world he saw many high barriers and threatening chasms. These were religious, socio-economic, and sexual in nature. All of these barriers had been broken down in the church.

Our modern world has these same barriers which separate, demean, and injure. Now that our world has been brought closer together and armed with the mighty power of its technology, the barriers can be so much more destructive than they were in the time of Paul. We need to hear the powerful gospel that tells us that our separation can be overcome, that we can be reconciled with God and each other. It is a tragic picture to see a church that has these barriers in its own life which negate the gospel it preaches and turn its pious and platitudinous words into hollow sounds.

While the double reconciliation between persons and God and between persons and persons, is of first importance, the other kinds of reconciliation are important, too, reconciliation within the personal life, reconciliation with nature, and reconciliation of cosmic forces.

We have referred to the conflict within Paul's life that made him cry out: "Wretched man that I am! Who will deliver me from this body of death?" He didn't find deliverance in positive thinking or a psychological gospel of hope. He found it in the grace of Christ. "Thanks be to God through Jesus Christ our Lord!" (Rom. 7:25).

Jesus told His disciples that His legacy to them would be peace. "Peace I leave with you; my peace I give unto you; not as the world gives do I give to you. Let not your hearts be troubled, neither let them be afraid" (John 14:27). And Paul's favorite greeting to the early churches was: "Grace to you and peace from God our Father and the Lord Jesus Christ" (Rom. 1:7).

The term *peace* had a broad meaning. It spoke of total well-being, and this certainly included inner peace. The grace of Christ could reconcile the warring powers of the human heart and heal the cleft will. The grace of Christ can take the life that is tempted to run off in all directions, thereby being torn and not at peace with itself, and make it one-directional.

We should be reconciled with nature. Reconciliation must not be thought of as being too spiritual, too abstract, and too ethereal. Reconciliation must be seen in holistic terms where the whole of existence is brought together in harmony and peace. This means that reconciliation will have a very natural, mundane, earthy quality. When reconciliation has run its full course, we will discover that we are at peace with nature. Then we will know that we are kin to nature, that the good earth is our mother, and that the beneficient forces of nature are like our brothers and sisters. Nature is our home, where we live, where the drama of our history unfolds. We should guard and keep it, heal its wounds, and enhance its beauty. We must make clean its air, pure its water, and sweet its soil. We should not turn its wealth into easy profits which would at last make us poor. We should make it more productive, and we should not forget that this earth will be the home of those who will come after us. We can then pass it on to them unspoiled.

Finally, we find joy in cosmic reconciliation. This is veiled in mystery, yet biblical faith bears testimony to it. There are warring powers beyond our time and space, and these are being reconciled. God created His universe for unity and wholeness. As I have already said, it is an uni-verse, one verse. Where it has been broken, God desires healing for it. This is being accomplished in Christ. Paul speaks of this: "For in him [Christ] all the fulness of God was pleased to dwell, and through him to reconcile to himself all things, whether on earth or in heaven, making peace by the blood of his cross" (Col. 1:19-20). Again, in the first chapter of Ephesians, he speaks of "a plan for the fulness of time, to unite all things in him, things in heaven and things on earth" (v. 10).

The Church and Reconciliation

It was reconciliation that brought the church into being and reconciliation is the primary business of the church. Indeed, a basic definition of the church might be something like this: The church is a fellowship of the reconciled, made possible by Christ, and sent by its Lord on a mission of reconciliation.

I have already mentioned the picture of the consummated church as given in the seventh chapter of Revelation. It is composed of a great host of people who come from every nation, from all peoples, from all classes, from all races, and from every conceivable background. They are dressed in white robes and they hold palm branches in their hands. The palm branches are symbols of peace which tell that the church has been about its primary task, that of reconciliation and peace making. The fact that the church is composed of people from everywhere, people who had once been hostile and separated, speaks eloquently of the church's fulfilling well its basic task.

Paul, in the fifth chapter of 2 Corinthians, tells why Jesus came into the world. He came on a mission of reconciliation. But He was not on a lonely isolated mission. God was in Him, working through Him, that men and women might be brought back in friendship to the God who made them, loved them, and would not give them up.

Here emerges one of the most exciting truths in the New Testament. God wants to continue the mission of reconciliation, begun in Christ, through the church. Let us note three things.

1. The church is to take Christ's place.

Let us observe two translations of verse 20:

"Now then we are ambassadors for Christ, as though God

did beseech you by us: we pray you in Christ's stead, be ye reconciled to God" (KJV).

"Here we are, then, speaking for Christ, as though God himself were making his appeal through us. We plead on Christ's behalf: 'Let God change you from enemies into his friends' " (GNB).

It is almost as if the church steps into the shoes of Christ. It represents Him, speaks for Him. We are His ambassadors.

2. The church has been given the word or message of reconciliation. "In Christ God was reconciling the world to himself, not counting their trespasses against them, and entrusting to us the message of reconciliation" (2 Cor. 5:19). The *Good News Bible* puts it this way: "And he has given us the message which tells how he makes them his friends."

What a message! What a powerful word! We have the best news the world has ever heard: God in Christ is making men and women His friends who have been His enemies. God is taking men and women, separated from Him by great distances and high barriers, and reconciling them to Himself in peace.

3. God has given His church, not only the word of reconciliation, but the ministry of reconciliation. Reconciliation is something we do. Reconciliation is more than a word we speak, it is a deed we perform.

I have put the word before the deed. But Paul uses the opposite order. He tells the church that they have been given the ministry of reconciliation, then he tells them about the word entrusted to them. Did he mean that we have to do the deed of reconciliation before we can speak effectively of it?

Let me mention two things about the modern church that should give us all concern.

1. We have often neglected preaching a double reconciliation in our evangelism. We have not failed to tell of God's gracious action in Christ to save us. And that is of first importance. There can be no evangelism without that. But we have often failed to tell that the Christ who reconciles us to God also reconciles us to our brothers and sisters. We have not spoken

of the social and ethical dimensions of evangelism as we should have. Some of the most passionately evangelistic churches I have known have at the same time been the most socially insensitive. There is something badly wrong there.

2. The church has failed to fulfill its role of reconciliation both in its own life and the life of the world.

Often we are almost as divided, fragmented, and hostile as the world. I think how often our gospel has been truncated, and how often we have reflected the brokenness of our world I remember that racism made one of its last-ditch stands in the church. That is a painful memory.

In a world with such deep hostilities, threatening divisions, and the temptation to misuse our awesome power, life on our planet could become extinct. Never have the deed and word of reconciliation been so urgent as now.

Thought Starters

A series of sermons on Our Tragic Separation.
A series of sermons on The Church as Reconciler.
Other sermons: Separation—Our Sad Story; The Inner Warfare; The Great Reconciler; Where We Stack Our Arms of Rebellion; Jesus' Legacy; The Church Reconciled and on a Mission of Reconciliation; Palm Branches in Their Hands; God Making Us His Friends; Taking Christ's Place; How Can a Broken Church Preach a Whole Gospel? Keepers of Nature.

Scripture

Genesis 3:1-24; 4:1-16; Acts 10:1-48; Romans 5:1-11; 7:13-25; 8:18-25; 2 Corinthians 5:16-21; Galatians 3:23-29; Colossians 1:15-23; Ephesians 1:1-10; 2:11-22.

Texts

Genesis 3:23-24; 4:16; 33:10; John 14:27; Acts 10:34-35; Romans 1:7; 5:10,11; 2 Corinthians 5:18,19,20; Galatians 3:28; Ephesians 1:10; 2:14, 16, 19; Colossians 1:19-20.

Illustrations

Reconciliation between Esau and Jacob (Gen. 33:1-11); Reconciliation between a father and Son (Luke 15:11-24); Reconciliation between Ananias and Saul (Acts 9:10-19); Paul and Mark reconciled (Acts 15:38-39; 2 Tim. 4:11); Reconciliation between Jew and Gentile (Eph. 2:11-22); All barriers broken down (Gal. 3:28); A rent veil: God accessible (Matt. 27:51); A broken down wall: Man accessible (Eph. 2:14); God and man reconciled (2 Cor. 5:16-21).

15
Redemption:
We Are Set Free

Redemption is one of the basic themes of the Bible. The terms *redeem, redeemer,* or *redemption* occur 130 times in the Old Testament. *Redeem* or *redemption* occur twenty-two times in the New Testament. Often where the terms do not occur, the reality is there. If the theme of redemption should be taken from our Bible, it would be decimated beyond recognition.

Like so many of our terms, redemption was originally secular. Then it became theological.

The basic meaning of redemption in the Old Testament was to buy back something you once owned. That applied not only to property but to persons. To redeem property was to get it back into its original hands. To redeem a person was to bring him back from slavery into his original relationship with his family. The redeemer was *goel,* meaning next of kin. The *goel* was under obligation to purchase back property a kinsman had lost (Lev. 25:25). Also, the *goel* was to buy back to freedom a relative who, because of debt, had been sold into slavery (vv. 47-49). When property was gotten back, it was redeemed. When a person was bought back to freedom and restored to his family, he was redeemed.

Here was imagery that could tell what God had done to free men and women from spiritual bondage, from alien hands. God had wrested them from those alien hands, given them freedom, and returned them to those to whom they belonged. In the New Testament the supremely liberating act had been done in Jesus Christ. Christ had freed people from dark and sinister powers and returned them to God and to the people of God to whom they belonged. Paul borrowed the term from slavery which was common in his world. When a slave was set free, he was redeemed.

Our Bondage

To speak of our liberation implies bondage, a time when we were not free. We have come quickly to the real tragedy of our lives: We are enslaved, we are in bondage. We are held in powerful hands that mean no good. Our gospel begins with that tragedy. It is bad news before it is good news. It is against this background of hopelessness that hope is announced.

But hands are too weak a metaphor to tell of our tragedy. There are walls much thicker and doors much heavier than those of a prison that lock us in. There are bars much stronger than prison bars that hold us in. There are forces more enslaving than clanking chains around our ankles. We are held in the terrible grip of dark and evil powers that intend to enslave us and then destroy us. Enslaving powers, like the darkness of a terrible night, have descended upon us, causing us to lose our vision and our way.

Who ever escapes this tragedy? It is not theoretical, but a fact of human existence. Who does not know what it is to be trapped, to be hemmed in? Who does not know what it is to have doors close on you, the combinations of which you do not know and therefore cannot open? This is obviously true of the drug addict and alcoholic. But in some deeper sense it is true of all of us. It is as if we are tied by chains to a self-centeredness, a grasping for power, and a narrow vision that does not allow us to see people and our world in the light of God.

The Liberator (Redeemer)

Against the long, dark, clammy night of bondage, a voice is heard, as if the voice of a watchman announcing the day: "The night is passing, the dawn is breaking, soon it will be day " Or there is another voice that calls: "Your bondage is almost over. The liberator is coming. Freedom is on its way."

So we have come to one of the overarching themes of the Bible, that of liberation, freedom, redemption.

I am looking for clues that will unfold the Bible in simple but basic patterns of meaning. Recently I came upon one of these clues, and my heart leaped up. The Bible is a story of three exoduses: The Exodus from Egypt, the exodus from Babylon, and the exodus from the bondage of sin and death made possible by Jesus Christ. Exodus in the biblical sense is going forth from bondage into freedom. It is redemption.

The first Exodus was the towering event of the Old Testament. When Israel wanted to establish her identity and understand her history, she always went back to that deliverance.

We always want to know the meaning of our history, else, we cannot understand the meaning of this journey we are on. We hope it has some purpose, that it is going somewhere. We want to believe that we are doing more than marking time, that the shuffling of feet we hear will not end in some dead-end street. Even a child will ask the meaning of history. He will do it in simple terms that are sometimes very profound. When a little Hebrew boy asked his father the meaning of their history, the father always told him that they had been Pharaoh's slaves in Egypt and that God had brought them out of Egypt with a mighty hand. Just as the landscape is seen in the light of the morning as one begins an early journey, so was Israel's journey seen in the light of that early liberating experience.

We have, in an earlier chapter, referred to what has been called Israel's creed in the twenty-six chapter of Deuteronomy. At the heart of this creed are these words:

"The Lord heard our voice, and saw our affliction, our toil, and our oppression; and the Lord brought us out of Egypt with a mighty hand and an outstretched arm, with great terror, with signs and wonders; and he brought us into this place and gave us this land, a land flowing with milk and honey" (vv. 7-9).

Israel never forgot to tell her story of redemption. It was

passed down from father to son, from generation to generation. She worked it into her liturgy, sang about it, and worshiped in the awareness that she was a redeemed people. Whatever her virtues were, she owed them all to God. It was He who had found them slaves down in Egypt, and had set them free from their bondage. Can you imagine how robustly and with what gratitude they sang?

> He rebuked the Red Sea, and it became dry;
> and he led them through the deep as through
> a desert (Ps. 106:9).

It is important to note that theirs was total redemption. It was social—they were no longer slaves, they were now a free people. It was political—they were no longer under the power of a cruel monarch, they were free to form and fashion their political life and government under God. It was economic— they were no longer forced to make brick without straw under the heavy hands of cruel taskmasters, they were now free to pursue their own trade and craft. And it was spiritual—they were now free to be God's people.

We should remember that in the Third World where people have been exploited, where they are poor, and where they have suffered many kinds of oppression, they have given us liberation theology. They are looking for total redemption. They want to be set free politically, socially, economically, and spiritually. They will not listen to some promise of ethereal redemption. Unless we know how heavy their chains are and show willingness to help free them of their oppression, they will not listen to our gospel.

Then there was the exodus from Babylon.

Jeremiah, with his nation, lived beneath the frightening shadow of the mighty Babylonian Empire. He predicted not only his people's bondage in Babylon but their exodus from it. "Therefore, behold, the days are coming, says the Lord, when men shall no longer say, 'As the Lord lives who brought up the people of Israel out of the land of Egypt,' but 'As the Lord lives

who brought up and led the descendants of the house of Israel
out of the north country and out of all the countries where he
had driven them. Then they shall dwell in their own land" (Jer.
23:7-8). They would be returning home to begin their history
over again. It would be redemption again.

Isaiah, too, felt that Israel would be redeemed from the Babylonian captivity. Therefore he began his magnificent fortieth
chapter like this: "Comfort, comfort my people, says your God.
Speak tenderly to Jerusalem, and cry to her that her warfare is
ended, that her iniquity is pardoned, that she has received from
the Lord's hand double for all her sins" (vv. 1-2).

We should observe that Isaiah uses the term *redeemer* more
frequently than any other writer of the Old Testament. God
was their redeemer. The following references are typical of
him:

> But now thus says the Lord,
>   he who created you, O Jacob,
>   he who formed you, O Israel:
> "Fear not, for I have redeemed you;
>   I have called you by name, you are
>   mine" (Isa. 43:1).

> Thus says the Lord, the King of Israel
>   and his Redeemer, the Lord of hosts:
> "I am the first and I am the last;
>   besides me there is no god" (Isa. 44:6).

Isaiah used the term *goel* for God as redeemer. The term
implied intimacy and personal responsibility. It was as if God
were their "next of kin."

We come now to the third exodus as deliverance from sin
and death.

There can be no doubt as to who the redeemer is. He is Jesus
Christ. He claimed this role for Himself: "Even as the Son of
man came not to be served but to serve, and to give his life as
a ransom for many" (Matt. 20:28; cf Mark 10:45).

In the eighth chapter of John, Jesus talks about committing
sin and thus becoming the slave of sin. He had come to deliver

men from this kind of enslavement: "If the Son makes you free, you will be free indeed" (v. 36).

In His inaugural address at Nazareth, Jesus talked about delivering captives:

> The Spirit of the Lord is upon me,
> because he has anointed me to preach good news to the poor.
> He has sent me to proclaim release to the captives
> and recovering of sight to the blind,
> to set at liberty those who are oppressed,
> to proclaim the acceptable year of the
>   Lord (Luke 4:18-19).

The early church certainly saw Jesus Christ as liberator or redeemer. Liberation is one of the great themes of the New Testament as it is in the Old. "They are justified by his grace as a gift," Paul wrote, "through the redemption which is in Christ Jesus" (Rom. 3:24). Or again, "He has delivered us from the dominion of darkness and transferred us to the kingdom of his beloved Son" (Col. 1:13).

It was a costly redemption: "You know that you were ransomed from the futile ways inherited from your fathers," Peter wrote, "not with perishable things such as silver and gold, but with the precious blood of Christ, like that of a lamb without blemish or spot" (1 Pet. 1:18-19).

Like the redemption from Egypt, the redemption of Jesus brought forth a new people. This is made plain in Titus: "Who gave himself for us to redeem us from all iniquity and to purify for himself a people of his own who are zealous for good deeds" (2:14). The doxology in the first chapter of Revelation says that Christ "made us a kingdom, priests to his God and Father" (1:6).

The redemption of Christ, like His reconciliation, had far-reaching effects. As we have seen, Jesus Christ, through His death, brought together in peace warring powers beyond our earth and history. So in like manner He will set all creation free from its bondage. Not only are human beings in bondage, not only is human history captive to evil powers, but all of creation is enslaved. It needs to be liberated. Therefore, Paul wrote that the whole creation will at last be set free by Christ's redemption: "Because the creation itself will be set free from its bondage to decay and obtain the glorious liberty of the children of God" (Rom. 8:21).

As has been indicated, the term *redemption* was lifted from slavery. When a slave was set free, he was redeemed. Paul had seen it happen at the auction block.

In the ancient world, often fine, aristocratic families were taken captives in war and subsequently sold into slavery. Therefore, in many households the slave might be the most gifted, best-educated, most cultured, and most morally sensitive member of the family. Often the finest specimens of young manhood were sold on the auction block. And as callous as that world was, it was not without compassion and caring. There were people who deplored what went on in the slave market.

It is easy to imagine Paul's visiting a slave market and seeing a sale. On the auction block was an outstanding young man. He was strong and graceful of movement. He was intelligent and the marks of culture were unmistakably on him. If he were free in a society that valued his life, he might be a prince, a scholar, or an artist. Too bad to waste a life like that. The bidding began. On the outskirts of the crowd was a gentle, soft-spoken man who consistently topped the bidding, and finally bought the young man. He took him aside and said: "I have bought you, not for myself but for yourself. I have redeemed you. You are free. Go in peace."

Paul believed that Christ had done something like that for us, yet in a much more wonderful way. Christ had freed us from the enslavement of sin and the bondage of death. Right at the heart of the Christian gospel is the proclamation that Christ has come to set us free from the ultimately enslaving powers.

Murdo Erven Macdonald is a very fine Scottish preacher. He was a chaplain during World War II and taken prisoner by the

Germans. He was with American prisoners since he had been lent to them as a chaplain. The British and American prisoner compounds were close to each other, being separated by a double apron of barbed wire. Often communication took place across that barbed wire. The British had an underground radio which allowed them to be in touch with BBC. A corporal on the British side spoke Gaelic, as did Macdonald, and kept him posted on the news. Macdonald, in turn, relayed it to the Americans.

Macdonald has never forgotten the momentous news of D Day when the allies were landing on the beaches of Normandy. Early that morning an American awoke him, shouting in his ear: "The Scotsman wants to speak to you. It's terribly important." Macdonald got into his clothes as quickly as possible and ran over to the barbed wire. Corporal MacNeil said only two words in Gaelic which meant: "They've come." Macdonald awoke the American camp and broadcast the news. He said their reaction was incredible. The men shouted for joy, hugged each other, leaped into the air, and rolled on the ground with wild abandon. The good news let them know that deliverance was on its way, that freedom was in sight.

The New Testament tells a story very much like that, except the good news is not, "They've come," but "He has come!" Christ has come to deliver us from the bondage of sin and death. "For the law of the Spirit of life in Christ Jesus," Paul declared, "has set me free from the law of sin and death" (Rom. 8:2).

Yet, there is a great difference between the two exoduses of the Old Testament and the exodus of Jesus. In the Exodus from Egypt, political slaves were delivered into freedom. In the exodus from Babylon, captives of war were allowed to return home. But no such deliverance is spoken of in the New Testament.

As a matter of fact, while slavery is mentioned in the New Testament, no hand was lifted against it despite the fact it must be the most evil institution of our designing. That was once very dillusioning to me, but I now understand it better than I once did. Slavery was so much a part of the economic and social structures of the ancient world that no one could attack it and survive. Paul understood that. Yet, I still wish he had said, even in one of his more obscure letters, that slavery is wrong. But he never said it.

What then do we have in the New Testament? We see deliverance taking place on a deeper level than the social and political orders. Men and women are being delivered from moral and spiritual oppression. You can say that they are being delivered from the bondage that lies behind bondage.

Back of all our historic bondages, whether political, social, or economic, lie sin and death. It is sin that causes men and women to misuse power in the exploiting and enslaving of others. That is understandable. But what is death's role in this? It seems much more elusive and difficult. Death speeds up the process. It says to men and women: "You live within the narrow confines of time. You don't have much time. What you do you must do quickly."

So Christ went behind the obvious bondages of our world to the bondage that lies behind them all in order to destroy it. But let it be said that when the freedom Christ gives has run its full course all shackles are struck whether they are economic, political, or social. He wants total liberation.

If Christ delivers us from the bondage that lies behind bondage, that makes our good news even better. What a gospel!

The Liberated (Redeemed)

As we have already seen, the redemption of Jesus Christ brought forth a new people just as the Exodus from Egypt did. The first redemption brought forth Israel as the people of God. The redemption of Jesus Christ brought forth another people, the new Israel or the church. We are the new people of God. We are the liberated ones.

What shall we say about the new people of God? What shall we say about ourselves? Let me suggest five things.

1. We make a confession: We are a servant people.

We do not belong to ourselves but to somebody else. "You are not your own," Paul wrote, "you were bought with a price" (1 Cor. 6:19-20). Or again, "You were bought with a price; do not become slaves of men" (7:23). We have been purchased with an ultimate price—with the death of Jesus Christ. When the church confesses, as it must, that Jesus Christ is Lord, it is at the same time confessing that we are His servants.

Paul would frequently introduce himself as a servant or slave of Jesus Christ.

I have often wished I could have been a part of the group approached by Paul, say in AD 60. There is a tradition that says he wasn't much to look at, did not have an imposing presence, was a hunchback, small of stature, with eyes so sick that they were repulsive. I would have looked at that odd, little man and dismissed him with the casual thought: *What a strange creature.* Then he would have begun to speak: "I want to tell you who I am. I am Paul, a slave of Jesus Christ." The atmosphere would have become electric. It would not have been hard to listen to him, but hard to keep from it, and I would have found myself clinging to every word, knowing that here was a man who did not belong to himself, he had given himself away. He belonged to Christ. Here was the secret of this man's life who, tramping across two continents, shook them to their foundations. He preached in the big cities, always leaving behind him little churches that changed the course of history.

Jesus Christ is our model. He was a servant, and the church is no better than its Lord. Jesus said about himself: "The Son of man came not to be served but to serve, and to give his life as a ransom for many" (Matt. 20:28).

The disciples could not forget the night a host forgot a common courtesy. He failed to provide a servant or slave for the comfort of his guests. So Jesus became a servant. He asked for a towel and basin of water. Tying the towel around His waist, He went by each disciple with the basin of water, and washed and dried his dirty feet.

While we are tempted to seek power and be a lordly people, we should resist it with all the strength of our lives. We must not be too proud to ask for a towel and basin of water nor too squeamish to mop the running sores of our world and heal its wounds. Unless we are willing to do that, we cannot be the people of Christ.

The church has a serving task.

2. We are a worshiping people.

Maybe worship is the first thing we do. We give thanks to our Liberator for our freedom. We are no longer slaves, but a free people; and free people should praise their Lord.

We should do what the Israelites did at the Red Sea, the place of their redemption. They worshiped. "Then Miriam, the prophetess, the sister of Aaron, took a timbrel in her hands; and all the women went out after her with timbrels and dancing. And Miriam sang to them:

Sing to the Lord, for he has triumphed gloriously,
the horse and his rider he has thrown into the sea (Ex. 15:20-21)."

The early church was a worshiping church. One of the loveliest doxologies, which enables us to feel the joy and lilting quality of that worship, is found in the first chapter of Revelation: "To him who loves us and has freed us from our sins by his blood and made us a kingdom, priests to his God and Father, to him be glory and dominion for ever and ever. Amen" (vv. 5-6). They worshiped as people who had been the slaves of dark and destroying powers but had been set free by the blood of Jesus Christ. There was great joy in their worship.

The most magnificient choral scenes in the world's literature are to be found in Revelation. We see great choirs singing moving anthems of praise. John tells us of a new song which is about liberation and its effects:

Worthy art thou to take the scroll and to open its seals,
for thou wast slain and by thy blood didst ransom men for God
from every tribe and tongue and people and nation,
and hast made them a kingdom and priests to our God (5·9-10)

The church has a worshiping task.

3. We have a message of liberation.

You remember how Paul said that God had given His church the message of reconciliation. He has also given it a message of liberation. We have good news to tell.

We speak to people who are morally and spiritually bound. Their bondage is as real as cuffs, chains, prison bars from which they cannot escape. We can say to them: "You don't have to stay that way. You can go free. Christ has come. He can snap those cuffs and tear away those bars."

I remember meeting a soldier returning home from Europe after World War II. We were on the same ship. Just a few weeks earlier he had been in a German prison camp. The marks of the privation of that experience were still on him. He told me about the day they heard the rumbling of tanks. When they learned that they were American tanks, the camp went wild. A joy swept that place which could not be suppressed. The soldiers wept and laughed, they prayed and danced for joy. While the setting was not a chapel, there was real worship—praise and thanksgiving that was deep and spontaneous.

Christians have heard the rumbling of God's grace in Christ, coming to set us free. The liberation He gives is as real as the liberation of that camp.

This is our evangelistic task. We have good news to announce.

4. We have been sent on a mission of freedom.

Just as God sends us on a mission of reconciliation, He sends us on a mission of freedom. We are in the business of breaking the bonds that hold people, sending forth their victims in freedom.

When Jesus raised Lazarus from the dead, he came out of the tomb, "his hands and feet bound with bandages, and his face wrapped with a cloth," and Jesus said to those who stood around, "Unbind him, and let him go" (John 11:44). We are like Jesus. We are in the unbinding and loosing business. Wherever men and women are bound we are to help set them free.

We must not forget that the liberation about which the New Testament speaks is first of all freedom from moral and spiritual bondage. Yet, as has already been said, the liberation of Christ, when it has run its full course, frees people from all kinds of bondage, be they psychological, social, political, or economic. Else, liberation becomes too ethereal, too far removed from the hard realities of our world. The liberation of the Israelites at the Red Sea was total deliverance. We must seek that in our own time. The hungry must be set free from the bondage of poverty, those who are discriminated against from the bondage of racism, little children from the bondage of abuse.

This is the prophetic task of the church.

5. We develop a new life-style.

As liberated people, we are to have a new life-style. We are to be different from the world, not for the sake of being different, but because we really are. And Jesus has told us what that difference is: "By this all men will know that you are my disciples; if you have love for one another" (John 13:35). We are to love with a new quality, care more deeply, accept more fully, and affirm more strongly than the world about us. Only then can we be like Jesus, only then will people take us seriously and listen to what we have to say.

This is the pastoral task of the church.

Redemption then is one of the basic themes of our Bible, rich in variation, which we often should preach.

Thought Starters

A series of sermons on The Three Exoduses of the Bible.
A series on The Marks of a Liberated People.
Other sermons: Like Chains About Our Ankles; Morning Is Breaking! The Redeemer Has Come! The Bondage Behind Bondage; Total Redemption; Freedom from Sin and Death; We Have a Worshiping Task; We Have a Serving Task; We Have an Evangelistic Task; We Have a Prophetic Task; We Have a Pastoral Task.

Scripture

Exodus 14:10-31; 15:1-21; Deuteronomy 6:20-25; Psalm 130:1-8; Isaiah 43:1-7; Jeremiah 23:5-8; Romans 3:21-26; Galatians 4:1-7; 1 Peter 1:13-21; Revelation 1:1-7; 14:1-5.

Texts

Exodus 12:42; 13:9; Deuteronomy 6:21; Psalm 130:7; Isaiah 43:1; John 8:36; Romans 8:21; Galatians 4:4-5; Colossians 1:13-14; 1 Peter 1:18; Revelation 1:5a-6.

Illustrations

The meaning of Passover (Ex. 12:26-27); When freedom is difficult (Ex. 16:3); Singing about Exodus (Ps. 114:1-8); Freedom that Christ gives (John 8:36); Set free from sin to become the slaves of God (Rom. 6:22); Creation to be redeemed (Rom. 8:18-25); A doxology of redemption (Rev. 1:5a-6).

16
Salvation:
We Are Healed

The earliest meaning of the Greek word, *soteria*, translated salvation, was health or wholeness. To be saved was to be restored to health, and this meaning is still inherent in the Christian use of the term. Our alienation, estrangement, bondage, and sin have made us sick, and to be freed from them is to become well, to have health and wholeness.

Yet, we don't usually think of salvation in those terms. The basic idea is that of deliverance. Even when salvation is thought of in terms of health and wholeness, the dynamic of deliverance is present. To have health is to be delivered from sickness, maybe even death.

In salvation, we are delivered from that which threatens us or holds us in its destructive power. To be saved in the distinctive Christian sense is to be delivered from the power of sin and death.

It is interesting to note that the term was secular before it was religious. Even the Bible speaks of being saved from hunger, physical danger, sickness, death, or the enemy. But this fact is not peculiar to our term *salvation*. Most of our theological words were secular before they were religious. Men and women have looked out upon their everyday lives and found experiences, words, and imagery that can tell of God's redemptive action. That tells us a great deal about our religion. God is not a despiser of mundane things. He is not only the God of altars, holy times, and esoteric experiences; He is the God of our world, our secular experiences, and our common life. He joins us along our dusty ways and tells us who He is. We dare use our common language to speak of Him and to tell what He has done.

The fact that the word *salvation* is so frequently and widely used in the Bible tells us that it is no ordinary term. The word *salvation* occurs 132 times in the Bible, *save* 148, *saved* 108, and *savior* 38 times. It is also one of the most widely used words in our theological vocabulary.

Salvation is an extremely comprehensive term, gathering up the meaning of several other basic theological words. For example, *reconciliation, liberation,* and *forgiveness* are under its umbrella of meaning. Salvation means having our separation and estrangement overcome. It is reconciliation. It means being set free from moral and spiritual bondage, from dark and enslaving powers. It is liberation. Salvation means deliverance from guilt, shame, and the penalty of sin. It is forgiveness.

Salvation Is of God

Let us make four observations about salvation being of God.

1. We cannot save ourselves.

The psalmist pleaded: "O grant us help against the foe, for vain is the help of man" (60:11).

The psalmist was probably thinking about some common foe, like enemies or military power, but the same truth holds when we think of our being delivered from moral and spiritual forces. "Vain is the help of man."

Jeremiah asked: "Can the Ethiopian change his skin or the leopard his spots? Then also you can do good who are accustomed to do evil" (13:23). Jeremiah knew how impossible it is for a black man to pluck the pigments from his skin and how utterly helpless a leopard is to change his spots. We cannot, even in our best effort, deliver ourselves from the power of sin.

All efforts at self-salvation are futile. They are like a man trying to lift himself up by his own bootstraps. The effort is doomed from the start. If he is to be lifted, some power outside him and from beyond him must bear him up.

Or again, such an effort is like an anemic person giving himself a blood transfusion. He draws blood from one arm and puts it in the other. But it is sick blood. There is no strength and vitality in it. Only healthy blood from another can help him.

Yet, we continue our futile effort to save ourselves. The more we try to free ourselves the more entangled we become. The harder we try the more deeply we sink into hopelessness. It is a story of guilt being heaped upon guilt, of despair being heaped on despair.

2. Only God can save.

If salvation in its deepest sense is deliverance from sin and death, then it is beyond anything I can do. I am free to sin but I am not free to cancel it out. I cannot negate its harmful effect. The word I spoke was so much more wounding than I had thought. I would like to call it back, but I can't. I would like to undo the foul deed and cleanse the stream into which it was cast. But I can do neither. Only God can forgive and deliver from sin.

I am so defenseless before death, and it comes inescapably upon me. It will destroy me and separate me from the things and people I love most. If there is any deliverance from it, it must come from God.

We can understand why the Bible tells us that salvation is with God alone. Only God can save.

The psalmist said: "Deliverance belongs to the Lord" (3:8). (See 25:5; 68:20.)

Isaiah heard God saying: "I, I am the Lord, and besides me there is no savior" (43:11).

Or again: "Turn to me, and be saved, all the ends of the earth! For I am God, and there is no other" (Isa. 45:22).

Andrew Blackwood, who taught preaching at Princeton Theological Seminary for many years, believed that Charles Haddon Spurgeon was the greatest preacher since Paul.

Spurgeon as a young man was driven one Sunday morning from the streets of London into a wayside chapel by a blinding snowstorm. The weather was so inclement that the pastor had been unable to get to the chapel, and a lay preacher was in the pulpit. Spurgeon remembered what a poor preacher he was, but he had a great text which he kept repeating over and over again. "Look unto me, and be ye saved, all the ends of the earth: for I am God, and there is none else" (Isa. 45:22, KJV). Spurgeon was greatly moved by the text. He felt as if God were paging him, calling him by name. By faith he looked to the great God of the universe with whom alone was salvation, and God saved him in great grace and mercy.

Thousands of mourners gathered to pay tribute at Spurgeon's funeral. When the casket was lowered into the grave, those who stood close by could see the Bible resting on top and opened to the passage that had led Spurgeon to salvation.

3. God's supreme act of salvation was in Jesus Christ.

Across Israel's long history, God had performed many saving acts, but His chief saving event was in Jesus Christ. The New Testament makes this perfectly clear.

The angel of the Lord said to Joseph: "She will bear a son, and you shall call his name Jesus, for he will save his people from their sins" (Matt. 1:21). (Jesus means *savior* or *salvation*.)

The Christmas angel announced: "Be not afraid; for behold, I bring you good news of a great joy which will come to all the people; for to you is born this day in the city of David a Savior, who is Christ the Lord" (Luke 2:10-11).

Jesus once defined the purpose of His life in terms of salvation: "For the Son of man came to seek and to save the lost" (Luke 19:10).

John wrote: "For God sent the Son into the world, not to condemn the world, but that the world might be saved through him" (3:17).

The early church certainly saw Jesus in this role. This is the way those first apostles preached: "And there is salvation in no one else, for there is no other name under heaven given among men by which we must be saved" (Acts 4:12).

The basic religious question was asked by the Philippian

jailer: "Men, what must I do to be saved?" and the answer was, "Believe in the Lord Jesus, and you will be saved" (Acts 16:30-31).

In some real sense, the great concern of every religion is salvation. Every religion has to answer the question: What must I do to be saved? If it cannot answer that question, it fails to meet the basic need of men and women. It must give some answer or be headed for extinction. Christianity answers it in terms of Jesus Christ.

4. God offers salvation to us through Jesus Christ as a gift.

God's salvation in Christ cannot be earned, merited, or purchased. It is of grace; therefore, it is a gift. The wealthiest cannot buy it. There are no price tags on salvation. Those who have scrupulously kept moral laws and religious rituals cannot exchange their virtue for salvation. It is a gift both to the best and the worst. Paul states this great truth very emphatically: "They are justified by his grace as a gift, through the redemption which is in Christ Jesus" (Rom. 3:24). Or again: "But the free gift is not like the trespass. For if many died through one man's trespass, much more have the grace of God and the free gift in the grace of that one man Jesus Christ abounded for many" (Rom. 5:15). Paul's clearest statement is found in Ephesians 2:8-9: "For by grace you have been saved through faith; and this is not your own doing, it is the gift of God—not because of works, lest any man should boast."

John Wesley in his *Journal* wrote about his preaching at Saint Ives: "In the evening we reached St. Ives. At seven I invited all guilty, helpless, sinners, who were conscious they had 'nothing to pay' to accept a free forgiveness. The room was crowded both within and without, but all were quiet and attentive."[1]

The gospel is addressed to people who have nothing with which to pay. But then they need nothing. Salvation is a gift.

Our Salvation Is Historical

When we say our salvation is historical, we mean that we are saved by the mighty historical action of God.

We are not saved by mysticism that lifts us out of this world into God, the experience of which is too ineffable to tell. We are not saved by universal truth that is inherent in the human mind. We are not saved by intuitive flashes of truth that break in upon our minds as if from nowhere. We are not saved by our rational powers. God is not found standing at the head of a stairway of logic.

We are saved by what God does along the common ways of our history. His salvation has dates, places, and faces upon it.

The great saving event of the Old Testament was the Exodus. It could not have been more historical. Just before Moses and the children of Israel crossed over the Red Sea, Moses said to them: "Fear not, stand firm, and see the salvation of the Lord, which he will work for you today; for the Egyptians whom you see today, you will never see again. The Lord will fight for you, and you have only to be still" (Ex. 14:13-14).

The psalmist saw salvation in historical terms:

> We have heard with our ears, O God,
>   our fathers have told us,
> what deeds thou didst perform in their days,
>   in the days of old (44:1).

Jesus Christ, our great Savior, is a thoroughly historical person. He was associated with places. His life is dated. We know when He was born and where. We know where He grew up, the setting of His ministry, where He was crucified, and where He was resurrected.

Jesus Christ, the Savior of the world, doesn't save us out of the world but in it. He doesn't save us out of history but in it.

A Japanese minister was serving at Christ Church in Cambridge, Massachusetts in 1943. That was a war year, and many military personnel attended Christ Church. Dr. Kitagawa, the minister, said that on a particular Sunday a young marine stopped to speak with him just after the worship service was over. The sermon that morning had dealt with the God-given unity of mankind as seen in the light of Jesus' teaching. The marine said to Dr. Kitagawa: "Father, I too believe what you said in your sermon is absolutely true. I'm glad I was in church this morning to hear your particular message." He paused momentarily and then continued: "I was trained as a violinist but that's all finished, for in the South Pacific my right wrist was permanently injured. When I was discharged, I vowed I would kill the first Japanese I met. You know, Father, you're that Japanese!" Having said that, he extended his injured hand to Dr. Kitagawa and left the church. We are saved in situations as concrete, personal, and social as that of the marine.

Total Salvation

Christian salvation includes the total life and also the corporate life.

All too frequently we have thought of Christ as saving only a part of the life—the part we call the soul. We speak of souls being saved. Christ does not envision a fragmented and broken salvation, rather He sees salvation in terms of wholeness. The whole life in its social setting is to be saved. To think of salvation in terms of only the soul being delivered from sin is more a Greek heresy than a Christian doctrine. The Greeks thought of the soul as being entrapped in the body, which was its prison. To be saved was to have the soul set free of the body. But in Christian salvation we envision even the body being reclaimed. Paul wrote: "When the perishable puts on the imperishable, and the mortal puts on immortality, then shall come to pass the saying that is written:

"Death is swallowed up in victory."
"O death, where is thy victory?
O death, where is thy sting?" (1 Cor. 15:54-55).

I think of Zacchaeus of Jericho whom Jesus met under strange circumstances when he was passing through that city. Zacchaeus, being small of stature and lost in the crowd, had climbed up into a sycamore tree so he could see Jesus. As Jesus came into the city, He looked up and saw the little man, perched like a bird on one of the limbs of the tree. Jesus told Zacchaeus to come down as He wanted to be a guest in his house. A great transformation took place in the life of Zacchaeus that day, and before leaving, Jesus said: "Today, salvation has come to this house, since he also is a son of Abraham" (Luke 19:9).

Zacchaeus's response to the grace, love, and acceptance he had found in Jesus was: "Behold, Lord, the half of my goods I give to the poor; and if I have defrauded any one of anything, I restore it fourfold" (v.8).

Zacchaeus was spiritually redeemed. But there was much more. His life in his social and economic relations was changed. He was given new values. People meant more, and money meant less. All of life was seen in a new light.

Zacchaeus had been a very bad man. He had cared more for money than human faces. He had exploited and used people through an oppressive tax system. His money was stained with human blood. He had gotten rich off the people of Jericho and they hated him for it. But the day he met Jesus he became a new man who set about redressing old wrongs and creating new relationships of justice and compassion. He was given a new life and with it a new pocketbook.

Several years ago I had a very interesting correspondence with an elderly woman in her nineties who was living in a nursing home in Washington, D.C. I never met her. She had picked up my name from an article I had written. She was a great admirer of Charles Haddon Spurgeon as a preacher. She especially appreciated the well-balanced gospel he preached. She told of one of his sermons she had heard in which as he came near the end he said, "May I never preach a sermon without a word to the unsaved." But earlier he had talked about weavers who wove expensive garments for the rich but were not paid a living wage. They could not afford the garments their hands had woven. He decried this social injustice. Miss Cunningham said that Spurgeon knew that salvation was both personal and social.

Beyond the personal life with its many social relations, Christ wants to save the corporate life. There we are most sinful and there the guilt of our sin lies most heavily upon us. Yet, it is there that we are least aware of our guilt. We have so individualized our salvation that we have almost lost sight of the corporate dimension. But the Bible does not make that mistake. It knows that God wants to transform the corporate structures of life.

Jesus announced the kingdom of God which is certainly a corporate reality. When the kingdom has fully come, all of life will be under the rule of God. Then the corporate structures will be more just, compassionate, and humane. Jesus prayed for the coming of the Kingdom of God: "Thy kingdom come, Thy will be done, On earth as it is in heaven" (Matt. 6:10).

As a sign that Christ takes corporate salvation seriously, we have the church as a reality of corporate redemption in the midst of our world. There is the new humanity that confesses Jesus Christ as Lord, that worships and serves, and that announces the good news of our salvation in Christ.

Salvation in Three Tenses

Our salvation is in three tenses. We have been saved, we are being saved, and we shall be saved. Emil Brunner once said that to be a Christian is to share "something which has happened, which is happening, and which will happen." Let us look at these three time dimensions of our salvation.

1. Salvation as Past.

Salvation in the past has two meanings: Something has been done in the past that made salvation possible, and our initial experience of salvation is in the past.

We look back to the gracious actions of God, especially the death of Jesus Christ, for the sources of salvation. Jesus while on the cross said: "It is finished" (John 19:30).

Scriptures are plentiful that tell of the past tense of our salvation: "Christ redeemed us from the curse of the law, having become a curse for us" (Gal. 3:13); "He has delivered us from the dominion of darkness and transferred us to the kingdom of his beloved Son, in whom we have redemption, the forgiveness of sins" (Col. 1:13); "In Christ God was reconciling the world to himself" (2 Cor. 5:19).

Also, we were saved in the past. Like all things personal and historical, there must be a beginning. The new birth, as well as the physical birth, takes place sometime. We sing: "O happy day that fixed my choice/On thee my Savior and my God!"

Some people have very dramatic experiences. They can pinpoint it in the past. They can tell you the day, the hour, and the place when the great burden of guilt was rolled away and they knew the peace of God.

Paul could have done that. He could have taken us to a roadside near Damascus, given the date, and then said, "It happened here on this spot at noon." He had no experience more dated than that.

John Wesley could have done that. It was at Aldersgate at 8:45 in the evening when he knew God had forgiven his sins.

Many cannot do that. They are Christians although they cannot date the experience of grace so precisely. But that it has happened is the great testimony of their lives.

2. Salvation as Present.

Paul felt that salvation is in the present. We are still being saved. "For the word of the cross," wrote Paul, "is folly to those who are perishing, but to us who are being saved it is the power of God" (1 Cor. 1:18). Or again, "Now I would remind you, brethren, in what terms I preached to you the gospel, which you received, in which you stand, by which you are saved, if you hold it fast—unless you believed in vain" (15:1-2).

Salvation in the present is a dynamic, vital experience, in which you are growing in grace.

I remember a bright young man we once had in our church. He became restless and unhappy with us, so I went to talk with him. He said something like this: "I don't like your concept of salvation. You think it is a point in the past, that it is static.

I see it as being present, vital, living, growing." I was able to say to him: "I would not want to argue with you about this. There is much in the New Testament that supports your way of thinking."

This growing experience in salvation is what we have called sanctification. It is growing in grace, becoming more like Jesus, and maturing in Christ. Paul tells us that we are to come to "mature manhood, to the measure of the stature of the fullness of Christ. . . . Speaking the truth in love, we are to grow up in every way into him who is the head, into Christ" (Eph. 4:13, 15).

One of the finest things about being a pastor is seeing people grow spiritually. Here is a man about whom you can say: "He is so different from what he was ten years ago. He is really not the same person." This is a man who knows salvation as a present experience. He is being saved.

Maybe you can say about yourself: "I am not the person I want to be, but I am certainly not the person I was." You are being saved.

3. Salvation as Future.

We shall be saved. "Since therefore, we are now justified by his blood," Paul wrote, "much more shall we be saved by him from the wrath of God" (Rom. 5:9).

One fifth of the 150 references to salvation in the New Testament have to do with salvation to be consummated in the last day. Full and complete salvation lies out there in the future. John tells us, "Beloved we are God's children now; it does not yet appear what we shall be, but we know that when he appears we shall be like him, for we shall see him as he is" (1 John 3:2).

"You . . . were sealed," Paul wrote, "with the promised Holy Spirit, which is the guarantee of our inheritance until we acquire possession of it, to the praise of his glory" (Eph. 1:13-14). The Holy Spirit is like a down payment which guarantees that God will eventually give us our inheritance in full.

We shall at last be fully saved from our sin and mortality,

not here but there. We shall have a new life in a new dimension, free from pain, suffering, tears, and death. We shall have new bodies befitting the new order, and we shall live in a new city without shadows and darkness. There will be no sin and death there. Work will be worship and worship will be work, for we shall serve God day and night in His temple. We shall offer God perfect service and we shall love our fellows with perfect love. Never before have we been able to do that. When all of this has come to pass, then can it be said that we have been fully saved. But we shall have to wait for it. It is out there in the future.

Do not forget that the most persistent religious question is: What shall I do to be saved? Speak often to that question.

Thought Starters

A series of sermons on Total Salvation.
A series on Salvation in Three Tenses.
Other sermons: The Most Persistent Religious Question; Only God Can Save; The Christian Meaning of Salvation; No Price Tags; For Those Who Cannot Pay; Saving the Whole Life; The Church as Corporate Salvation.

Scripture

Psalm 3:1-8; 27:1-14; Isaiah 1:1-20; Luke 19:1-10; Acts 16:25-34; Romans 5:1-11; 8:18-25; 10:5-13; 13:8-14; 1 Corinthians 1:18-31; Ephesians 2:1-10; 1 Timothy 1:8-17; Titus 2:1-15; 3:1-11; 1 Peter 1:1-9; Revelation 7:9-17.

Texts

Isaiah 45:22; Matthew 1:21; Luke 2:11; 19:10; Acts 4:12; 15:11; 16:31; Romans 1:16; 5:15; 8:24; 10:12-13; 13:11; 1 Corinthians 1:18; Ephesians 2:8; 1 Timothy 1:15; Titus 2:11; 3:4-5; 1 Peter 1:5; Revelation 7:10.

Illustrations

Exodus as salvation (Ex. 14:13-14); Morality will not save us (Mark 10:17-22); A man whose whole life was saved (Luke 19:1-10); Salvation as a free gift (Rom. 5:15-17); Salvation as past (Rom. 8:24); Salvation as present (1 Cor. 1:18); Salvation as future (Rom. 13:11, Phil. 1:6; 1 Pet. 1:5; 1 John 3:2).

Note

1. *Wesley's Journal:* Selections, Edited by Hugh Martin (London: SCM Press LTD, 1955), p. 59.

17
Evil and Suffering:
The Two Great Enigmas

We are baffled more by evil and suffering than anything else. They cause more painful and unanswerable questions than all other things. You have heard people, face to face with some stark evil or unbearable pain, cry out: "Why did it happen?" It is such an anguished question. Therefore, we are speaking of evil and suffering as the two great enigmas of human existence. They are the two treacherous shoals on which faith makes shipwreck of itself more often than any other place in human experience.

A nationally known rabbi, at the close of World War II, lost his faith and gave up his rabbinate. He reflected morbidly over the extinction of 6 million Jews under the Nazi regime in Germany and elsewhere. Where was God when the Jews were being uprooted from their homes, herded into concentration camps, and thrown into torture chambers? Why would God allow such unbridled evil and inhuman suffering? These questions smoldered in his soul until they left him a burned-out spiritual hulk. He gave up his faith in God. There must not be a God, but, if there were, He would be unworthy of his faith, love, and worship.

If I have not wrestled with this problem, I am not prepared to be either a pastor or a preacher.

I want to speak about the problem, the sources of evil, and look toward a solution

The Problem

The problem arises at the point where, in the face of so much evil and so much pain, we make the claim that God is both perfectly good and all-powerful. Standing face to face with the harsh realities of life, we are tempted to feel that if God is perfectly good He could not be all powerful; if all-powerful He could not be perfectly good. If God is perfectly loving, why does He allow so much evil and suffering; if almighty, why doesn't He do something about it? If God were missing in one or both of these qualities, we would not have such a serious problem.

C. S. Lewis has written: "If God were good, He could wish to make his creatures perfectly happy, and if God were almighty, He would be able to do what he wishes. But the creatures are not happy. Therefore God lacks either goodness, or power or both! That is the problem of pain in its simplest form."[1]

I remember the great catastrophe in Bangladesh in 1970 when 300,000 people were destroyed by tidal waves and high winds within a few hours. My son, then a bright boy in grammar school, asked: "Daddy, where was God when all of this was taking place?" And I couldn't tell him.

Please never give cheap answers when you stand in the presence of almost insufferable pain, and often you will stand there. I have frequently had to say something like this: "So far as I can see there is no answer. But at times like this we cling most strongly to the faith that says God is good and loving and that sometime, somewhere, He will shed light on the mystery of pain and redeem all tragedy."

Sources of Evil

While suffering and evil are sometimes related, being inextricably bound up together, they are not identical. If you had to choose which is the greater of the two problems, you would certainly have to say that evil is. Let us look at the sources of evil.

Evil obviously has three sources—inside us, outside us, and above us.

1. There is evil inside us. There is a proneness to evil within us, a moral gravity that pulls us downward. In the fall, there was something within Adam and Eve that drove them to power, that made them want to be like God. All of us are power prone and power happy. We reach readily for handles of power.

Hear how evil is spoken of in the sixth chapter of Genesis: "The Lord saw that the wickedness of man was great in the earth, and that every imagination of the thoughts of his heart was only evil continually" (v. 5).

Jeremiah could say: "The heart is deceitful above all things, and desperately corrupt; who can understand it?" (17:9).

Paul, in telling of the fierce warfare that went on in his life, speaks of the evil inside him: "Now if I do what I do not want, it is no longer I that do it, but sin which dwells within me. So I find it to be a law that when I want to do right, evil lies close at hand" (Rom. 7:20-21).

Let us hear James: "But each person is tempted when he is lured and enticed by his own desire. Then desire when it has conceived gives birth to sin; and sin when it is full-grown brings forth death" (1:14-15). Or again: "What causes wars, and what causes fightings among you? Is it not your passions that are at war in your members? You desire and do not have; so you kill. And you covet and cannot obtain; so you fight and wage war" (4:1-2).

2. There are sources of evil that lie outside of us.

In the fall the serpent represents evil. Where does he come from? The story does not tell us, but he is not the creation of Adam's and Eve's imagination. He is there, an objective reality. And the tree of good and evil, with its strange appeal to our forebears, is an objective reality. The serpent and the tree were sources of temptation that lay outside those who were tempted and who yielded.

One of the most obvious sources of evil that lie outside of us is bad men who not only do evil but build it into our social structures, even in the best and most acceptable of them. I remember how Reinhold Niebuhr used to tell us that human justice, even the best of it, would corrupt itself.

It is significant to note that the Bible usually sees the city as a place of evil. There is evil in its life and power structures.

You remember the parting of Abraham and his nephew, Lot, which was painful, especially for Abraham. Lot looked to the east and saw the well-watered and fertile valley of the Nile. He moved in that direction, while Abraham remained in the less promising Canaan. The comment is made in the story: "Now the men of Sodom were wicked, great sinners against the Lord" (Gen. 13:13).

In the eighteenth chapter of Revelation the destruction of Rome is dramatically told. She is extremely wicked and likened unto a harlot. (See Rev. 18:1-24.)

Then nature is another source of evil outside us which we call natural evil.

We do not mean that nature is evil and immoral. She is amoral, we never arraign nature before a court of law. Yet, think of floods, winds, tornados, earthquakes, disease, pestilence, and famine. The effects of nature can create evil and inflict pain.

Pompeii was a Roman city of 18,000 people located on the southwest coast of Italy at the beginning of the Christian era. In AD 79 Mount Vesuvius erupted and within a few hours buried Pompeii beneath twenty feet of ash and cinder. Its life was snuffed out. Think of the suffering and evil that nature caused.

In the thirteenth chapter of Luke Jesus talks about both kinds of evil that lie outside us—moral and natural.

There were the Galileans whose blood Pilate mingled with

their sacrifices. This was moral evil that lay in the will of a Roman governor who was suspicious and insecure.

Then Jesus told about the eighteen who sought shelter and protection at the base of the tower of Siloam in Jerusalem during a storm. The tower toppled over and crushed them beneath its rubble. While neither the storm nor the tower was evil within itself, think of the pain and tragedy they caused.

3. There is evil that comes from above us.

Many of us have visited Hitler's concentration camps in Germany. Years have passed since the terrible atrocities occurred, and redemptive symbols such as chapels have been built in some of these camps, yet there hovers over those places a terrible darkness and evil that nothing can ever eradicate. One cannot help wondering about the source of such depravity. You look at the German heart, sinful like all human hearts, but no adequate explanation is found there. You look at German society, the structures of which were terribly evil during the Nazi regime, yet it fails to offer a satisfying explanation. It was as if a terrible evil, darker than the blackest midnight, had settled over the camps, deranging human minds and destroying all decency. It was as if a dreadful evil, too terrible to describe, had come upon them from beyond.

Paul, speaking of the Christian warfare, said: "For we are not contending against flesh and blood, but against the principalities, against the powers; against the world rulers of this present darkness, against the spiritual hosts of wickedness in the heavenly places" (Eph. 6:12).

They were not wrestling merely with evil within themselves or evil in the social, political, and economic structures, but with great powers of darkness that came upon them from beyond. This is supernatural evil which has terrifying power.

Peter wrote: "Be sober, be watchful. Your adversary the devil prowls around like a roaring lion, seeking some one to devour" (1 Pet. 5:8).

Or John: "We know that we are of God, and the whole world is in the power of the evil one" (1 John 5:19).

Toward a Solution of the Problem

Let me say five things, knowing that we cannot come upon a complete solution of this problem. Mystery will always hang over it.

1. God did not create evil and suffering.

C. S. Lewis has written that we must guard against two sub-Christian doctrines of the origin of evil: monism, a single reality that created both good and evil; and dualism "according to which God produces good, while some equal or independent power produces evil."[2] Monism is too simple, not taking into account the complexity of evil. In dualism, we can never be sure which force will win.

The Bible leaves no doubt as to who will win. God will win. Goodness will overcome evil and light will conquer darkness.

I heard the late John Baille speak only once. That was in a chapel service in Union Theological Seminary in New York City. It was in early 1941, England's darkest hour in the war. Baille said he couldn't tell us how this war would end. (I have often wondered if he didn't believe England would lose.) But he knew how the last one would end. God would win that one.

God didn't create evil, His creation was good. Yet, it must be said that He created a world where evil could occur. This was possible because God made creatures to whom He gave free will. This was risky business. What if they should misuse their freedom, disobey, and rebel against God? This happened on the historical and human level, but what about the supernatural? What about Satan? He certainly does not coexist eternally with God; therefore he is not independent of God. The devil or Satan is most likely a semidivinity who misused his freedom, rebelling against God and seeking to establish himself over God's creation. This he can never do. He is fated for defeat.

Reinhold Niebuhr has written of the devil: "To believe that there is a devil is to believe that there is a principle or force of evil antecedent to any evil human action. Before man fell the devil fell. The devil is, in fact, a fallen angel. His sin and fall consists in his effort to transcend his proper state to become like God. This definition of the devil's fall is implied in Isaiah's condemnation of Babylon, in which the pride of Babylon is compared or identified with Lucifer's pride: 'How art thou fallen from heaven, O Lucifer, son of the morning! how art thou cut down to the ground. . . . For thou hast said in thine heart, I will ascend into heaven, I will exalt my throne above the stars of God. . . . Yet thou shalt be brought down to hell.' "[3]

Neither does God create suffering, but life is filled with it.

Suffering, like evil, has always been such a baffling reality. It would not be so confusing if there were some kind of justice that meted out suffering fairly for one's sins. While sin and suffering are sometimes related, they are never related in an exact way. Sometimes they are not related at all, so far as we can see. The fact that the innocent suffer constitutes one of our greatest problems.

We find a theology in the Old Testament that sees suffering as a punishment by God for sin, while health, prosperity, big family, and long life are the favor of God bestowed on the righteous. It was believed that those who suffered were sinful.

The Book of Job was meant to destroy that kind of theology. Job is described as a man who "was blameless and upright, one who feared God, and turned away from evil" (1:1). Yet, he was a great sufferer. He lost his wealth, his children, and his health, holding on to life with a fragile thread of strength.

The great question of suffering is never answered. Suffering is left a mystery, but Job made a great discovery: God is knowable:

> I had heard of thee by the hearing of the ear,
>   but now my eye sees thee;
> therefore I despise myself,
>   and repent in dust and ashes" (Job 42:5-6).

It was enough to know God. Job could then bear suffering, even though he could not explain or understand it. It was better to have the power with which to bear suffering than to have the explanation of it. This is something that we moderns need to learn from Job.

2. We need to learn to use suffering creatively.

To begin, let suffering test and discipline us.

Suffering can make us bitter and cynical but that need not be true. Suffering can test us, making us stronger. It can be like a refining fire that burns away the chaff and dross of our lives.

> And I will put this third into the fire,
>   and refine them as one refines silver,
>   and test them as gold is tested.
> They will call on my name,
>   and I will answer them.
> I will say, "They are my people";
>   and they will say, "The Lord is my God"
>   (Zech. 13:9).

Again, let suffering create a social sensitivity.

Humanity is a fellowship of suffering. Because I suffer, I can become more aware of and more concerned about my suffering brother.

I knew a woman who lost her only son in a plane crash. Rather than making her cynical, it made her extremely sensitive to the suffering of others. I have never known a person who could minister to others the way she could. Without being self-conscious she could walk through the doorway of another's pain and be at home there because she had been a great sufferer herself. There were so many ways she could say: "I know. I understand. I am with you."

One of the great things about Israel was that her suffering in Egypt, rather than making her bitter and antisocial, heightened her social awareness. She never asked: Why me? (She asked that about her being chosen as a special people but never about her privation from slavery.) Israel was especially careful about the uprooted, the homeless, and the sojourner.

"When a stranger sojourns with you in your land, you shall not do him wrong. The stranger who sojourns with you shall be to you as the native among you, and you shall love him as yourself; for you were strangers in the land of Egypt: I am the Lord your God" (Lev. 19:33-34).

Further, turn suffering to an advantage.

Paul was able to do this. While in prison he wrote to the Philippian Christians:

"I want you to know, brethren, that what has happened to me has really served to advance the gospel, so that it has become known throughout the whole praetorian guard and to all the rest that my imprisonment is for Christ; and most of the brethren have been made confident in the Lord because of my imprisonment, and are much more bold to speak the word of God without fear" (Phil. 1:12-14).

The rattling chains, the prison bars, the confinement, and the denial of freedom all worked to the advantage of the gospel and Paul's influence.

Leslie Weatherhead dedicated his book, *Why Do Men Suffer?* to his mother and sister in their struggle against suffering:

Dedicated
In unfolding remembrance
to Elizabeth Mary Weatherhead, my mother
and to
Muriel Weatherhead, my sister
whose bodies were defeated in battle against painful
disease, but who, from that defeat, wrested a spiritual
victory which challenged and inspired all who knew them,
and made glad the heart of God. And to all proud
suffers who, with broken bodies and unbroken spirit, are
seeking to achieve for themselves and for others
The conquest of suffering.[4]

Ralph Sockman was one of the great preachers of the generation that has just passed. I met a graduate student who was doing a biography of him. Sockman had experienced a great tragedy when his son committed suicide. The student said it was at this point that a new quality appeared in Sockman's preaching: There was a warm, compassionate element he had never been able to express before

Still further, know that suffering can be redemptive.

The fifty-third chapter of Isaiah may be the highwater mark of the Old Testament. There we are told, God's Servant will redeem the world through suffering.

> But he was wounded for our transgressions,
>   he was bruised for our iniquities;
> upon him was the chastisment that made us whole,
>   and with his stripes we are healed (v. 5).

This is the way Jesus redeemed. He was God's Suffering Servant. His cross bears witness to it.

Suffering as redemption can work on a human level. It can happen where one human being freely and lovingly takes into his own life the pain and tragedy of another and suffers for him. Such suffering can turn a person from his tragic ways and heal his wounds. This, of course, can never be a substitute for redemption wrought by divine suffering.

Finally, suffering can bring glory to God.

The story of Jesus' healing a blind man is told in the ninth chapter of John. The disciples clung to the old theology that said illness is the punishment for sin. Therefore, they asked: "Rabbi, who sinned, this man or his parents, that he was born blind?" And Jesus answered: "It was not that this man sinned, or his parents, but that the works of God might be made manifest in him" (vv. 2-3).

I remember a regular visit I was making in the hospital. There was nothing special about it, yet it became special. I visited a member of our church who told me she was incurably ill and that she would suffer the rest of her life. Then she said: "I would like to offer God my suffering for his glory if he can use it." That hospital room became an altar.

3. We should know that evil has opposition.

I want to mention some opposing forces.

Evil is self-opposing.

There is conflict within evil. It is set against itself. Death is built into its life.

The psalmist knew this:

> He makes a pit, digging it out,
>   and falls into the hole which he made.
> His mischief returns upon his own head,
>   and on his own pate his violence descends (Ps. 7:15-16).
>   (See also Ps. 9:15; 57:6b.)

There is a moral law within us that opposes evil.

Paul is very clear about this: "For I delight in the law of God, in my inmost self, but I see in my members another law at war with the law of my mind and making me captive to the law of sin which dwells in my members" (Rom. 7:22-23).

There was the law of God in his inmost self that opposed the lawlessness of sin in his life.

Further, there is a moral structure within the universe that opposes evil.

Paul wrote: "Do not be deceived; God is not mocked, for whatever a man sows; that he will also reap. For he who sows to his own flesh will from the flesh reap corruption; but he who sows to the Spirit will from the Spirit reap eternal life" (Gal. 6:7-8).

The law of the harvest is as great a reality in the moral world as it is in the physical.

In addition, God opposes evil.

> For the eyes of the Lord are upon the righteous,
> and his ears are open to their prayer.
> But the face of the Lord is against those that do
>   evil" (1 Pet. 3:12).
>   (See also Ps. 5:4; Jer. 21:10.)

God has set Himself against all darkness and all evil. He has cast the mightiness of His life, like a giant battalion, on the side of righteousness.

4. Evil has been crippled and mortally wounded.

Christ in His life, death, and resurrection has dealt evil a mortal blow.

The overcoming of demonic power was a sign that the kingdom of God was at hand. One day when Jesus had cast out a demon, He said: "But if it is by the finger of God that I cast out demons, then the kingdom of God has come upon you" (Luke 11:20).

You remember the seventy returning from their mission in great triumph and joy. The story is concluded like this: "The seventy returned with joy, saying, 'Lord, even the demons are subject to us in your name!' And he said, 'I saw Satan fall like lightning from heaven'" (Luke 10:17-18).

We know, of course, evil doesn't look as if it is near its demise. It remains dreadfully powerful. But it is like a big animal that has been mortally wounded.

5. Power has been given us.

We want answers, many of which will never be given to us here, but we have something better than answers. Power, which enables us to cope in our kind of world, has been given to us.

Christ loves us with a love from which we can never be separated, and He has set us in a new relationship with God— the one relationship that can never be broken.

Paul could ask: "Who shall separate us from the love of Christ? Shall tribulation, or distress, or persecution, or famine, or nakedness, or peril, or sword? . . . [Nothing] will be able to separate us from the love of God in Christ Jesus our Lord" (Rom. 8:35,39).

Christ has entered our world. He has not been spared pain nor the worst evil can do. Yet, He has won, and He is with us in the most painful and tragic situations of our lives. He doesn't give us answers so much as He does His presence and power.

When I heard that the two children of one of our families had been killed in an automobile accident, along with two other young people, I remembered Job. The messages those parents received were like the one Job received. (See Job 1:18-19.)

I remember the funeral with those caskets before us. I was able to say to the grieved parents and friends: "God understands your pain, loss, and grief. He has suffered the way you are suffering. He lost His only Son." There may not be an answer in that, but there is something better than an answer. Grace and power are in it.

You will have to face the reality of these two great enigmas in your preaching and pastoral work. There is much you cannot say since often pain and evil are shrouded in mystery. But there is much you can say. You can tell them that this world belongs to God, that He loves it, and that He has not escaped its pain and tragedy. You can tell about Christ's entering our world, suffering the worst that evil can do, and bearing the greatest pain. You can say He won, not only for Himself but for us, and that He is with us.

Thought Starters

A series of sermons: Where Does Evil Come From?

A series of sermons: Looking for a Solution to Evil and Suffering.

A series of sermons: Using Suffering Creatively.

Other sermons: The Problem of Evil and Suffering; The Corrupted Heart; Held in the Grip of Dark Powers; Evil Has Been Mortally Wounded; Who Will Win the Last Battle? When Suffering Makes Us More Socially Aware; When Weakness Is Strength; Healed By His Stripes; When Evil Is Self-Opposing; Our Universe Has a Moral Structure; Not Answers, But Power.

Scripture

Genesis 3:1-7; 4:1-11; Job 21:1-34; Psalms 5:1-6; 73:1-28; Isaiah 29:11-16; Jeremiah 12:1-4; 17:1-10; Matthew 2:1-19; Luke 13:1-5; John 9:1-41; Romans 7:13-25; Galatians 6:1-10; Ephesians 6:10-20; James 1:12-14; 4:1-10; Revelation 18:1-24; 21:1-27.

Texts

Genesis 3:1-2; 4:6-7; Psalms 5:4; 7:15-16; Jeremiah 17:9; Matthew 2:19-20; Romans 7:24-25; Galatians 6:7; Ephesians 6:13; Revelation 7:16-17; 18:10; 21:4, 27.

Illustrations

The mystery of evil in a snake (Gen. 3:1); Corporate evil as represented by the city (Gen. 13:10-13; Rev. 18:1-24); God using evil and tragedy (Gen. 50:15-21); Why is a just God silent? (Hab. 1:13); When evil people prosper (Job 21:7-16; Ps. 73:4-14); The self-destruction of evil (Pss. 7:15-16; 9:15; 57:6); When God seems to hide (Ps. 10:1); God against evil (Ps. 5:1-6); How long? (Ps. 13:1-2); Evil powers subject to Jesus (Luke 10:17-20; 11:19-23); When suffering glorifies God (John 9:1-12); Doing battle with evil (Eph. 6:10-20); Turning tragedy to an advantage (2 Cor. 12:7-10; Phil. 1:12-14); A city without evil and suffering (Rev. 21:1-27); Three sources of evil: inside (Gen. 5:1; Rom. 7:17-18; Jas. 1:14-15; 4:1-2); outside (Rev. 18:1-24); above (Eph. 6:11-12).

Notes

1. C. S. Lewis, *The Problem of Pain* (New York: Macmillan Publishing Company, 1962), p. 26.
2. Ibid., p. 69.
3. Reinhold Niebuhr: *The Nature and Destiny of Man*, Volume 1 (New York: Charles Scribner's Sons, 1941), p. 180.
4. Leslie Weatherhead, *Why Do Men Suffer?* (Nashville: Abingdon Press, 1936).

18
Hope:
Affirming Life
in Spite of Everything

The Bible is a book of hope. Through the darkest night it urges us to look for the morning. It sets our faces to the future without despair. Such hope allows us to affirm life's meaning and purpose in spite of everything.

The New Testament is especially a book of hope. There is more hope in it than in any of the world's literature. Hope sweeps in upon you like a mighty stream. You cannot stop it. You may as well try to shout back the incoming tide. No matter how loud you cry it keeps on coming in, floating cargo and lifting stranded barges stuck in the sand.

Hope as Indispensable

We can't live without hope. When hope dies, something in the person dies. When the light of hope flickers and goes out, we are plunged into darkness, sometimes into death.

A proverb says: "Hope deferred makes the heart sick" (Prov. 13:12). It is not the absence of hope, it is hope delayed, hope put off. But even hope deferred makes the heart sick, the ancient wisdom tells us. It is so. But what about hope when it is not merely delayed, when it is absent?

A friend told me about a young mother in her late twenties. He said he had never felt such total despair in a person's life. The light of hope had gone out and she could not stand the darkness that engulfed her. So she took her life.

Hopelessness can cause despair and death. "Hell is hopelessness," Jurgen Moltmann has written. "It is not for nothing that at the entrance to Dante's hell there stand the words: 'Abandon hope, all ye who enter here.' "[1] There is a sense in which Moltman is right. Hell can be hopelessness.

But as long as there is hope we can continue with life. It may be nothing more than a flicker of light in the darkness but it is enough to enable us to continue the journey. We go on hoping that the flicker will become a dawn.

At the end of World War II, the state of North Carolina converted part of the facilities at Camp Butner into an alcoholic rehabilitation center. Those who planned the center knew how indispensable hope was if healing were to take place there. No matter how well trained the personnel and how adequate the facilities were, sick men and women who went there sick would leave sick if they could not have hope. Knowing this they devised a simple symbol, a three-point star, to tell their story. The message of the star was: Let all who enter here know that there is hope.

Paul could say: "For in this hope we were saved" (Rom. 8:24). Maybe nothing more radical and profound has ever been said about hope than that.

Hope in Spite of Everything

The hope of the Bible is not fair-weather hope. Often it is hope that comes out of the night. How often you find hope where there are no signs of hope.

You remember Abraham who was without an heir. God promised him a son when he was an old man and when Sarah, his wife, was beyond the age of childbearing. Paul says of him: "In hope he believed against hope, that he should become the father of many nations" (Rom. 4:18). He had hope when there were no signs of hope. So much of the hope of the Bible is like that. It is hope of the night, not of the day. It is hope born in the shadows, not on the sunlit slopes of morning. It is hope in spite of everything. The meaning of this is that hope is essentially in God's hands, not ours.

Let us look at several more examples where hope occurred

when there were no signs of it, when the situation argued against hope.

In the eleventh chapter of Isaiah, where the new age of peace is pictured, Isaiah began like this: "There shall come forth a shoot from the stump of Jesse, and a branch shall grow out of his roots" (v. 1). He wasn't speaking of a mighty oak, but the dead stump of a tree. What could be more unlikely?

In the fifty-third chapter of Isaiah, where Isaiah pictured the Suffering Servant, he wrote: "For he grew up before him like a young plant, and like a root out of dry ground" (v. 2). He would not spring up from fertile and well-watered fields, but from the dry ground. Once more there was hope without its signs.

Isaiah lived through a troubled time when the shadow of the Assyrian Empire lay across his little land. Sooner or later his nation would be overrun. Jerusalem with the Temple would be destroyed, the land despoiled, and many of the people taken away into captivity. The lights were going out, yet there was hope. There would be a remnant returning, the nation would be reborn, and life would start over again. "In that day," he wrote, "the remnant of Israel and the survivors of the house of Jacob will no more lean upon him that smote them, but will lean upon the Lord, the Holy One of Israel, in truth. A remnant will return, the remnant of Jacob, to the mighty God" (Isa. 10:20-21).

But the most radical expression of hope without the signs of hope is the story of the valley of dry bones found in the thirty-seventh chapter of Ezekiel. There Ezekiel, in a vision, looked out upon an ancient battlefield where the victor and vanquished had left their dead. The only reminder of that faraway battle was bleached bones on desert sands. The prophet had never looked upon such a desolate scene. There was no sign of life. There is nothing so dead as bleached bones on desert sands. God asked Ezekiel: "Son of man, can these bones live?" And Ezekiel, evading the question, answered, "O Lord God, thou knowest." Then there was the blowing of the wind, and the bones came together forming skeletons which were covered with flesh, muscle, sinew, and skin. The valley was filled with perfectly formed bodies but there was no vitality in them. Everywhere were seen forms of life without life. So God breathed His breath into them "and they lived, and stood upon their feet, an exceedingly great host" (v. 10).

Ezekiel's nation was like bleached bones upon desert sands. The nation was saying, "Our bones are dried up, and our hope is lost; we are clean cut off" (v. 11). But there was hope! The nation would live again.

In the New Testament you find the same kind of thing. First Peter was written to encourage Christians undergoing persecution. Peter spoke of "the fiery ordeal" (4:12) through which they were going. There was reason for pessimism and despair, yet the epistle is sometimes called "the letter of hope." Peter introduced his theme of hope like this: "By his great mercy we have been born anew to a living hope through the resurrection of Jesus Christ from the dead" (1 Pet. 1:3).

Often we hear stories from modern life with the same theme —hope without the signs of hope. We are always excited by them.

Archibald Rutledge tells about sailing down the Santee River in South Carolina with Sam Singleton when, in an hour of great danger, he learned the meaning of hope.

They left home at one o'clock on a winter morning to paddle down the Santee to a point appropriately called Tranquility. There they would shoot ducks for a few days. They had planned to drop down ten miles or so with the tide, hoping to reach their destination at dawn. The stars were shining when they left home but they soon became obscured by a fog so dense that they could scarcely see the bow of their little boat. Going with the tide they felt secure about their general direction, but they soon came upon looming shores and landscapes with which neither was familiar. Then for an hour there was no visible land. They knew they should soon be at their destination, but waves, suspiciously like sea waves, began to roll their canoe. The roar of the surf, which they had heard for a long time, became more clamoring. The tide was now turning, and try as hard as they might, they could not reach either shore. The canoe shipped gallons of water, and the mist blinded them. It was obvious they were in great danger, so they began to make preparation for the worst. Rutledge, in a very mild voice, told Sam that in case the canoe was swamped they must turn it over and cling to it. Then like a voice of hope the humble boatman said: "Never mind, Cap'n. It will be daybreak soon." In their plight, there was only one thing they could certainly count on: the coming of light—daybreak, sunrise.

Archibald Rutledge, often in his dark hours, remembered that experience. "And even now," he wrote, "after all these years whenever the shadows are deepest and most impentrable I seem to hear, out of the dim celestial past, the quiet voice of Sam Singleton saying to my doubting and besieged heart, 'Never mind, Cap'n, it will be daybreak soon.' "[2]

Reasons for Hope

There are basic reasons why we can hope. Our hope is not grounded in fantasy but in reality.

1. We can hope because of the nature of our God and who He is.

He is the God of creation. God created our world in love and has infused it with purpose. Our world is not blind and we do not walk with aimless feet. History is on the move. It is not going round and round, it has destiny.

He is the God of the Exodus. Therefore, He is the God of redemption and liberation. He is the God of covenant, and His covenant love is called steadfast love. God remains faithful amid all our faithlessness.

He is the Father of our Lord and Savior Jesus Christ. God is like Jesus Christ. In Christ's face we have seen God, in His voice we have heard God speak, in His touch we have felt God's healing. Jesus taught us to call God Father. We remember how winsome Jesus was, inviting perfect trust. God is like that. In that trust we can find hope as nowhere else.

Even the poor, oppressed, and disinherited can hope, since God looks upon them with special favor. We can even speak of God's bias—His concern for the disadvantaged. Many are the admonitions in the Old Testament concerning the poor and helpless. Deuteronomy 15:7 is typical: "If there is among you a poor man, one of your brethren, in any of your towns within your land which the Lord your God gives you, you shall not harden your heart or shut your hand against your poor brother."

James Muilenberg has written about the compassion of Israel's God: "Nothing is more clear than that the God of Israel has a special concern for the weak, the poor, the disinherited, the alien, and all who stand in need. He is concerned for the welfare and well being of all. Special provision must be made for the landless, the widow, the orphan, and for all who have no power in themselves to press their claims."[3]

We remember the solicitude Jesus had for the poor and disadvantaged who loved and followed Him. Jesus in His inaugural address at Nazareth told how His ministry would be concerned with the poor, the captives, the oppressed, and the blind. (See Luke 4:18-19.)

It is little wonder then that Israel looked to her God for hope. Such an expression as this is typical of Israel's faith: "And now, Lord, for what do I wait? My hope is in thee" (Ps. 39:7). (See Ps. 130:7 and Jer. 14:22.)

A common refrain in Israel's worship was: "For his steadfast love endures forever." It occurs twenty-six times in Psalm 136.

"God, we believe, loves us better than we love ourselves," John Baille wrote. "Our deepest interests are safer—beyond imagination safer—in His hands than they would be, had we ourselves the most unrestricted guardianship over them. And all things that matter in the universe are safer in His hands than they could ever be in ours. Justice is safer. Friendship is safer. Love itself is safer. The cherished gains of the past are safer;

and so also the promise of the future. 'So the all-great were the all-loving too.' The omnipotence behind the universe is our Father and our Friend."[4]

Such a God can be trusted, and in that trust we can hope.

2. We can hope because of the possibilities of life and history under God.

The Bible does not see life reaching its highest possibilities in its own effort nor history coming to fulfillment under its own momentum. Life and history are fulfilled under God, and both under Him have great possibilities.

You recall Jeremiah's parable of the potter. God told him to go down to the potter's house, so Jeremiah did and found the potter working at his wheel. The vessel the potter was making was spoiled while still in his hands. The sides became bashed in and the vessel lost its symmetry and beauty. The potter did not cast it aside in anger. No, he did a wonderful thing. He pressed it again to the wheel and remade it, a vessel that was both beautiful and useful.

It was a parable concerning the nation which was ill-formed like a piece of pottery. God said: "Behold, like the clay in the potter's hand, so are you in my hand, O house of Israel (Jer. 18:6). God would make Israel over again so she would be a fit instrument for God's use in history.

This remaking and reshaping, if it can apply to a nation and history, is certainly applicable to the individual. God can remake us and give us new life. We can become new creations in Christ. We don't have to remain the same. God offers us new life for the old. There is always hope for the sickest and most broken.

D. L. Moody was a great American evangelist during the last quarter of the last century. He was a Presbyterian layman, and was never ordained. Moody had a popular singer by the name of Ira Sankey. They traveled not only across our nation but held evangelistic crusades in the British Isles. One day while they were in England they passed a group of Gypsies bivouacked on a hillside. Sankey suggested that they stop and hold a service for them. The idea appealed to Moody so he read Scripture and preached and Sankey sang. At the close of the service, a little boy whose face was blackened by the sun and who was dressed in tattered rags came to Sankey and looked up at him. Sankey looked down into the face of the lad through his black eyes into his soul and said: "Son, God can make a great man of you." And God did. That little boy became the great Gipsy Smith, who was one of the most effective preachers of the church across its long history and who claimed seven continents as his parish.

3. We can hope because of the Christ event.

John tells us that "In him was life, and the life was the light of men. The light shines in the darkness, and the darkness has not overcome it" (John 1:4-5). Those are such wonderful verses. Let us hear them in several different translations.

"In him appeared life and this life was the light of mankind. The light still shines in the darkness, and the darkness has never put it out" (Phillips). "All that came to be was alive with his life, and that life was the light of men. The light shines on in the dark, and the darkness has never mastered it" (NEB). "All that came to be had life in him and that life was the light of men, a light that shines in the dark, a light that darkness could not overpower" (The Jerusalem Bible).

Men and women who live in the shadows of death look to Jesus because He is life. People who walk in darkness look to Him because He is light.

Paul Tillich told about the doctoral ring that was presented to his father by the theological faculty of the University of Berlin. On it were inscribed the Greek words phos and zoe'— light and life. The meaning was: Let the light shine in order that life may abound! The same can be said about Jesus Christ, yet in a much more wonderful way.

We can be sure that the life that is in Him will conquer all death and the light that is in Him will at last drive away all darkness.

4. We can hope because of the resurrection.

We cannot say the resurrection is more important than the birth, life, and death of Jesus Christ. All of these are indispensable for the gospel. But what has to be said is that without the resurrection all would have been lost. Without the resurrection there would be no living Christ, no cross with power, no gospel, no church, no New Testament.

It is significant that all the gospel writers have daybreak as the setting of their resurrection stories. The women went to the tomb of Jesus in the early morning, the freshest and most beautiful time of the day, just at dawn. Day was breaking and the light was driving away the darkness of night and the shadows of the early morning. But the light was more than luminous energy. It had theological meaning. Hope was breaking over a despairing world and life was being given to men and women held in the grip of death.

Peter, writing to a persecuted church, spoke of how they had been born to a living hope through the resurrection. (See 1 Peter 1:3.)

The New Testament is indeed a book of hope. There are many sources of that hope, but the chief one is the resurrection. The stream of hope that flows from that open tomb cannot be stopped. It keeps coming in. You might as well attempt to stop the dawn by throwing up a screen on your back porch as to try to hold back the hope of Easter. The morning light comes on, overrunning your little screen and everything around it, driving away the shadows from the valleys and lifting the mist from the hills and flooding the earth with the light of day. Just so with Easter. Its hope is indomitable. You cannot stop it.

5. We can hope because of the promise of the future.

Biblical faith is future oriented. That was true of Israel and it is true of Christians. We are not so much moved by the past as we are pulled by the future. The past is the threshold of the future.

James Muilenburg wrote of Israel's future-oriented faith: "The God who comes in the present has come in the past, and in the present he recalls the past; but what is more important is that he points to the future. . . . The future is therefore the center of gravity of Israel's faith. . . . The orientation of Israel's faith is to the future. The past is prologue to what is yet to come."[5]

Greece had a golden age, but it was in the past. Israel's golden age was in the future. She looked for a new age, the messianic age. And even in her darkest night she could, by faith, see its dawning. The great prophets would not let her forget the coming of the new age. Therefore, they kept hope alive in Israel's heart. The prophets had a kind of formula by which they introduced the hope of the new age. When a prophet talked like this: "In the latter days" (Mic. 4:1; Isa. 2:2), "In that day" (Isa. 4:2), "in those days" (Jer. 31:29), "And it shall come to pass" (31:27), "Behold, the days are coming" (Jer. 23:7; 31:27,31,38), the hearts of the people leaped up because they knew the prophet was going to talk about the future age. Even in the most despairing night, hope was kindled like a flame in their lives.

There were certain characteristics of the new age. Let me mention four of them.

1. It would be an age of peace. Shalom would be realized. Even nature would be transformed, losing its venom and hostility. (See Isa. 11:6-8.) Not only would nature be at peace but there would be peace among men. (See Isa. 2:4.)

2. It would be an age of justice. Righteousness would reign. (See Jer. 23:5-6.)

3. It would be the age of the Spirit. God would pour out His Spirit upon all His people, from the highest to the lowest (Joel 2:28-29).

4. There would be a universal knowledge of God. God would be known everywhere and by all people. (See Isa. 11:9; 45:22; 55:1.)

Just so with us Christians. We have much to remember but we have even more to hope for. We are like travelers who keep glancing back over our shoulders to remember where we have come from and what has been done for us while our faces are set steadfastly to the future.

We believe the future is malleable and that we can bring about a better world which is more humane and more just. But our hope lies beyond that. We believe that Christ will return to consummate history, seeing that it will end the way God has planned it.

The most glorious part of our salvation lies in the future. We shall be saved. We have just gotten the first installment here. The best is yet to be. (See 2 Cor. 5:5; Eph. 1:14; 1 John 3:2; 1 Cor. 15:54.)

We look for a new order with a new heaven, a new earth, and a new city. Within the new order will be a radically new life which will be too wonderful to describe. (See Rev. 21:1-27; 22:1-5.)

You will often stand before hopeless and despairing people. Therefore, preach often on hope.

Thought Starters

A series of sermons on Hope Where the Sign Does Not Appear.

A series on Sources of Hope.

Other sermons: Hope Is Indispensable; Hopelessness Is Hell; Bleached Bones on Desert Sand; The Remnant—Where Life Begins Over Again; God's Bias: Concern for the Disadvantaged; Jesus' Inaugural Address; The Steadfast Love of God; Like Bashed-in Pottery; New Creation in Christ; Daybreak —The Setting of Easter; The Tides of Hope Keep Sweeping In; Life and Light; Pilgrims Whose Faces Are Set to the Future; Light in Our Darkness, Hope in Our Despair; The Last Installment of Our Salvation; New Life in the New City.

Scripture

Psalms 39:1-11; 71:1-6; Isaiah 2:1-5; 10:20-27; 11:1-9; Jeremiah 18:1-11; Ezekiel 37:1-14; Amos 9:11-15; Micah 4:1-13;

John 11:17-44; Romans 4:13-25; 8:18-39; 2 Corinthians 1:8-11; 4:7-18; Ephesians 4:1-6; 1 Peter 1:1-12; Revelation 21:1-27.

Texts

1 Kings 8:56*b;* Psalms 65:5*b;* 71:5; Proverbs 13:12; Isaiah 40:22,31; Romans 4:18; 7:24-25; 8:24; 1 Corinthians 15:54-55; 15:57; 2 Corinthians 4:16; Ephesians 1:12; 1 Thessalonians 5:8; 1 Timothy 1:1,15; 1 Peter 1:3; Revelation 7:14; 21:1.

Illustrations

God keeps His promises (Josh. 23:14); Hope beyond judgment and tragedy (Jer. 31:31-34; Amos 9:11-15); The new age: hope for the future (Isa. 4:2; Jer. 23:7-8; 31:27-29,38); A shoot from a stump (Isa. 11:1); God renews us in our weariness and fatigue (Isa. 40:31); A piece of pottery remade (Jer. 18:1-11); The purchase of land in hope (Jer. 32:6-15); Deliverance in Christ (Rom. 7:24-25); Three reasons for hope: Scriptures, God, Power of the Spirit (Rom. 15:4,13); Hope when despairing of life (2 Cor. 1:8-11); Indiscourageable hope (2 Cor. 4:7-18); Hope because of Christ's power (Phil. 4:13).

Notes

1. Jurgen Moltmann, *Theology of Hope* (New York: Harper and Row, 1967), p. 32.
2. Archibald Rutledge, *It Will Be Daybreak Soon* (New York: Fleming H. Revell Company, 1938), p. 39.
3. James Muilenburg, *The Way of Israel* (New York: Harper Torchbooks, 1961), p. 72.
4. John Baille, *And the Life Everlasting* (New York: Charles Scribner's Sons, 1933), p. 194.
5. Muilenburg, p. 129,131.

19
Prayer:
The Soul's Upward Thrust

There is nothing more native to the human heart than prayer. The human spirit is constantly trying to break out of its flat, space-time dimension. The soul is constantly making an upward thrust toward God.

There is nothing more universal than prayer. It is like laughter and weeping. You hear a child laughing and you know what he is doing. Laughter speaks an universal language. You hear a woman sobbing and you know what she is doing. Weeping uses a universal language. You see a man on his knees or with his hands uplifted and you know what he is doing. He is praying. Prayer, like laughter and weeping, speaks a universal language.

What Is Prayer?

1. Prayer is many things but basically and foremost it is being with God, listening to God, talking with God. It is fellowship with God, communion with God.

The fact that God would enter into communion with us staggers the imagination. He is creator, we are creatures. He is eternal, we are mortal. He is perfect, we are marred and broken. But what if it is God's basic nature to desire communion with us, even to need it? I am suggesting that He does.

I remember working with children during the pre-Easter season. I pictured men and women in rather dismal ways, telling of their greed, selfishness, and pride. I spoke of how, with awesome power in our hands, we could, and may, destroy life on our planet. Then I asked why God would bother to make such creatures. I sometimes think that a little girl, in responding to that question, may have spoken one of the most profoundly theological words I have heard. "God was lonely," she said, "and needed somebody to talk to." I have never forgotten that.

James Weldon Johnson in his book, *God's Trombones,* tells us the same thing. God, one day, said, "I'm lonely," and He began to create. He created the heavens, spangling them with the stars. He created the earth and the seas with their myriad forms of life. But God couldn't have fellowship with His vast creation. He was still lonely, and said "I'll make me a man!"

If prayer is essentially communion with God, it may follow that prayer's best gift is God's sharing Himself.

Augustine once said: "Give me thine ownself, without whom, though thou shouldest give all that thou hadst made, yet could not my desires be satisfied."

George Matheson wrote: "It is thee and not thy gifts I crave."

We would all, no doubt, find prayer much more satisfying, if we prayed: "If thou shouldst give us all thou hast made and withhold thyself, we would be poor indeed. But if thou shouldst withhold all that thou hast made, and give thyself, we would be rich indeed."

This manner of thinking about prayer would help correct an inadequate view of it; namely, that prayer is a way of getting things. That is how we thought about prayer as children, but unfortunately for many of us, long after we have passed into adulthood, this childish view of prayer stays with us. We remember, and believe, the words of Jesus: "Ask, and it will be given you; seek, and you will find; knock, and it will be opened to you" (Matt. 7:7). However, in prayer we ask for things we do not get; we seek for things we do not find; and we knock upon doors that do not open. Still, we believe, as we should, that Christ is faithful. We may try to assuage the disappointment by saying that we asked for the wrong thing or that God made us some better gift. This does not cause the problem of unanswered prayer to go away, but it would not be so painful and puzzling if we believed that God is His own best gift. When prayer is seen as communion, God does in fact give Himself.

2. Beyond prayer as communion with God, it is adoration and praise of God.

We adore and praise God because of who He is. He is back of us as the source of life, He is above us like the vast heavens, He is ahead of us as the end of all our journeying, He is beneath us like the solid earth, He is beside us like a faithful and tireless friend, and He is inside us like some deep, innermost thought.

The best that we know here are but pale pointers toward God. Goodness, truth, beauty, and love are all made perfect in Him. He is not broken, there are no blemishes on Him, and no shadow lies across His life. Yet, these qualities do not remove Him from us. He is no serene God dwelling in the perfect peace of heaven beyond the turbulence of history and our human existence. He is touched by our pain, He is in the midst of our tragedy.

And God is holy. That is what makes Him God. He is all that we can never become. Isaiah in the Temple heard the seraphim singing:

> Holy, holy, holy is the Lord of hosts;
> the whole earth is full of his glory (Isa. 6:3).

That is perfect adoration and perfect praise.

3. Prayer is also thanksgiving.

We adore God and praise Him for what and who He is. We thank God for what He gives.

God's gifts are innumerable. We give God thanks for the beauty of the earth and for the plentitude of harvest; for family who, knowing us as we really are, still love and accept us; for friends who affirm us, who often see goodness in us we cannot see in ourselves, who, when we have lost faith in ourselves, allow us to go in the trust they put in us until we can believe in ourselves again. We give thanks for honest work to do, for the comradship of fellow laborers. We give thanks for freedom, justice, human dignity, and the privilege of service. We give thanks for institutions like churches and schools that have challenged us, calling forth the best that is in us. Above all things else we give thanks to God for Jesus Christ, His "unspeakable gift" to us.

I heard O. T. Binkley say that he lived by grace and gifts, from God and others. Who does not know what he meant? It is so right that we offer thanks to God.

> Enter his gates with thanksgiving,
>   and his courts with praise;
>   Give thanks to him, bless his name!
>
> For the Lord is good;
>   his steadfast love endures for ever,
>   and his faithfulness to all generations
>   (Ps. 100:4-5).

4. Prayer is confession. This is such an important part of prayer.

The harsh word I spoke yesterday was much more wounding than I thought it would be. The foul deed today corrupted life beyond my imagining. I would, if I could, call back the word and the deed, but I can't. They are now on their way, beyond me, doing their hurting and corrupting work. I feel guilty and I feel helpless. To seek to redress the wrong is not enough. I still feel guilty and burdened. Is there forgiveness, is there hope? Yes, in the grace and mercy of God. I ask for His forgiveness and beg Him to heal the wounds I have inflicted and to cleanse life where I have besmirched it.

Confession is so important that in corporate worship I feel we should have a separate confession and with it the assurance of pardon for all who truly repent of their sins and ask for forgiveness.

Such assurances of forgiveness as these can be helpful:

> Come now, let us reason together, says the Lord:
>   though your sins are like scarlet,

they shall be as white as snow;
though they are red like crimson,
they shall become like wool (Isa. 1:18).

"If we confess our sins, he is faithful and just, and will forgive our sins and cleanse us from all unrighteousness" (1 John 1:9).

We confess our personal sins—those sins that are often hidden, known only to us and to God. And we should confess our corporate sins—those sins we do together, sins committed by family, business, industry, community, state, and nation.

We should be like Isaiah who confessed both personal and corporate guilt:

"Woe is me! For I am lost; for I am a man of unclean lips and I dwell in the midst of a people of unclean lips; for my eyes have seen the King, the Lord of hosts!" (Isa. 6:5).

5. Prayer is intercession. We bring a brother or a needy situation into the presence of God. I shall later speak of the social effect of prayer, but let me say here that prayer cannot be selfish. We are concerned not only for ourselves but for others.

We pray for the sick, the bereaved, the weak, the lonely, the aged, the discouraged, the depressed, the poor, the hungry. We pray for those who are sinful who are in need of forgiveness, for the estranged who are in need of reconciliation.

I had a rather strange habit of visiting the hospital on Saturday evening, a time usually reserved by pastors for study and preparation for Sunday. I went for one reason, essentially, to tell our sick members that their church would be remembering them in prayer on Sunday. I was never rebuffed by any member. Rather, their eyes lighted up when I told them their church would be praying for them.

Not only do those for whom we pray need our prayers of intercession, we need them too. They help take us out of ourselves.

6. Prayer is petition.

While prayer is not essentially a way of getting things we

want, yet it is certainly permissible to ask for those things we need and cannot get in our own effort. We should ask for strength in our weakness, peace in our anxiety, love in our bitterness, faith in our doubts, hope in our despair. Jesus taught us to ask for things as mundane and common as bread: "Give us this day our daily bread."

The Model Prayer takes the form of petitions—six of them: three concern God and three concern us. Two things should be noted about the petitions we make on our behalf and the behalf of others: First, nothing is asked for ourselves alone; second, no trivial requests are made—only those things people desperately need.

Jesus and Prayer

Jesus was a man of prayer. There was a rhythm about His life. He moved between work and prayer, from the busy life to the solitary place. He walked from the presence of God into the presence of men and from the presence of men back into the presence of God.

You remember how the disciples would sometimes awake in the early morning and find Jesus missing and then track Him to a solitary place of prayer. One of those incidents is recorded in the first chapter of Mark:

"And in the morning, a great while before day, he rose and went out to a lonely place, and there he prayed. And Simon and those who were with him pursued him, and they found him and said to him, 'Every one is searching for you. And he said to them, 'Let us go on to the next towns, that I may preach there also; for that is why I came out' " (vv. 35-38).

Jesus went out "a great while before day." He gave time to prayer and He gave the best hours—the time of the early morning when the day was freshest and He was strongest and most alert. He was no recluse, and the desert was not a place of escape from the busy, noisy, demanding world. Jesus said to them: "Let us go on to the next towns." It was from the quiet desert place back to the jostling streets of the busy town, from the presence of God into the hurry and rush of men. There was this basic rhythm in His life.

Jesus' prayer life was spontaneous, private, and public.

His prayer was often spontaneous, unplanned, unrehearsed. Sometimes He prayed with the busy crowds milling about Him, for example, the prayer recorded in the eleventh chapter of Matthew: "At that time Jesus declared, 'I thank thee, Father, Lord of heaven and earth, that thou hast hidden these things from the wise and understanding and revealed them to babes; yea, Father, for such was thy gracious will' " (vv. 25-26).

Jesus' prayer was frequently private. The incident referred to in the first chapter of Mark was private prayer. He was away from the crowds, alone in a solitary place. Luke says of Him: "But he withdrew to the wilderness and prayed" (Luke 5:16). (See also Luke 6:12; 9:18; 22:41.)

Jesus also regularly engaged in public prayer and corporate worship. Jesus was a regular attendant at the synagogue. When He gave His inaugural address, He went home and delivered it at the synagogue which was dear to His heart. No place provoked such sacred memories in the mind of Jesus as did that house of prayer. Luke, in telling this story, introduced it like this: "And he came to Nazareth, where he had been brought up; and he went to the synagogue, as his custom was, on the sabbath day" (Luke 4:16). Jesus was always in the synagogue at its appointed hours of worship.

There in the synagogue Jesus prayed the prayers His people had prayed for generations and heard the stories of redemption they had been telling for centuries. People struck cadence with Him in His spiritual pilgrimage. Jesus knew the value of this.

A final observation needs to be made about Jesus and prayer: He met the crises of His life with prayer. He prayed at His baptism (Luke 3:21-22). He spent a whole night in prayer before choosing His disciples (Luke 6:12-13). The night before His crucifixion He prayed in the garden of Gethsemane (Luke 22:42). He prayed twice from the cross (Luke 23:34,46). And

Jesus prayed just before He ascended to His Father (Luke 24:50).

The Effects of Prayer

Since prayer is a spiritual exercise, one of its effects will obviously be spiritual in nature. Prayer lifts us to a spiritual vantage point. It gives us a spiritual perspective on life we can get nowhere else. In prayer, more than at any other time, God, as it were, calls us to Himself, and says to us: "Stand here. I want you to see life as I see it." Standing there, amid the jarring and discordant notes of life, we hear harmony and melody. Light breaks into the shadows and darkness of life, and the broken, ill-fitting pieces are brought together into a pattern of meaning. There life makes sense more than anywhere else and we are able to declare the beauty, value, and purpose of life. There, despite its pain and tragedy, we thank God for life as a gift from His own hands.

In the seventy-third Psalm, we see a man who is baffled and confused by the mystery of evil. The rich, while being wicked, prosper and grow richer. The psalmist had tried to keep his hands clean and his heart pure, yet he had come upon evil times, and moreover had lost his health. It was only as he went into the sanctuary of God to pray that the situation made any sense at all. There he saw life with clearer vision. He wrote:

> When I thought how to understand this,
> it seemed to me a wearisome task,
> until I went into the sanctuary of God;
> then I perceived their end (vv. 16-17).

Prayer also has its personal effect. How often a person rises from his knees in strength, hope, courage, peace, and forgiveness. He knelt one kind of person and arose a different kind.

Brother Lawrence prayed: "Lord make me according to thy heart." And God answered his prayer. He became more and more like Jesus. The light that shone in the eyes of Jesus was in his face. The love of Jesus was in his heart, and the peace of Christ was in his life.

And prayer has a social effect. In authentic prayer, conscience is quickened, social consciousness is aroused, and awareness of our brothers and sisters is heightened.

I often think of the Model Prayer. It can be said privately, but it is much more effective when it is shared with fellow believers. The reason for this is that the Lord's Prayer has a social and corporate dimension. There is not a first person singular pronoun—not an I, or a me, or a my in it. They are all plural—us and our. It is "our Father," not "my Father." It is "give us this day our daily bread," not "give me this day my daily bread." It is "lead us not into temptation," not "lead me not into temptation." It is "forgive us our trespasses," not "forgive me my trespasses." The Lord's Prayer links us in a kind of solidarity with all who lift hands to God in prayer.

In prayer a hand reaches out to me. God says, "Do you see that hand?" "Yes, Lord, but it is a deformed hand. You know how squeamish I am about withered hands." And God says: "Take that hand. It is your brother's hand." And there is a voice that speaks. "Do you hear that voice?" God asks. "Yes, Lord, but it is a strange voice. It has a funny accent. I don't like it. It is not my kind." God's voice, growing more imperious, insists: "Listen to that voice. It is your brother's voice. He is in trouble, he needs you. Do not turn a deaf ear."

We should remember that our people will often come to our worship making the same request the disciples made of Jesus: "Lord, teach us to pray" (Luke 11:1*b*). We should often address the issue of prayer, and, in doing so, know that we will be speaking to deep spiritual needs of our people.

Thought Starters

A series of sermons on What Is Prayer?
A series on Prayer and Its Effects.
A series on Jesus' Use of Prayer in Crises.
A series on The Great Prayers of the Bible.

A series on The Benedictions of the Bible.
A series on The Doxologies of the Bible.
Other sermons: The Universal Language of Prayer; Confession
and Assurance of Forgiveness; A Basic Rhythm in the Life
of Jesus; God's Best Gift Is Himself; Living by Grace and
Gifts; Failing to Become Mature in Prayer.

Scripture

Exodus 32:25-34; 1 Kings 8:22-53; Psalm 100:1-5; Habakkuk
3:1-19; Matthew 6:9-13; Mark 1:35-39; Luke 4:16-30; 6:12-16;
22:39-46; 23:32-49; John 17:1-26; Romans 8:26-30; Ephesians
3:14-21.

Texts

Genesis 12:7; Exodus 32:31-32; 2 Chronicles 7:14; Psalms
19:14; 65:2; Mark 1:35; Luke 6:12; 22:42; 23:34; John 17:20-21;
Ephesians 3:14-15.

Illustrations

Abraham and his altars (Gen. 12:7; 13:4); Moses' great in-
tercessory prayer (Ex. 32:31-32); Life looks different from the
vantage point of worship (Ps. 73:16-17); Thanksgiving for a
good harvest (Ps. 65:9-13); The model prayer (Matt. 6:9-13);
When prayer is painful (Mark 14:34); Prayer that does not give
up (Luke 11:5-13); Great prayers of the Bible (Ex. 32:32; 1
Kings 8:22-53; Hab. 3:1-19; Matt. 6:9-13; 26:39; Luke 18:13;
23:34; John 17:1-26; Eph. 3:14-19); Benedictions (Num. 6:24-
26; Rom. 16:20b; 2 Cor. 13:14; 2 Thess. 3:18; Heb. 13:20-21;
Jude 24-25; Rev. 22:21); Doxologies (1 Chron. 16:36; Ps. 41:13;
72:18-19; 106:48; 150:1-6; Rom. 16:27; Eph. 3:20; 1 Tim. 1:17;
1 Pet. 4:11b; Rev. 1:5a-6; 5:12).

20
Love:
The New Life-Style

Christians were first called those of "the Way" (see Acts 9:2). Why that epithet? Likely because the world was impressed by the way the Christians lived. They must have had a unique life-style which judged the moral decadence of their world and at the same time held out hope for a better way of life. The world could not help taking notice that the Christians were a new morally innovative force. Someone has said that they outthought, outloved, and outlived the world about them. The most impressive thing was that they outloved those about them.

We are living through a time when we desperately need moral renewal. Walter Russell Bowie tells the story of Armistice Day, 1948, when General Omar Bradley said:

"With the monstrous weapons man already has, humanity is in danger of being trapped in this world by its moral adolescents. Our knowledge of science has clearly outstripped our capacity to control it. We have many men of science; too few men of God. We have grasped the mystery of the atom, and rejected the Sermon on the Mount. Man is stumbling blindly through a spiritual darkness while toying with the precarious secrets of life and death. The world has achieved brilliance without wisdom, power without conscience. Ours is a world of nuclear giants and ethical infants. We know more about war than we know about peace, more about killing than we know about living. This is our twentieth century's claim to distinction and progress."[1]

Our science has outdistanced our social progress, our ethics lag far behind our technology. Our moral vision is so blurred that we see poorly the social ends of life. We hold awesome power in weak ethical hands. One of the overarching questions of our time is: Can we catch up ethically with our scientific progress? Can we have a moral rebirth?

We as Christians have a demanding task. We need to bring our lives under the Christian ethical imperative and let it shape a moral life-style that knows what it is to live in the modern world.

The New Life-style

What is the new life-style of Christians? It is a life-style shaped by the spirit of Jesus which is love. The Christian ethic is an ethic of love.

Jesus said: "A new commandment I give to you, that you love one another; even as I have loved you, that ye also love one another" (John 13:34).

What was new about the new commandment? Certainly the first part was not: "that you love one another." People before Christ and those who have never heard of Him have known that it is better to love than to hate, just as they have known that it is better to tell the truth than to lie, better to work than to steal, better to protect property than to destroy it, and better to save life than to kill.

What then is new about it? The second half: "even as I have loved you, that you also love one another."

The world saw a radically new kind of love in Jesus which it had never seen before. The love gave a new kind of wistfulness—maybe men and women after all could be better.

What kind of love is this? The New Testament calls it *agape*. This love never depended on the beauty, health, or goodness of the object. It depended solely on the subject from whom love flowed spontaneously like an artesian well. Jesus loved the poor, the outcast, the ugly, the marred, the sick, and the sinful. He loved those who were not loved by the world, who hated and despised themselves. His love was never calculating or utilitarian, it was never degrading or manipulative. It never turned people into things or used them as tools. It was a love that gave with no thought of return. It was an extravagant, reckless, sacrificial love. Some thought it was irresponsible. There was no price too great for love to pay and no shame too shameful for it to bear in order to find the lost, heal the sick, and set free those who were in bondage.

This kind of love became the great Christian cardinal virtue which gathered up into itself all other moral values, completed them, and allowed them to be fulfilled. Jesus spoke of the love of God and love of neighbor as the two greatest Command- ments and said "On these two commandments depend all the law and the prophets" (Matt. 22:40). Paul wrote: "For the whole law is fulfilled in one word, 'You shall love your neigh- bor as yourself' " (Gal. 5:14). Or again: "Owe no one anything, except to love one another; for he who loves his neighbor has fulfilled the law. The commandments, 'You shall not commit adultery, You shall not kill, You shall not steal, You shall not covet,' and any other commandment are summed up in this sentence, 'You shall love your neighbor as yourself.' Love does no wrong to a neighbor; therefore love is the fulfilling of the law" (Rom. 13:8-10).

In the light of this we are not surprised that Jesus told how His followers and His church would be identified through the ages: "By this," He said, "all men will know that you are my disciples, if you have love for one another" (John 13:35).

One is shocked at first when one realizes that this is an ethical identification. One would expect a more spiritual and theological badge of identification. Yet the shock is eased when we realize, as we shall later, that the ethical life rests upon theological foundations. This ethical life-style grows out of who God is.

The early church took seriously this ethical injunction. Paul wrote the church at Ephesus: "And walk in love, as Christ loved us and gave himself up for us, a fragrant offering and sacrifice to God" (Eph. 5:2).

The longest and most adequate statement about this kind of love in the New Testament is found in the thirteenth chapter of First Corinthians. There Paul speaks of the superiority of love, the behavior of love, and the permanence of love. We can be sure that he had before him the mental image of Jesus Christ. It is interesting to observe how Paul describes the behavior of love. He observes fifteen qualities: Love is patient, is kind, knows no envy, is not a braggart, is not inflated with its own importance, is not rude, does not insist upon its own rights, does not fly into a temper, does not store up hurtful memories, finds no pleasure in evildoing, rejoices in the truth, endures everything, is completely trusting, never ceases to hope, bears everything in strength.

Jesus had given a face, hands and feet, voice, and vision to this love, and He had given it a heart. He had incarnated *agape*. It is little wonder that our world cannot escape His influence.

Jesus Christ calls His followers to incarnate this love. Our incarnation will be much more limited and incomplete than His, never as full and as absolute. Yet, it must be real. And when it is, great power is released from our lives.

In 1941, at Auschwitz, the most inhuman of Hitler's concentration camps, a prisoner escaped. When this happened, ten men were arbitrarily chosen for execution. One of the ten was a Polish man with a wife and children who, upon hearing the fateful news, wept. Father Maximillian Koble stepped forward to take his place, which was allowed. Before they were sent into the death chamber where they would die from thirst and starvation they were stripped naked as a prelude to their final dehumanization. Father Koble ministered to the starving and dying men. When the others had died, he was still alive. There was a quiet and peaceful look in his eyes which so haunted the guards that they commanded him to look toward the floor when they entered the chamber. Finally, they put him to death with an injection. What was the secret of Father Koble's rare strength? The love of God which made him really care for his brother. He incarnated the love that was first seen in Jesus, *agape* love.

Is it strange to you that Jesus never commanded people to tell the truth and be honest? He never mentioned the homely American virtue of hard work, thrift, and frugality. What He did tell the people to do was to love. The world knew about these other virtues, but they didn't know about *agape*. That was new. And Jesus knew no other authentic virtues would ever be violated if love were the controlling force and that no other virtue could ever be fulfilled apart from love.

Augustine once said: "Love God and do as you please." He was probably right. If you genuinely love God, you will not want to violate His laws and injure His children. Love sets its own limits and boundaries beyond which we should not go.

I have mentioned how effectively Paul wrote about love, yet it should be observed that John, more than any other New Testament writer, stressed the importance of love. John, who accounts for one tenth of the New Testament, provides one third of the references to love.

C. H. Dodd said John's outstanding contribution to Christian theology is the sublime sentence in the First Letter: "God is love." A. M. Hunter once said that the fourth chapter of 1 John is the Johannine equivalent to the thirteenth chapter of 1 Corinthians.

A rather authentic tradition says that John spent his last years in Ephesus. He lived to be a very old man and at last his disciples had to carry him on a stretcher to the small groups of Christians in Ephesus. John would always say to them: "Little children, love one another." He was so repetitious that one of his disciples became aggravated with him and one day asked the aged man: "Tell me, why do you always say to your disciples, 'Little children, love one another'?" And the apostle answered, "If they would but love one another, it would be enough."

It is important to say that love has a theological foundation. Its source is not in man, not even in the moral structure of the universe, but in God. Christian ethics is a flower that grows from a religious soil that affirms that God is love. It matters not how lovely the flower—and the Christian ethic of love is indeed a lovely flower—it will die if cut from the soil that has nurtured and sustained it.

When life seems to argue against a God of love, we still hold on to this magnificient claim. When nature is violent, when famine stalks the earth, when there are wars and rumors of war, we still say that at the heart of the universe there is love—the kind of love we have seen in Jesus Christ.

When Love Is Missing

What happens when love is missing? Let me suggest three things.

When love is missing, virtues, even the best of them, are hollow and empty.

Paul, in the thirteenth chapter of 1 Corinthians, talks of five things that meant a great deal to the Corinthian church—tongues, prophecy, knowledge, faith, and generosity. The Corinthians took pride in all of these, but without love, Paul told them, these would be hollow and meaningless:

"If I speak in the tongues of men and of angels, but have not love, I am a noisy gong or a clanging cymbal. And if I have prophetic powers, and understand all mysteries and all knowledge, and if I have all faith, so as to remove mountains, but have not love, I am nothing. If I give away all I have, and if I deliver my body to be burned, but have not love, I gain nothing" (vv. 1-3).

This series hits you with surprises. They are even shocking, especially in the climatic statement when Paul says though you make the ultimate gift of life and become a martyr for your faith, that, too, is meaningless unless it is motivated by love.

While love is the cardinal virtue, there are other virtues, such as truth, humor, dependability, the worth and dignity of persons. But these are like spokes in the ethical wheel which has love as its hub. And all these virtues are empty unless they are infused with love.

Again, other virtues without love will eventually become vices. No virtue is safe except in the keeping of love.

Truth is a great virtue but can become a great evil if not spoken in love. You can destroy a person with the truth unless you love him. Paul said, "Speaking the truth in love, we are to grow up in every way into him who is the head, into Christ" (Eph. 4:15). He knew how important it is to speak the truth in love. Beauty is good, but a woman can destroy a man with her beauty if she does not love him. Honor is a virtue, but without love you can sacrifice people on the altar of honor.

The elder son in Jesus' story of the prodigal son is an example of a person who took virtues and turned them into instruments of injury. His virtues became vices. He indeed had been a "good" boy. He had stayed home, worked hard, and been a dutiful son. When his father went out to entreat him, urging him to help celebrate the safe return of his younger brother, he said to his father: "Lo, these many years I have served you." And his father did not dispute him. He had indeed been loyal, faithful, and responsible, yet, his virtues had made him proud, heartless, and loveless. His virtues, born of legalism, had dried up the springs of compassion in his heart. He ignored his brother, rejecting him. News telling of his brother's death would have been preferable to finding out that he was alive.

Finally, when love is missing, life is turned into a kind of hell.

Zossima in *The Brothers Karamozov* says: "What is hell? I maintain that it is the suffering of being unable to love."[2]

Thomas Merton once said: "Hell is where no one has anything in common with anybody else except the fact that they hate one another, cannot get away from one another and from themselves."

Where there is no love the vacuum is filled with hate, and hate is an inferno that burns up the interior life. It can be like a volcano, the pressure of which builds up and eventually erupts, destroying the person and injuring those about him.

I remember in a counseling session a counselee saying, "But I cannot love." I still feel the anguish in her voice. Her pain was almost insufferable. She was in a kind of hell.

Hell can be defined as separation from God, the brother, and the sister. Hate, which fills the vacuum love has abandoned, leads to rejection, estrangement, loneliness, and death. Is there anything worse than that?

Keeping the New Commandment

Who can obey the new commandment? It seems to be an impossible commandment. We often find it hard to give common, ordinary love. How can we love one another the way Jesus has loved us? The truth is we cannot in our own effort. If left to our strength alone, the commandment would be a crushing burden. Rather than Jesus delivering us from the enslavement of the law, He would be imposing a law much more severe than the law of Moses. Rather than being a liberator, Jesus would be an impossible taskmaster. But we are not left in our own strength. Power from beyond us is given us so that the impossible becomes possible. Yet we can never live that commandment as perfectly as Jesus did. At best, it will be an approximation of that love. Yet, there can be that quality in our life-style that reminds the world of Jesus.

Paul Engle, founder of the University of Iowa writers' program, when an old man said: "The most important and profoundly felt thing is that to my surprise I came to the end of my life convinced that love is indeed possible in a basically unlovely world. It seems to me that love is not only possible, but it is the ultimate reason for life on earth."[3] We might have to speak more guardedly than Engle, yet I believe he is basically right.

Let me mention several things that will at least help to approximate the new commandment.

1. To begin with, God has loved us first. "We love," John tells us, "because he first loved us" (1 John 4:19).

We could never have loved unless somebody had loved us first. We learn to love by accepting love, returning it, and sharing it.

In my earliest moments of consciousness there was the awareness that there was somebody with me who loved me. My mother was there. She touched me gently, spoke softly to me, held me firmly to herself, and put forth every effort for my comfort and welfare. Because she loved me there was the possibility that I might love. Here is one of the most redemptive things in life: the earliest experience normally confirms the presence of a person who loves and cares for us. Nothing is so important as that.

God has loved us first, and He has loved us in a very concrete, personal way. He has loved us in Jesus Christ. While all human love is imperfect and broken, even the best of it, God has loved us with perfect, unbroken, and unsparing love in Jesus. Because He has, I can love Him and I can share His love with others.

2. The grace of Christ is always available.

We are saved by grace and the grace that saved us is always with us. There are new meetings with Christ and new gifts of grace. Christ's grace is always with us to steady and support us, and when we fall on our faces it is there to stand us on our feet and give us a new start. The gift of grace is a gift of strength.

Paul, one of the towering giants of history, was a man of weakness. He suffered much from exposure to the elements and from the hands of fellow countrymen and others. He knew what it was to be exhausted, with his energy spent. He experienced depression so deep that he despaired of life (2 Cor. 2:8). He had an illness, whether physical or emotional we do not know, that sapped his strength. But through it all Christ told Paul that His grace was sufficient for him and Paul found that it was (see 2 Cor. 12:8-10).

The grace of Christ in us enables us to be gracious. It turns us outward, making us sensitive to the need and pain of others. It enables us to love as Christ has loved us.

3. The Holy Spirit gives us the power to love.

We all know how unruly our hearts are. Who can control an angry and hostile heart? Today has been a bad day. I have been angry and have nursed wounded feelings all day long. I know how destructive this kind of thing is. I say to myself: "It is such an irrational thing. This hostility is like an inner volcano which someday will erupt and destroy me. Today has been bad but tomorrow will be better. Tomorrow I will not hate, I will love." I awake the next morning, and what is the first thing in my consciousness? The same old bitterness and hatred. My heart is so unruly, I cannot manage it. Who will deliver me from my own heart?

If I cannot manage my own heart, is there help from beyond me? Yes, the Holy Spirit can enable me to love. Paul wrote: "God's love has been poured into our hearts through the Holy Spirit" (Rom. 5:5).

The image could be that of the heart as a cup which is filled with all kinds of negative thoughts, jealousies, and hostilities. Then the Holy Spirit begins to pour in the love of God, and as He does, the negative feelings are gradually displaced and the heart is eventually filled with the love of God. The Holy Spirit does what we cannot do, and it does it in grace. The love of God is a gift.

4. There is the church which is a loving, accepting, and affirming fellowship. It will help us to love.

Because of the nature of the Christian fellowship, Paul could admonish the church at Ephesus: "Be kind to one another, tenderhearted, forgiving one another, as God in Christ forgave you" (Eph. 4:32).

There are always those in the church who will allow us to unmask ourselves, be who we are, confess that we are sinners and not saints, and who will still, rather than reject us, accept us and love us. They will help siphon off the hate and bitterness so the inner life can heal. They will walk with us, pray for us, and steady us when we are weak. In such a fellowship, we can learn to love.

Love in Our Kind of World

What about the kind of love I have been talking about in our kind of world? Is there a place for it? Is it too idealistic? It must be confessed that Christian love has a hard time in our world. It is still rejected, injured, and put to death. But the world can no more destroy it than it can Christ. And it is relevant. It touches our world where it is most confused and where it is suffering most. It is our world's best chance of survival. Love alone can give an adequate evaluation of the worth and dignity of human life, set in motion those forces that can make for peace, minister to our world so its wounds can be healed, define adequate social ends for life. And only love can drain off the bitterness and hatred that threaten to destroy us. Love knows how to listen and keep open channels of communication. We must never make the mistake of believing that love is a gushing sentimentality. It is not weak. Because it is not loud and noisy and does not strut, do not believe that it is without strength. Although it is gentle, it is capable of being tough without being ruthless and merciless. It is like Jesus Christ who made tough decisions. On His last journey to Jerusalem, knowing what awaited Him there, He set His face like a flint toward the city. Jesus was no sentimentalist, no idealist with His head in the clouds. He was a realist in touch with life. He faced realities as hard as Roman nails, Roman swords, and a Roman cross, and did not turn from them.

Love is called on to make hard ethical decisions. It knows for the most part that the choices are not between black and white, but more often in the gray zone. Frequently it is called to make choices in black zones, as in war, where often whatever choice is made will be wrong. Then it is careful to choose the least wrong, and always it is open to healing, forgiveness, and reconciliation.

For the first time we have power to destroy life on our planet. The shadow of a nuclear war lies across the face of our earth. Whatever our agendas are, the top priority of them all must be peacemaking. If we can't achieve peace, then nothing else will matter. If love cannot point the way, there is no hope for us.

We are called on to preach and live the good news that God loves us and our world, that His love has appeared in Jesus Christ, and that it is possible for us to love.

Thought Starters

A series of sermons on The Thirteenth Chapter of 1 Corinthians.

A series on The Fourth Chapter of 1 John.

A series on Resources for the New Commandment.

A series on When Love Is Missing.

Other sermons: The People of the Way; Nuclear Giants, Ethical Infants; Lagging Behind Our Scientific Progress; The Christian Ethic; The New Commandment; The Radically New Love in Jesus; I Must Always Be in Debt (Rom. 13:8); The Incarnation of Love; Cut Flowers; The Holy Spirit and Love.

Scripture

Proverbs 25:21-22; Matthew 5:43-48; 22:34-40; Mark 10:17-22; John 13:31-35; 21:15-19; Romans 12:9-21; 13:8-10; 1 Corinthians 13:1-13; Ephesians 4:11-16; 5:1-14; James 2:8-17; 1 John 2:7-11; 4:7-21.

Texts

John 13:34,35; Romans 12:9-10; 13:8; 1 Corinthians 10:24; 12:31; 13:13; 16:14; 2 Corinthians 2:8; 6:11; Ephesians 1:15; 4:15; 5:2; 6:24; Colossians 3:14; James 2:8; 1 John 4:7,16,18, 19,20-21.

Illustrations

Supporting another (Ex. 17:8-13; Job 4:3-4); Identification (Job 29:15-16); Two better than one (Eccl. 4:9-12); Love of enemies (Matt. 5:43-48); When love is extravagant (Mark 12:41-44; 14:3-9); Love knows no social boundaries (Luke 10:29-37); The new commandment (John 13:34); How the world will know the disciples of Jesus (John 13:35); Love's priority (John 21:15-19); Two great principles—love of God and love of brother (Rom. 14:5-21); Love that enables us to identify (1 Cor. 9:19-23); Loving the unlovable (2 Cor. 2:5-11); Love allows us to give ourselves (2 Cor. 8:3-5); Love as the fulfillment of the law (Matt. 22:40; Rom. 13:8-10; Gal. 5:14); The social test of spiritual religion (1 John 4:20-21).

Notes

1. *The Interpreters Bible*, Vol. 1 (Nashville: Abingdon Press, 1952), p. 592.

2. Fedor Dostoyevsky, *The Brothers Karamozov* (New York: Vintage Books, 1950), p. 387.

3. *Time*, September 27, 1982, p. 73.

21
The Kingdom:
God's Order

The kingdom of God is certainly one of the great themes of the Bible. It is the predominant theme of the Synoptic Gospels. About this there is little dispute among scholars. And while the term is not so frequently used in the rest of the New Testament or in the Old Testament, the great truth of the kingdom is there.

Mark introduced Jesus' great Galilean ministry like this: "Jesus came into Galilee, preaching the gospel of God, and saying, 'The time is fulfilled, and the kingdom of God is at hand, repent, and believe in the gospel'" (Mark 1:14-15). The kingdom was the heart of His preaching. God, through His gracious and mighty action in Jesus Christ, had brought in the new age. The kingdom of God was at hand.

Luke tells us that Jesus in His postresurrection appearances "presented himself alive after his passion by many proofs, appearing to them during forty days, and speaking of the kingdom of God" (Acts 1:3). He talked with them about the kingdom of God which had been His theme before His crucifixion.

The kingdom of God was also the theme of the disciples' preaching. Luke tells us that Jesus sent forth the twelve "to preach the kingdom of God and to heal" (9:2). And Jesus instructed the seventy: "Whenever you enter a town and they receive you, eat what is set before you; heal the sick in it and say to them, 'The kingdom of God has come near to you'" (10:8-9)

Jesus taught us to pray for the coming of the kingdom of God when His will would be done on earth as it is in heaven.

What Is the Kingdom of God?

When I speak of the kingdom, I am thinking essentially in terms of the kingdom of God on earth, in our history.

Jesus, in His Model Prayer, told us what the kingdom of God is:

Our Father who art in heaven,
Hallowed be thy name.
Thy kingdom come,
Thy will be done,
On earth as it is in heaven (Matt. 6:9-10).

The kingdom of God is God's will being done on earth as it is in heaven. It is the rule of God in all spheres of life—the personal, social, economic, political, and religious. The kingdom is God's order.

The kingdom occurs when men and women, because of God's gracious action in Christ, turn from their false gods, giving up their idols, and acknowledge the true God, the God of our Lord and Savior Jesus Christ; when men and women seek to do, not their own will, but the will of God; when people are willing to sacrifice all their values so they can have the one value of supreme worth which is the kingdom of God. (See Matt. 13:44-45.)

It should be said at this point that we have great difficulty in understanding the kingdom of God because we associate power, especially political power, with the idea of kingdom. This is why the disciples also found it so hard to understand the kingdom Jesus was bringing in. They could never disassociate it from political power. They dreamed of a king, marching armies, military victories, and a nation free and independent. Although Jesus tried hard to tell them His kingdom would be different, they clung to their old idea to the end. On the day of His ascension they were still asking: "Lord, will you at this time restore the kingdom to Israel?" (Acts 1:6).

The third temptation in Matthew's order was the devil's taking Jesus to a very high mountain and letting the kingdoms of earth pass before His vision. There they came in power, pomp, ceremony, and glory. These he would give Him, the devil said, if Jesus would fall down and worship him. The temptation was the alluring appeal of an intense, nationalistic hope that dreamed of military conquest and political independence. It was indeed powerful.

As has been suggested, we find the kingdom of God mysterious, elusive, and hard to understand because of our concept of power. We associate power with big, bulky, measurable, and clamoring reality—reality that is ostentatious, that is pompous, that struts. We see nothing of this in the kingdom Jesus brings and we are confused.

It should help us to realize that even physical power is not always loud and clamoring. The incoming tide quietly lifts the stranded barge. The morning breaks without the blast of trumpets, flooding the earth with energy, light, and life. The universe shifts its mighty tides of power on our planet with the changing of the seasons. While there are signs of the change, they are never loud or noisy.

We have to understand that the power of the kingdom of God is moral and spiritual in nature. Such power is not big, bulky, or loud. It doesn't shout or strut. It doesn't have to, knowing that it alone is strong. We can never appreciate the kingdom of God until we realize that the great power that runs through history and courses through the universe is moral and spiritual. This is so because God is moral and spiritual in His nature.

Jesus and the Kingdom

The New Testament makes the staggering claim that the kingdom of God made its advent with the coming of Jesus Christ. This does not mean that God had not been sovereign of the universe and history before Jesus came. God had always been sovereign of the universe. He had created it, and history, in its wildest and most destructive hours, had been under His control. But it did mean that God was establishing His rule in the sphere of history in a fresh, new way in the coming of Jesus of Nazareth. The birth, life, death, and resurrection of Jesus Christ were such powerful events that they made possible the coming of the kingdom. The kingdom for which prophet, seer, and saint had prayed and hoped had happened in Jesus of Nazareth. What a claim! Yet, that is what the New Testament says.

As stated above, that is what Jesus announced at the beginning of His great Galilean ministry. He said the time was fulfilled and the kingdom of God was at hand.

What kind of time was fulfilled? *Kairos,* not *chronos* time, which is qualitative time. It eludes all our instruments of measurement. It is eventful, crisis, creative time. It is pregnant time, ready to give birth to something great. It is time that offers history a new chance, that sets it in a new direction. *Chronos* time is quantitative, ordinary time, the kind we measure on our calendars and watches.

In this momentous time Jesus appeared, initiating the kingdom. In the light of this unprecedented event, people were not to remain passive. Decisive action was called for: "Repent and believe the gospel." They had to repent, to do the strong turning of mind, heart, and will. They had to set their faces in a new direction, giving up their false gods and false hopes. And they had to believe. Faith was more than intellectually affirming the kingdom. It was committing their lives to it, living in its hope, walking in its light, and submitting to its authority. The kingdom was beating upon the doors of their time and place. They must respond to it.

What was Jesus doing essentially to bring in the kingdom of God? He was disclosing the real nature of God, forgiving sins, setting in motion the most powerful moral force in the universe which is love, and breaking the power of evil.

Special attention must be given to Jesus' breaking the power of evil. It is evil that obstructs the will of God, that prevents

His will being done on earth as it is in heaven. Until this obstruction is removed, the kingdom cannot come.

Jesus, in casting out demons, said: "But if it is by the finger of God that I cast out demons, then the kingdom of God has come upon you" (Luke 11:20).

Jesus sent the seventy on mission. "The seventy returned with joy," Luke tells us, "saying, 'Lord, even the demons are subject to us in your name!' and he said to them, 'I saw Satan fall like lightning from heaven' " (10:17-18).

Jesus went so far as to give a constitution or guidelines for those of the kingdom. These guidelines are the Sermon on the Mount. Here we have the world's finest body of ethical teaching. But it was not for everybody. It was for the citizens of the kingdom. You remember how Matthew introduces the Sermon on the Mount: "Seeing the crowds, he went up on the mountain, and when he sat down his disciples came to him. And he opened his mouth and taught them" (5:1-2). He left the crowds behind him at the base of the mountain and moved on up its slopes with the inductees of the kingdom. The ethical instruction would be for them.

The early church therefore felt a new age was upon them, the age of the kingdom.

Israel thought of history as one age following another. It was like a succession of waves. It was as if they stood where an old wave was lapping to an end, being followed by another mighty wave that was moving in. That new wave was indeed the wave of the future, the kingdom of God. Or to use another metaphor: They felt they were standing where the shadows of an old age were being driven away by the dawn of a new one. What a place to stand! And, the early church felt it was standing there.

At Pentecost Peter saw Joel's prophecy of the messianic age being fulfilled:

> But this is what was spoken by the prophet Joel:
> "And in the last days it shall be, God declares,
> that I will pour out my spirit upon all flesh

and your sons and your daughters shall prophesy,
and your young men shall see visions,
and your old men shall dream dreams" (Acts 2:16-17).

The new age had come and the Spirit, being poured out on all people, was a sign of it.

The Kingdom in Three Tenses

Like salvation, the kingdom has come, is coming, and will come.

The kingdom has come. The early church was sure Jesus Christ had ushered in the kingdom. Through His life, death, and resurrection He had brought in the new age. It was an accomplished reality. It had been done, it was back of them. It could have been said: "Thy kingdom has come."

Yet the kingdom had not only come, it was still coming. It was not a static reality located exclusively in the past. It was a throbbing, dynamic, growing reality. To understand the kingdom it had to be experienced in the present moment. It could not be fully grasped when seen only in the past. Jesus stressed this in His parable of the seed.

"The kingdom of God is as if a man should scatter seed upon the ground, and should sleep and rise night and day, and the seed should sprout and grow, he knows not how. The earth produces of itself, first the blade, then the ear, then the full grain in the ear. But when the grain is ripe, at once he puts in the sickle, because the harvest has come" (Mark 4:26-29).

There is growth, progression, becoming, just as with the kingdom. The kingdom not only has come, it is coming now.

Whenever men and women respond to Christ's love and grace, allow Him to break the power of evil in their lives, submit their wills to God's will, reach out in love and affirmation to their brothers and sisters, and seek to establish justice and goodwill, the kingdom comes.

This, however, is not the full story about the time dimension of the kingdom. The past and the present cannot fully explain it. It has a future: The kingdom will come.

The kingdom of God never completely comes on earth in its purity, fullness, and perfection. Jesus talked about the imperfection of the kingdom in His parable of the dragnet.

"Again, the kingdom of heaven is like a net which was thrown into the sea and gathered fish of every kind; when it was full, men drew it ashore and sat down and sorted the good into vessels but threw away the bad. So it will be at the close of the age. The angels will come out and separate the evil from the righteous, and throw them into the furnace of fire; there men will weep and gnash their teeth" (Matt. 13:47-50).

The kingdom net in history catches all kinds of men and women, good and bad. They will be separated only at the end of history when the kingdom comes in its fullness and purity. The kingdom will come in power and glory. The kingdom will be consummated, but only at the end of history and beyond the end of history.

It is sin that frustrates the will of God in history. It is evil that does not allow God's kingdom to come fully on earth. We saw that as Jesus broke the power of evil it was then the kingdom drew near. But Jesus never claimed to completely destroy evil on earth and in history. As already suggested, we believe that He mortally wounded the powers of darkness and evil and that they are doomed to perish. Like a wounded animal that must die, evil may seem to become more ferocious, even more powerful, but it knows its end is certain. With the second coming of Christ, history will be brought to an end, there will be a new heaven and a new earth, and evil will have been completely destroyed. Evil can no longer frustrate God and block His will. Then the kingdom will come in all its glory and perfection. But that is in the future. It is not here, but there.

John says that in the new Jerusalem, darkness, which is a symbol of evil, will have passed. There shall be no shadows, darkness, or night there. The city will be perfectly lighted for "the glory of God is its light, and its lamp is the Lamb. . . . Its gates shall never be shut by day—and there shall be no night there. . . . Nothing unclean shall enter it, nor any one who practices abomination or falsehood, but only those who are written in the Lamb's book of life" (Rev. 21:23,25,27).

The Strangeness of the Kingdom

You would probably have more difficulty in defining the *kingdom of God* than almost any other theological term. There is something elusive about it, almost indefinable. Part of the problem lies in our concept of power, but there are also other reasons. There is a strangeness about the kingdom, and recognizing this is the first step in understanding it. What makes it strange? Let me suggest three things.

1. There is the strangeness of grace.

We can understand justice better than grace; achievement better than gift. The kingdom of God is essentially a kingdom of grace. We enter it, not because of who we are or because of our moral achievement. Christ forgives us in grace, affirms us in grace, and accepts us into the kingdom of God in grace.

I have in an earlier chapter talked about two parables of Jesus—the workers in the vineyard and the prodigal son—as illustrations of the strangeness of grace. Let us here refer to an incident from the life of Jesus.

The scribes and Pharisees brought to Jesus a woman caught in the act of adultery. Then follows one of the tenderest scenes from Jesus' life. Those who brought her were legalists and they were prepared to stone her. She had been caught in the act of adultery, and the law of Moses commanded that such a person should be stoned. She had violated the law and that was that. Now let her pay the penalty with her life. You remember what Jesus did. He accused the legalists of their own sins while He dealt in grace with this poor woman. He was so gentle with her. "Woman, where are they?" He asked. "Has no one condemned you?" "No one, Lord," came the reply. Then the words of grace: "Neither do I condemn you; go, and do not sin again" (John 8:1-11).

It is easy to feel that Jesus was too lenient with this woman, that He should have been more severe with her. A mentality shaped by legalism will ask: Does not that kind of acceptance ignore moral values and flaunt ethical standards? Grace is indeed strange.

Paul, the great preacher and teacher of grace, discovered how vulnerable grace is. It was strange that this should be true. Because it was vulnerable, it was open. It was not standoffish but accessible, close to life's hurt, pain, and tragedy. One of its sources of strength was its vulnerability. Grace was easily hurt and easily misused.

Paul talked about the flagrant misuse of grace in the church at Rome. He had told them that where sin increased, grace did much more abound (Rom. 5:20). No matter how much sin there was more grace was available. Some in the church saw this as cutting the moral nerve of life. They were now free to do as they pleased. No matter if they satiated themselves with sin, they could easily be forgiven since there was always a surplus of grace. Paul was shocked. Having died with Christ in baptism, how could they go on sinning? (See Rom. 6:1-4.)

Rather than grace cutting the moral nerve in life, it becomes the greatest motivator in ethical behavior. We are no longer goaded by law, we live the good life out of gratitude for what has been done for us. We seek no reward for what we do. We have already been rewarded. Such is the ethical life in the kingdom. To many, it does indeed seem strange.

2. There is the strangeness of the people who belong to the kingdom.

A man who sat at dinner with Jesus said to Him: "Blessed is he who shall eat bread in the kingdom of God" (Luke 14:15). And Jesus responded by telling a story about a great banquet to which many were invited. At the time of the banquet the host (a householder) sent his servant to those who had been invited, saying, "Come; for all is now ready." And they began to make excuses and would not come. Then the host, in anger, said to his servant: "Go out quickly to the streets and lanes of the city, and bring in the poor and maimed and blind and

lame." Still there was room. "Go out to the highways and
hedges," the host commanded, "and compel people to come in,
that my house may be filled." The highways and hedges were
beyond the city wall where the most unacceptable people
lived, among them being the Gentiles and the social outcasts.

If you could have been there and looked into that banquet
hall, you would have been surprised at the people who were
seated at those tables. It would have all been very strange.
People you would have expected to be there were not, and
people you would not have expected were there. So being
members of the kingdom is not determined by who you are,
how educated or ignorant, how powerful or how weak. It all
turns on the question: Will you accept grace? Many people—
the kind we often see at the banquets of our world—will not
be there. They are too proud to accept grace.

3. There is the strangeness of paradox.

Let me mention some paradoxes that are related to the kingdom.

First of all, the kingdom has come, yet it is to come; the
kingdom is present, yet it is in the future.

Again, the kingdom is in the world, yet not of it.

Jesus set forth this paradox in His high priestly prayer: "I do
not pray that thou shouldst take them out of the world, but
that thou shouldst keep them from the evil one. They are not
of the world, even as I am not of the world" (John 17:15-16).
Jesus did not want His disciples to be escapists, to be recluses.
He wanted them to stay in the world, to be in the midst of life
with its striving, pain, and suffering. Yet, He did not want
them to succumb to the false values and idolatry of the world,
or to be destroyed by the evil that is so rampant in the world.

Jesus prayed that God's kingdom would come, not in some
distant and ethereal realm, but on earth where we work, toil,
and sweat. Yet the kingdom is never comfortable in the world.
There is always tension between the two. The kingdom feels
it is in an alien place.

Jesus, who prayed that the kingdom would come on earth,

said to Pilate: "My kingship is not of this world; if my kingship were of this world, my servants would fight, that I might not be handed over to the Jews; but my kingship is not from the world" (John 18:36).

Paul wrote: "For though we live in the world we are not carrying on a worldly war, for the weapons of our warfare are not worldly but have divine power to destroy strongholds" (2 Cor. 10:3-4).

We sing:

> For not with swords' loud clashing,
> Or roll of stirring drums;
> With deeds of love and mercy
> The heav'nly kingdom comes.

Finally, we work for the coming of the kingdom, yet it is a gift.

Jesus worked hard and so did His disciples. They were not idle, loitering the time away, waiting for the kingdom to come. No, they were busy men. Jesus said: "We must work the works of him who sent me, while it is day; night comes, when no one can work" (John 9:4).

We must be busy establishing justice, showing compassion, and creating humaneness in our world. But we must never believe that by doing these things we can bring in the kingdom. We can't. In more optimistic times, some believed that if we worked hard enough in the right way we could bring in the kingdom. We know better now. In the final analysis, the kingdom is God's gift.

"Fear not little flock," Jesus said, "for it is your Father's good pleasure to give you the kingdom" (Luke 12:32). And Paul said: "He has delivered us from the dominion of darkness and transferred us to the kingdom of his beloved Son, in whom we have redemption, the forgiveness of sins" (Col. 1:13-14). The kingdom is something God provides, it is His great gift.

It is our privilege to preach on the kingdom which is God's

order. It touches and intersects all our temporal orders, judging and redeeming them. We can preach on it with hope.

Thought Starters

A series of sermons on The Kingdom of God in Three Tenses.
A series on The Strangeness of the Kingdom.
A series on The Paradoxes of the Kingdom.
Other sermons: The Kingdom Is at Hand; "Thy Kingdom Come"; What Kind of Power Is This? The Constitution of the Kingdom; Who Are the Citizens of the Kingdom? Grace Is Strange; Grace Is Vulnerable; When Jesus Seems to Be too Soft; "Not with Swords Loud Clashing."

Scripture

Matthew 3:1-6; 4:12-22; 6:5-15; 13:1-51; 20:1-16; 25:1-46; Mark 4:1-34; Luke 15:25-32; 17:20-37; John 18:22-38; Romans 14:13-23; 2 Corinthians 10:1-6; Ephesians 4:1-10; 1 Peter 3:13-22.

Texts

Matthew 3:2; 6:10; 7:21; Mark 1:14-15; Luke 17:21; John 18:37; Acts 28:30-31; Romans 14:17; 1 Corinthians 4:20; 2 Corinthians 10:3-4; Revelation 11:15; 12:10.

Illustrations

Sermon on the Mount: life in the kingdom (Matt. 5—7); Stories about the kingdom (Matt. 13:1-51); The kingdom has small beginning (Matt. 13:31-32); The kingdom has supreme worth (Matt. 13:44-46); The kingdom and grace (Matt. 20:1-16); Sign of the kingdom: destruction of evil powers (Luke 11:14-23); Doing, not words, is what matters (Matt. 7:21-27; Rom. 2:13); Weapons of the kingdom (2 Cor. 10:1-6).

22
History:
The End and Beyond

Christianity does not make sense without history since it is in history that God discloses Himself. And it is just as true to say that history does not make sense without Christian faith, the light of which falls along its way, telling us the meaning of history, where it is going, and its end.

Yet, history is not forever. It comes to an end which is caught up and fulfilled beyond itself. The temporal and shadowed vistas of history are at last fulfilled in eternal light and life. The technical term for what happens at the end of history and beyond is *eschatology*.

History and the End

History has meaning because God has created it and chosen to meet us there. God has not shoved history up blind alleys and dead-end streets. History has not been caught in revolving doors, going round and round. It does more than repeat itself and mark time. The Christian interpretation of history does not reflect the thought of the writer of Ecclesiastes, in the cynical phase of his pilgrimage of faith: "What has been is what will be, and what has been done is what will be done; and there is nothing new under the sun" (Eccl. 1:9).

God has put history on a main thoroughfare that is going somewhere. Its movement is linear and it has an end. Yet, it is true that history misses its way, gets sidetracked, may even regress. Its line is not always onward and upward; it is broken and jagged with depressions and peaks. Yet, history will reach its end.

Revelation does not come to us in a celestial glow. It occurs in the dust, grit, and gravel of history. As we all know, the great revelatory event of the Old Testament was the Exodus. It is a dated event that occurred at a particular place. We hear the rumbling of chariot wheels, the cursing of cavalry officers, the shuffling of masses of feet, and the groaning of people longing to be free. The great revelatory event of the New Testament—yes, of all time—was the advent of Jesus Christ, His birth, life, death, and resurrection. We can trace His ways along the dusty paths of history. He was no phantom. He was a flesh-and-blood person, He was historical.

History occurs in the space-time dimension, and both space and time are temporal. They will pass away. (See Heb. 1:11-12 *a*; 2 Pet. 3:10; and Rev. 10:6, KJV).

History can never fulfill itself in its own power and momentum. It will not end with a bang, nor will it fizzle out. Christ will come again to complete history. We speak of His second coming as the Parousia.

The Parousia has an Old Testament background, as do so many of the ideas of the New Testament. The people of the Old Testament, whose thinking had been shaped by the mighty acts of the Exodus, awaited expectantly a further deliverance in the future. This expectation frequently had a nationalistic hope but sometimes it took a cosmic dimension. Such terms as "the Day of the Lord," or "the latter days," or "that day" were used to express the expectation of deliverance. The New Testament held on not only to the concept, but to the language as well. The Day of the Lord or its equivalent occurs frequently in the New Testament. (See, for example, 1 Cor. 1:8; 5:5; Phil. 1:6,10; 2:16; 2 Pet. 3:10.)

The New Testament church never doubted that the same Jesus who had lived, died, and was resurrected would come again to fulfill and complete history, bringing in the kingdom of God fully. (See Acts 1:11.) The hope was such a lively one in the New Testament. (See, among others, Mark 8:38; 9:1; 10:37; 13:6-7,24 ff; 14:62; 1 Thess. 1:9-10; 2:19; 3:13; 4:13 to 5:10; 5:23.)

There were many in the early church who expected Jesus to return upon the clouds in their generation. Some of them thought it was so close at hand that they gave up their jobs and waited for His return. Paul was very severe on these people. (See 2 Thess. 3:7-12.) Most generations since have had people who looked for Jesus' return in their time. They have gone so far as to set the date and place. Historically such intense expectation has occurred in crisis time, when history was unmanagable. In our time, one of these frightening periods of history, there are those who look for the return of Jesus before the end of this century. While most of them do not set places and dates, they come close to it. It is too bad that we have not heard and heeded the words of Jesus: "But of that day and hour no one knows, not even the angels of heaven, nor the Son, but the Father only" (Matt. 24:36).

Beyond History

History ends, yet it does not end. It is fulfilled beyond itself, its meaning being gathered up into a greater dimension.

What lies beyond history? Let me speak of four things: judgment, the resurrected life, heaven and hell, and the new order.

1. There will be judgment.

We have seen how God is active in judgment in history. His judgment will come to a grand finale in the great last judgment which Jesus depicted in the twenty-fifth chapter of Matthew. Jesus began by picturing His own return as the Son of man, coming in glory and sitting upon His imperial throne. Before Him will be gathered the nations of earth and history, and He will separate them one from the other like a shepherd dividing his sheep from the goats. He will put the righteous on His right hand and the unrighteous on His left. And the unrighteous will "go away into eternal punishment, but the righteous into eternal life."

This parable has great homiletical possibilities, especially when you become aware of its surprises. We are shocked by the contrast between the Christ of judgment and the humiliated Jesus on Good Friday, stumbling beneath His cross through the streets of jeering and scoffing people. They are the same person, yet they seem to be so different and so far apart. Then the witnesses are a surprise. They are not the kind of people I would have chosen. I would have selected cultured, refined, middle-class people. But not so in this scene. For the most part they are the kind of people we associate with the Third World. They are the poor, the hungry, the naked, and the homeless. And there are the sick and prisoners. One wonders if the poor and starving of our world will rise up before us in the day of judgment and say to us: "I was hungry and you gave us no food." Again, we are surprised by the questions that will be asked. They are social questions, not theological ones: Did you feed the hungry, clothe the naked, take in the homeless, and visit the sick and prisoners? It should be said that nowhere is it suggested that we are saved by doing these humanitarian things. We are saved by grace, but the grace that saves us expresses itself in gracious behavior. The evidence of our salvation is not some verbal confession but deeds of loving-kindness.

We are further surprised that Christ, with these poor and hungry people before Him, never says that they are hungry but that He was. "I was hungry and you gave me food." This tells a wonderful thing about Jesus: He is so identified with those who suffer that He takes into His own life their pain. We remember the risen Christ confronting Saul of Tarsus on the Damascus road. "Saul, Saul," he asked, "why do you persecute me?" Saul could have so easily remonstrated: "Jesus, how can you say that I am persecuting you. I have never met you. I did not accuse you, neither did I throw the purple robe around your shoulders or press the crown of thorns upon your head.

I did not drive the spikes into your hands or pierce your side with the sword." That was true but Jesus was so identified with those who confessed His name that when Saul whipped them the lash that fell on them cut the shoulders of Jesus, when he put them into prison Jesus was with them behind bars.

Finally, we are surprised that these righteous people, in doing the deeds of mercy, were not self-conscious about it. They performed them without being aware of what they were doing. Such behavior had become second nature for them. In great surprise, they asked: "Lord, when did we see thee hungry and feed thee, or thirsty and give thee drink?" Here is the ultimate in Christian behavior: to do the deed of mercy and grace without seeking approval or congratulations, indeed not to be self-aware of what you are doing. That is to be gracious like our Lord.

2. There will be the resurrected life.

The emphasis of Christianity is not on immortality, but on resurrection. We live again by the mighty act of God, not because we have an indestructible spark within us known as a soul.

The most decisive event of the New Testament is the resurrection of Jesus. It is as if it is the hinge on which history turns. It is that pivotal. Paul could say: "If Christ has not been raised, then our preaching is in vain and your faith is in vain" (1 Cor. 15:14). If Christ has not been resurrected, there is no good news, no gospel, and faith is a hollow and empty thing.

The two great events which formed the heart of early preaching were the death and resurrection of Jesus, and both bore stigmas. The death of Jesus was such a shameful event. How could the life of the mighty Son of God end on a thing as shameful as a Roman cross? Many made fun of the idea. "We preach Christ crucified," declared Paul, "a stumbling block to Jews and folly to Gentiles" (1 Cor. 1:23).

The resurrection of Jesus was just as offensive as His cross. The ancient world was suffused with a Greek mentality that saw the body as being cheap and evil. How credulous it was to believe that a thing as worthless and as evil as a body would be resurrected. To many it was pure nonsense. You remember that Paul got along well with his sermon on Mars Hill until he came to the resurrection: "Now when they heard of the resurrection of the dead, some mocked; but others said, 'We will hear you again about this' " (Acts 17:32). They scoffed him down that hill. Possibly Paul was never more humiliated.

The New Testament is sure that the resurrection of Jesus was historical, real, and objective. It was more than the fantasy of tired, sick, and disillusioned minds. They were not seeing something that did not exist, they were looking at reality, a real body that asked for bread.

Because Christ has been resurrected, those who believe in Him may expect to be resurrected. He who conquered the grave will not leave us in the dust. Paul, in the fifteenth chapter of 1 Corinthians, where you find his classical statement on the resurrection, sees our future life in relation to the resurrection of Jesus Christ. The future life will be a resurrected life.

Paul related our resurrection to Christ's: "But in fact Christ has been raised from the dead, the first fruits of those who have fallen asleep. For as by a man came death, by a man has come also the resurrection of the dead. For as in Adam all die, so also in Christ shall all be made alive. But each in his own order: Christ the first fruits, then at his coming those who belong to Christ" (vv. 20-23).

Paul goes on to speak about the nature of the resurrected body: "So is it with the resurrection of the dead. What is sown is perishable, what is raised is imperishable. It is sown in dishonor, it is raised in glory. It is sown in weakness, it is raised in power. It is sown a physical body, it is raised a spiritual body. If there is a physical body, there is also a spiritual body" (vv. 42-44).

The resurrected life is spoken of throughout the New Testament. (See Acts 24:15; Rom. 6:5; Rev. 20:5.)

It is easy for us to slip into an ancient heresy—a dichotomy of life. We may think of life as being divided between soul and body, with the soul being immortal and the body being perishable. But biblical faith will have none of this. The body and soul are one, a unity, and a whole. So it will be in the future life. There will still be unity and wholeness. We shall still have bodies, albeit spiritual ones.

The resurrected life has two basic meanings: We shall have bodies preserving the wholeness of life, and we shall live again because of the mighty act of God. Not even Jesus came forth from the tomb by His own power. He was resurrected by the mighty doing of God. Paul could speak of "the immeasurable greatness of his power in us who believe, according to the working of his great might which he accomplished in Christ when he raised him from the dead" (Eph. 1:19-20). We shall live again because God chooses for us to and because He acts mightily on our behalf in a resurrection deed.

There are few things that are more comforting than our faith in the resurrected life. Death looks so final. The face that was so friendly just a few hours ago is now so expressionless, the hand that was so warm is now so cold, the voice that was so vibrant is now so silent, and the body that was so vigorous and active is now so still. It is easy to believe that this marks the end, that death speaks the last word.

A cynical soldier in World War II struck a match and blowing it out said to me: "Chappie, isn't that what happens to us at death?" The soldier would probably have been right were it not for the love of God and His mighty resurrection power.

3. There will be a heaven and a hell.

We look for a heaven. Underlying the hope of heaven is the assurance of the life everlasting. God has set the longing for eternal things deep within our hearts. And He has put upon our lips praises for the life that shall be. We do not believe that God will deny that which He has planted so deep within our hearts. We are not like lonely, flickering lights burning in a cold night, soon to be blown out forever by a careless and impersonal wind. We are not like bits of foam heaved up for a moment by a great wave only to be lost in a vast, impersonal sea. No, God loves us and He will not discard and cast aside that which He loves. If I, broken and sinful as I am, love my child and am willing to make any sacrifice that his life may come upon worthy fulfillment, how much more will God make provision for our highest fulfillment? But what about heaven? What will it be like?

The Bible does not think abstractly but vividly and concretely. It uses spatial terms, and is rich in imagery, metaphor, and simile. The fact that the Bible uses imagery lends greater credence to it, since such language tells truths that elude our more prosaic ways of expression. The Bible speaks of heaven as a place. Indeed, the most beautiful and extravagant language in the world's literature is used to describe heaven as a place. John, in the twenty-first chapter of Revelation, pictures heaven as a city, the New Jerusalem. The foundations of the city are garnished with all manner of precious stones. Its walls are jasper. The twelve gates are pearls, the streets are of pure gold. John, no doubt, meant to tell us that heaven is more wonderful than we can imagine. There are surprises in God's providence that lie beyond our imagination: "What no eye has seen, nor ear heard, nor the heart of man conceived, what God has prepared for those who love him" (1 Cor. 2:9). Or again, "Beloved we are God's children now; it does not yet appear what we shall be, but we know that when he appears we shall be like him, for we shall see him as he is" (1 John 3:2).

But we shall probably come nearer the truth if we think of heaven more as a relationship than a place. Jesus told His disciples in one of their loneliest and most depressed moments: "And when I go and prepare a place for you, I will come again and will take you to myself, that where I am there you may be also" (John 14:3). What was so important was not the place but the fact that they would be with Him. John, in Revelation, speaking of heaven as a relationship, wrote: "He who sits upon the throne will shelter them with his presence" (Rev. 7:15b). It is significant that John, before describing the New Jerusalem, spoke of a new relationship with God: "Behold, the dwelling of God is with men. He will dwell with them, and they shall be his people, and God himself will be with them" (Rev. 21:3).

Much has been said in this book about the importance of relationship. The tragedy of life is that basic relationships are broken, while salvation is having those broken relationships healed. Heaven will have no broken relationships, all will be made whole.

My life is fulfilled in God and my brother and sister. It is never perfectly fulfilled here because I cannot offer a perfect love to either. But in heaven it will be different. The God whom I have dimly seen on earth I shall see face to face. The God to whom I have, at best, given a broken loyalty I shall offer a perfect obedience. The God whom I have loved so poorly I shall love with perfect love.

I shall do more than love my brother as myself. My self-love has always been corrupted by my ego. But in heaven I shall love my brother and sister with selfless love. There life will come upon high fulfillment. No person will be hated or despised, no one turned aside because of one's skin or accent. The strong will not oppress the weak, and no one will be treated as if one were a cheap and worthless thing.

But what about hell? What will it be like? There is no way of wishing it away, however much we would like to. The Bible speaks of hell as plainly as it does heaven.

The Old Testament uses the term *Sheol* which is sometimes translated hell. It was the place of the departed dead, with a shadowy, eerie, half-human existence where there was a total forgetfulness of God. Everyone upon death, whether saint or sinner, went there.

The New Testament translates two terms, *Hades* and *Gehenna,* hell. Hades literally means the abode of the dead, and, like Sheol, was a place of hopelessness and despair.

Gehenna is the Greek for the Hebrew word meaning "valley of Hinnom" which was a ravine to the south of Jerusalem. It was an infamous place. Centuries before Jesus a religious cult flourished there which sacrificed children to a god called Moloch. During the time of Jesus it was the city dump. The garbage, refuse, and waste of the city was carried there. A fire burned day and night, consuming the waste of the city. Vermin, maggots, and worms crawled among the refuse. In the time of Jesus, Gehenna was spoken of symbolically to indicate hell. A Jew, speaking of hell, would call it Gehenna. Jesus sometimes used the term. (See Mark 9:47.)

There are many who believe in a literal, physical hell. Such a position is not without Scripture support. (See Matt. 13:42,50; 18:8; 25:41; Luke 16:24; Rev. 20:14; 21:8.) It is beyond human imagination to envision the suffering of such a hell. I can't stand to touch my little finger to a candle flame. Imagine being engulfed by flames forever!

There are those who envision hell basically as separation and alienation from God. If heaven is where relationships are whole, hell is where relationships are tragically and irreparably broken. Moreover, hell is a kind of wasteland as Gehenna was a place of waste. Here is the destination of lives that could have been productive of love, beauty, and goodness, but have not been. It is a place of empty, hollow people. It is where people burn with hatred, bitterness, remorse, and torturing memories. It is darkness and not light.

4. There is a new order.

John in Revelation introduces the new order like this: "Then I saw a new heaven and a new earth; for the first heaven and the first earth had passed away, and the sea was no more" (21:1).

In some prophetic passages of the Old Testament, there is a vision of a transformation of the present heaven and earth, not a new creation. In some apocalyptic literature, we are told that after the destruction of the world and the judgment, the first heaven will pass away and a new heaven will appear in its place.

In 2 Peter 3:10,13 the meaning is clear: The first heaven and earth are to be destroyed by fire, and according to promise, a new heaven and a new earth will appear in their place.

In Revelation 21, John envisions more than a transformation of the old order lifted up into a new dimension. He shares Peter's thinking: the first heaven and the first earth have been destroyed and a new heaven and a new earth have replaced them. John writes that He who sat upon the throne said: "Behold, I make all things new" (v. 5).

God will sustain a new relationship with the new earth and His people. He will no longer be transcendent, faraway, and unapproachable. He will be in the midst of them. They will be His people and He will be their God. (See Rev. 21:2-3.)

Further, there will be a new life befitting the new order. The new life will be saved from the weakness of the old—no more tears, no more suffering, no more death. (See Rev. 21:4.)

Again, there will be triumphant moral powers. God will have triumphed over Satan, light over darkness, and goodness over evil in all its forms. The city will be perfectly lighted and nothing unclean will enter it.

Finally, a new phase of salvation will be experienced—the final and last. You remember how salvation occurs in three tenses—past, present, and future. The future tense of salvation will become a reality. There we shall be fully saved.

Let me make one more observation about the new order. John uses no esoteric language to tell about the new order. He uses familiar language. He speaks of a city, light and darkness, life and death, and a river with trees along its banks. He even mentions precious stones. This tells us an important thing about the language we use in speaking of our faith and theology. We speak of God in terms of human experience, of the eternal in temporal terms, of heaven in the language of earth. Limiting? Yes. But it is a limitation we have to live with, and it is not too crippling.

It is our privilege to help people plodding their way, often tiresomely and painfully, on earth to see by faith the shimmering light of the eternal city and be made glad.

Thought Starters

A series of sermons on What Lies Beyond History?
A series on Surprises of the Last Judgment.
A series on The New Order.
Other sermons: On a Main Thoroughfare; Evidence of Our
   Salvation; The Power of Identification with Others; The
   Resurrection—No Illusion; Two Basic Meanings of the
   Resurrected Life; Christ Will Come Again; Gracious Like
   Our Lord; Resurrection Not Immortality; Resurrection—The
   Pivotal Event; What Is Heaven? What Is Hell?

Scripture

Matthew 24:1-51; 25:31-46; Mark 13:1-37; Luke 21:5-36; 1
Corinthians 15:20-28, 35-57; 2 Timothy 3:1-9; 2 Peter 3:8-13;
Revelation 7:9-17; 19:11-16,17-21; 20:7-15; 21:1-27; 22:1-21.

Texts

Job 14:14; Matthew 24:36; 25:31-33; 1 Corinthians 15:24,54;
2 Corinthians 5:1; Revelation 7:15; 21:3,4,5,25; 22:4.

Illustrations

The last judgment (Matt. 25:31-46); Watchfulness (Luke
12:35-38); No timetable (Matt. 24:36); What kind of body? (1
Cor. 15:42-50); Life's final shout of victory (1 Cor. 15:54); From
tent to house not made with hands (2 Cor. 5:1); All things new!
(Rev. 21:5); Life in the new order (Rev. 21:1-27); We shall see
Him face to face (Rev. 22:4); The last great invitation (Rev.
22:17).

Notes